DOUBLE EXPOSURE

A Twin Autobiography by

GLORIA VANDERBILT and
THELMA LADY FURNESS

In 1921 there burst upon the New York social scene the famous Morgan twins, Thelma and Gloria, whose names in the decade that followed came to spell glamour and excitement in that magic world of the "international set." Two continents thrilled to Thelma Furness's romances with Richard Bennett, Lord Furness, the Prince of Wales, Aly Khan, and Edmund Lowe. The whole world followed with bated breath the searing custody trial over young Gloria that pitted mother against daughter and shook the Vanderbilts and society. While much has been written from the outside about all of this, the two principals have never before disclosed the real truth behind the rumors and the headlines. And exciting as are their personal adventures and escapades, their story is also a portrait of an era.

In every age there have been certain women who through a combination of beauty and personality have attracted the love and admiration of rich or famous men, and who seem to be the embodiments of the feminine charm

(Continued on back flap)

DOUBLE EXPOSURE

*Life is mostly froth and bubble.
   Two things stand like stone:
Kindness in another's trouble,
   Courage in your own.*

DOUBLE EXPOSURE

A Twin Autobiography

by

GLORIA VANDERBILT

and

THELMA LADY FURNESS

DAVID McKAY COMPANY, INC.
New York

To Tony and Gloria

Foreword

Why a twin autobiography? A good question and one we have often been asked. Well, in the first place we are identical twins. Indeed, we looked so much alike when we were children that even our parents were hard pressed to tell us apart. Then, too, our lives have been curiously intermingled in spite of the very different paths we have trod. At nearly every important crisis either of us has been confronted with, the other has been on hand to help. Thus there has been an intertwining of our lives, a pattern and a continuity rarely experienced by sisters however close.

But above all there is an empathy, an understanding, between us that borders on telepathy. For example, when we were little girls of thirteen living in Hamburg, where our father was Consul General, I, Thelma, bought a birthday present for Gloria. It was a statuette of a Dresden dancing girl, and I carefully wrapped it and hid it so Gloria wouldn't know what I intended to give her. When finally the day came and we exchanged our presents, I was crushed to see the look of disappointment on her face when she opened her package. However, when I opened mine from her I understood; she had given me the identical figurine, purchased secretly at a different store at a different time. She had thought I was giving her back her own gift!

When Thelma was expecting her child, I, Gloria, was in New

FOREWORD

York. The baby was not due until May, and I had made steamer reservations in what seemed ample time to be with her. On the last day of March I had a luncheon engagement; but about an hour before I was to leave the house I developed violent abdominal pains, so severe in fact that I had my maid telephone to say I should have to cancel. I remember saying to her, as she started for the phone, that if I didn't know such a thing was out of the question I would think I was having a baby. I finally dozed off under the influence of a sedative; when I awoke some hours later, I felt completely recovered. On the bedside table was a cable from Lord Furness announcing the premature birth of Thelma's son, Tony.

When Gloria married Reggie Vanderbilt, she had a very sore throat; she kept her condition a secret from everyone in order not to be persuaded to postpone the ceremony and disappoint Reggie. I, Thelma, was in Europe with my father and mother to establish residence for a divorce on the breakup of my first marriage, and thus could not come back to New York for the wedding and therefore knew nothing of all this. But I did develop a sore throat that persisted until I received the cabled news that Gloria had a severe case of diphtheria.

These are but a few of innumerable instances of this strange sharing of each other's thoughts and feelings. Thus, while we differ in many ways, there is this psychic bond, this common entity, which is in many ways the strongest influence in our lives —almost as if we were Siamese twins without the physical connection. Since this is the way it is with us in life, so in the telling— we can't imagine doing it any other way.

GLORIA VANDERBILT
THELMA FURNESS

Contents

I	The Twins	3
II	Hither and Yon	19
III	America, Here We Are	43
IV	We Become Two	62
V	We Become Four	74
VI	New Horizons	100
VII	Heyday	108
VIII	Movies and Moving	120
IX	Duke	133
X	"I'll See You Tomorrow"	148
XI	Stormy Weather	169
XII	Honeymoon	192
XIII	Friedel	206
XIV	Wings of Love	215
XV	Renunciation	222
XVI	Enter the Prince	229

CONTENTS

XVII	The Trap	239
XVIII	Quick Sand	254
XIX	Royal Romance	274
XX	"Take Care of Him"	305
XXI	Little Gloria Grows Up	315
XXII	Dick	320
XXIII	Little Gloria Marries	331
XXIV	Spanish Interlude	340
XXV	The Maestro	346
XXVI	Together	358

Illustrations

following page 84

Our father, Harry Hays Morgan
Mamma
Our mother's family
Double exposure
Little Gloria and her mother
Little Gloria and her father
The Breakers
Mrs. Vanderbilt
Thelma in Hollywood
Presented at court
With Duke and Tony
Burrough Court
Averill
The Prince of Wales
Christmas presents for the staff at the Fort
Friedel Hohenlohe
Margarita and Friedel with their son
Entrance to Schloss Langenburg
Young Gloria at sixteen
Young Gloria's wedding
Elizabeth Wann, a faithful friend
Thelma and Edmund
Tony
Dick
Our sister, Consuelo
Gloria
Thelma

DOUBLE EXPOSURE

CHAPTER I

The Twins

Thelma

One early summer morning at 2 A.M., at the Hotel Nationale in Lucerne, Switzerland, one could have heard a proud and nervous father say to the maid standing patiently by, "The baby is here. Bring the bottle of champagne. We must celebrate."

When the champagne was brought to him, the door opened. From the next room a nurse came in, a baby girl in her arms. "You'd better sit down, Mr. Morgan," said the nurse gently as she placed the baby in his arms. Looking at the bottle of champagne, she said, "You'd better order another bottle; there is another baby on the way." It must have been quite a shock for Papa and Mamma. They already had Harry and Consuelo. Harry, five; Consuelo, two; and now twins.

Our father, Harry Hays Morgan, was American Consul at Lucerne, Switzerland. Papa came from a long line of diplomats who had served their government well. Our grandfather, Philip Hickey Morgan, was a judge of the Supreme Court of the State of Louisiana and was later appointed the first judge of the International Court of Alexandria, Egypt, and after that was given the post of American Minister to Mexico. Our father was born at Baton Rouge where his family owned a plantation called The Aurora.

Much of our family's background was chronicled in items Mamma kept in her scrapbook—a record we had no opportunity to examine carefully until a few weeks before her death. Here is one item, an account of Mamma and Papa's wedding, that appeared in the New York *Herald* in 1897:

> The bride became suddenly imbued with the idea that the sum of her happiness would be complete if she could only secure a foreign appointment which would carry her abroad as soon as she was married. Her father, General Kilpatrick, and Vice-president Hobart had been intimate friends. She called on Mr. Hobart and blushingly explained the object of her visit, an appointment for her prospective husband. He gallantly offered to aid her and, as a first step, introduced her to the President. When the President argued that there were a few others who wanted foreign appointments, she answered gently that there were none surely more deserving than he. The President surrendered completely and promised that before her wedding was celebrated, Mr. Morgan should have a desirable appointment abroad. From the hands of President McKinley himself, Mr. Morgan received the commission of Consul to Berne, Switzerland, an appointment with a salary of $2,000 a year.
> "This is your bride's wedding gift," said the President. "I know you will prize it as much as you love and cherish her."

How we managed to salvage this scrapbook from Mamma, we will never know. A few weeks before she died we found her amidst all sorts of papers torn up in little pieces at her feet: letters written to her father, General Kilpatrick, by Abraham Lincoln, General Sherman, General Custer, General Grant, President Taft, Vice-President Hobart, Attorney General George B. Wickersham, and many, many more who had made history. We pleaded with Mamma not to destroy these records, but it was too late. She kept slowly tearing one after the other. After a while, with a deep sigh, she said, "No, darlings, I don't intend to leave my past behind me."

Mamma's obsessive pride in our ancestry and Papa's frequent change of consular posts were two factors that had a profound effect on our childhood. We were raised as children with an enormous pride in our background, but nevertheless children with no fixed home, no identification with a single country, no mother tongue. To this day, American as we are, we still speak English with a slight but odd mixture of French and Spanish accents.

Our childhood properly began in Holland. We had moved to Amsterdam from Lucerne when we were still in our toddling period. Then, a few years later, Mamma burst into our nursery, exuberant, her eyes bright with excitement. "Twins, twins!" she shouted.

"What is it, Mamma?" we asked in duet.

"Oh, my darlings," she said, taking us in her arms, "your Mamma is the happiest woman in the world." She explained that our father, who was then the American Consul in Amsterdam, had been transferred to Barcelona. "Think, darlings," she went on ecstatically, "we are going to Spain—the land of my birth."

We appreciated our mother's enthusiasm, but even at that age we were quite well aware that Mamma had been born in Santiago, Chile, where her father, General Judson Kilpatrick, had served as American Minister, and where he had later married Louisa Valdivieso, our grandmother. We had never known our grandmother, but Consuelo, our older sister, told us that when she saw her—when Consuelo and her husband, Benjamin Thaw, went to Chile—she looked and dressed like a duchess in one of Goya's paintings. Her beautiful white hair, when loosened, tumbled almost to the floor. She was scarcely five feet tall, but her hair, worn in braids around her head, formed a crown that added at least four inches to her height. According to Consuelo's report, our grandmother never for a moment let you forget that she was a descendant of the grandees of Spain.

The same concern for ancestry, developed to the point of megalomania, was a lifelong characteristic of our mother; and in dramatizing her background, fantasy and invention never cowered before the rigors of fact. Her sudden claim to ancestral bonds with Spanish royalty was a case in point; but at this moment we did not care. Mamma was happy. She rose, danced around the room humming and singing snatches of Spanish songs.

We stood quietly by watching her. We did not want her to stop. She was a different Mamma, one we had never seen before—gay, lighthearted. Then she stopped, out of breath, and sat on the sofa. "Come, twins, come and sit beside me." Taking us again in her arms, she whispered, "Now you will know who your Mamma really is. We will place flowers on the graves of Ferdinand the Third, King of Castille and León, Prince Manuel of Castille and his beautiful wife, Beatrice of Savoy, and on the grave of Pedro Ponce de León, Lord of Villagareia." Who were all these people, we wondered? What had they to do with Papa's appointment to Barcelona? But Mamma was happy and we did not care. She rose and posed for a moment, her head high.

My curiosity outweighed my discretion. "But why, Mamma," I asked meekly, "why must we put flowers on all those graves?"

Mamma looked at the two of us in amazement. "Why?" Her voice cut like a file. "Why? Because they are my ancestors." No queen ever left a room more arrogantly.

We had never before, and have never since, given much thought to our ancestors. Our attitude in this area was probably shaped by Papa, who once said, "Those who brag about their ancestors are like potatoes—the only good thing about them is underground." But Mamma had different ideas. She believed that the blood which flowed in her veins—and ours—had a direct intravenous connection with the scores of Spanish and other royalty who spanned the generations between ours and those of the Byzantine emperors.

The house in Amsterdam now became a hub of excitement. Trunks to be packed. Furniture to be shipped. Silver to be put into their little blue flannel jackets. Mamma interfering with everybody. Having given one order, she would countermand it. "No, you fool," she would say in Spanish to a poor Dutch maid,

THE TWINS

"not there, here." Spanish now was the only language she would allow spoken. Our Spanish was not too good at that time, but we understood enough to keep out of her way.

Mamma's irritability was hard to understand. On the slightest provocation she would fly into terrible tempers. A nail file borrowed from her dressing table and not put back would cause a storm. An answer not given quickly enough would bring forth an "Answer your mother" that would send us flying from those terrifying, flashing dark eyes. These violent storms, like most storms, did not last long. She would then take us in her arms with tears and embrace us, forgive us. Half the time we did not know what we were being forgiven for, but as long as Mamma said we were forgiven, we were happy. We are sure now that an old-fashioned spanking for any wrongdoing would have been much better for us than those emotional outbursts of Mamma's. Yet with all of this we loved her.

At best Mamma was a disorganized traveler, and any move with her was a major one. Papa declared that he knew what Napoleon meant when he said he would rather move his entire army than Josephine and her bundles.

We departed calmly enough from the consulate. Papa, our nurse Jeanne, and we were in one carriage; my brother Harry, Consuelo, Mamma, and the maid followed with the hand luggage in another. At the Centrale Station Mamma sent us on to the train with Jeanne while she, Papa, Harry, and Consuelo looked after the luggage. They missed the train. Fortunately, Jeanne had our tickets with her. A telegram at the next stop reassured us that they would be on the next train.

We arrived in Barcelona early in the morning. In the excitement of seeing a new and very different city for the first time, we became dumb. Our knowledge of Spanish was of no help to Jeanne. In desperation she handed the driver a slip of paper with our new address, 234 Calle Mallorca, and with the clip-clop of the horses' hoofs, we were off to our new home.

Barcelona is a beautiful city. Long, wide avenues called *ramblas* are bordered on either side with magnificent old trees. The one we loved best of all was the Rambla de las Flores, the avenue of flowers. Every day under the trees the flower vendors set up their stalls and if you went there very early in the morning, before the city really woke up, you could make yourself believe you were in a beautiful long garden. We went there often to buy armfuls of mimosa, pinks, carnations, tuberoses, anything that was in season. We were thankful we could get these exquisite flowers for practically nothing, for we had to buy them out of our pocket money. Unlike us, Mamma did not like flowers; she considered them a waste of money. "Tomorrow or the day after they will all be dead and wilted. Then what will you have to show for your money?" Many a time we saw Mamma open a large box of beautiful flowers sent to her as a gift. Without even looking at the flowers she would take out the card, read it, replace it with her own; then, turning to the butler, she would say, "Take these around to Mrs. So-and-So."

Mamma's distaste for flowers was more than counterbalanced by her affection for superstitions. Whatever practice had been established by Spanish legends, whatever had been sanctioned by old wives' tales was Mamma's—to cherish, to follow, to preach as infallible doctrine.

Among other things, she frowned upon roller skates. "Mamma," I said to her one day, "won't you buy us skates? All the other children have them." The question came to her as a shock. She stopped what she was doing, her hand poised in midair; she looked at me incredulously—it did not seem possible to her that she had heard aright. "Roller skates? Of course not. My darling grandmamma always said young ladies did not run, jump, roller-skate, climb trees. Those were for boys to do." Mamma looked at us adoringly. "Why, if I let you skate your muscles would develop; they'd grow knotty and large. Do you want to look like acrobats when you grow up? You know, twins, my grandmamma always said, 'Dainty little hands are a woman's greatest asset.' This is why Jeanne has instructions to cream your hands at night and put your little white cotton gloves on when you go to bed." Smilingly she added, "How I love my dear, dear grandmamma!" Mamma may have loved her dear, dear grandmamma, but at that time we wished dear, dear grandmamma had never been born.

Our earliest recollections of Mamma were of a very dainty woman, very short, and with an exceedingly small waist. She had dark brown eyes which she used expressively and constantly to telegraph her moods. Sometimes she would hide them coquettishly behind a fan; sometimes she used them to flash bitterness and anger. Before we asked a favor, we invariably and carefully checked the state of Mamma's eyes; experience taught us to use them as oracles. Her hands and feet were minuscule, in keeping with her size. Her mouth was thin; when she was angry, it would seem to disappear almost entirely. Her nose was long and thin—probably an inheritance from some Iberian ancestor. "Roman," she called it.

One day Mamma announced that she was going to Paris to buy her wardrobe for the forthcoming visit of Sir Thomas Lipton, who, we were told, was to be Papa's and Mamma's house guest. We were eagerly awaiting this visit. Sir Thomas was arriving on his famous yacht, the *Erin*. We had never been on a yacht before and could not wait to go aboard.

"Now, twins, don't get into any mischief while I'm away or I won't give you the pretty dresses I hope to get for you in Paris."

"Oh, no, Mamma," we murmured, "we'll be as good as gold."

With a hug and a kiss for each of us, she sailed out to the carriage, followed by Maria, her maid, carrying her many bags and bundles.

"There goes Josephine," Papa said under his breath, as Mamma stepped into her carriage.

"Oh, no, Papa," I said, correcting him. "That was Mamma." Papa only smiled.

With Mamma gone, time hung heavily on our hands. The house was so quiet. There were no storms, no tearful embraces, no words of unnecessary warning, no reminders of past glories. We missed Mamma; for with all her faults and affectations, we adored her. She was a possessive woman; and all possessive people —most of all a possessive parent—develop an abnormal sense of dependence in those close to them; without her we were lost. To fill the vacuum, Gloria and I spent hours in the drawing room gazing at her portrait—a life-sized portrait showing her leaning soulfully against a pillar, her eyes, sad, looking beyond the horizon, as if contemplating the tragedy she was eventually to bring to Gloria. Her hair in the portrait was auburn, although she was to change its color many times in later years.

Eventually Mamma came back, bringing us each a blue organdy dress she had bought for us in Paris. The dresses had short puffy sleeves trimmed with lace. We were happy with Mamma back; happy with the dresses—which we considered good compensation for our loneliness.

The following week we heard a great commotion in the main hall. We heard a man's deep, booming voice; we heard Papa's soft, modulated tones, and Mamma's airy responses. There was the sound of servants scuttling across the tile floors and the scraping of luggage. Gloria and I raced down the stairs to investigate the hubbub.

In the middle of the front hall, surrounded by Mamma, Papa, and the servants, stood a giant of a man, with a sailor's weather-beaten, ruddy complexion. His blue eyes were framed by crow's feet. His gray hair curled. His mustache had a flourish. There were brass buttons on his double-breasted blue flannel jacket. In his hand he held a yachting cap. We landed with a hop, skip, and a jump at his feet. "Bless me," he cried, holding out his arms, "if here aren't the looking-glass girls."

"Twins," reproved Mamma, "how often have I told you not to run and jump? Where are your manners? This is Sir Thomas Lipton." We curtsied.

He turned to Mamma. "They'll be beauties, Laura."

Mamma sighed. "They'll be beauties only if I last long enough to make them so. Right now, I doubt it."

We liked this tall man with an aura of the sea about him. We each took him by the hand and led him to the drawing room. As he sat down, he cupped our chins. "I'd say they bear more resemblance to Harry than you"—he patted Mamma's arm—"more's the pity, probably. You're such a dainty mite. Pocket size, huh, Harry? But they've got your big brown eyes, and I think they'll be tall like you."

Sir Thomas held us at arm's length. "Which is Thelma and which is Gloria?"

We winked at each other, suppressing giggles. Papa looked at us for an instant and said, "The one on the right is Gloria."

We shrieked. Papa, as usual, was wrong.

For a whole week the sound of laughing voices filled the house. There were endless parties—luncheon parties, dinner parties. How we wished we were old enough to join the gaiety. But our day came. We were allowed to accompany the family and Sir Thomas to see his first bullfight. It was to be a gala affair: one of the bulls was to be dedicated to Sir Thomas—a mark of respect often given to visiting celebrities. A few days before, we heard Papa say he had taken a box at the back of the arena.

The rear box had apparently been chosen by Papa out of consideration for Sir Thomas, who was a reluctant recipient of the honor which was to be shown him. "You know, old boy," Papa said to Sir Thomas, "these bullfights can get pretty gory. They do things to the pit of your stomach."

But Gloria and I were innocents; all we knew was that bullfights were gala festivities. We wanted to be in the center of the fun. "Oh, no, Papa, please!" we pleaded. "Let's sit in the *barreras*. The boxes are so far away no one can see anything."

"Now look here, Harry"—Sir Thomas turned to Papa with a twinkle in his eye—"this is my looking-glass girls' day, too, and where they want to be, I want to be."

We ran and threw our arms around him. From then on, he was our hero.

The great day came. A cloudless blue sky greeted us when we awoke. Our little blue dresses Mamma had brought from Paris were waiting to be put on. "Look," Gloria said, "they are as blue as the sky."

Dressed and ready to go long before we were supposed to, we sat bolt upright in our chairs, not daring to move lest we crumple our dresses. Hours seemed to pass before Mamma came to get us. She stood in the doorway; we had never seen her looking more beautiful. A lovely red ruffled dress was topped by a magnificent old white lace mantilla, held up by an enormous shell comb under which red roses had been tucked. Soft lace framed her face and fell to beyond her waist. Tapping her fan impatiently, she said, "Come, twins, it's time to go. You both look very pretty." We were ecstatic; we had the most beautiful mother in the whole world; and loved and admired, we were going to climax our excitement by going to a bullfight with her, and with our hero.

The arena was packed; the crowd was lighthearted and festive. The band filled the air with the gay, teasing rhythms of the *paso doble*. And like the wings of thousands of giant, varicolored butterflies the women's fans fluttered in the boxes and *barreras*, creating iridescent ripples. We looked at Sir Thomas. He was beaming. "How colorful all this is," he said, turning to Mamma.

We held our breath. The *corrida* was about to begin. Matadors, toreadors, banderilleros—all in their superb costumes—were standing under the president's box, waiting for the toss of the key that would officially open the *corrida*. The president rose. The key flashed in the sunlight as it arced into the ring. There were loud shouts of *Olé!*—and the crowd settled down to watch the spectacle.

Bullfighting is not everybody's sport. To most Americans and Englishmen it is distasteful and cruel. And although it is as thrilling to Spaniards as is the World Series to us, or a Derby at Epsom Downs to Englishmen, Sir Thomas, it became apparent, had not the temperament that creates an *aficionado*. He was the kind of Englishman who believes that sporting contests are contests between equals; and that a bull, by rights, should have his own picadors and his own sword.

By the time the third bull was brought in for dexterous slaughter Sir Thomas had lost much of his enthusiasm. This bull, the biggest and presumably the best of the day, was to be fought in honor of the distinguished guest—Sir Thomas. Gloria and I stole furtive looks at our hero. He was not smiling now and his ruddy complexion had turned slightly green. In time a great roar went up. The matador had made a superb kill.

"Thank God, that's over," we heard him whisper, almost to himself.

Then we saw the matador striding toward us.

A matador who has made a brilliant kill is awarded the ears of his bovine adversary. The matador, in turn, usually makes the macabre but gallant gesture of presenting these to the prevailing or presiding woman of his choice. This afternoon, however, it was no woman who was so honored; the favor was bestowed on Sir Thomas. The matador stood proudly in front of our seats, bowing. Two bloody ears were cradled lovingly in the fold of his satin cape. The crowd rose, roared, rained flowers into the arena. The band struck up its liveliest and most triumphal music. On all sides people were shouting, "*Olé, olé*"—and Gloria and I *oléd* louder than anybody else. But by now Sir Thomas had turned completely green. Nevertheless he rose, bowed to the matador, bowed to the twenty thousand spectators, and graciously accepted the ears.

Many years later in London, when I was a grown woman, Sir Thomas made a singular confession. "Thelma," he said, "I wish I had listened to your father that day in Barcelona, and sat in a rear box. I have never in my life come so close to being sick in front of twenty thousand people."

As the years passed, Gloria and I began to grasp the fact that Mamma's mind had strange, dark, labyrinthine windings. Our understanding developed slowly. Although it was not until we were fully grown, and each of us had had a child of her own, that this quality was revealed to us in all its twisted glory, incidents occurred from time to time which revealed only too clearly the warped, obsessive impulses that defined her character. One of these centered about money. There was, for example, the day of our First Communion.

The great day had arrived, the most important day in young lives. We wanted to look like all the other little girls who were to receive their First Communion—in their long white dresses that reached to the ground. They all looked like little brides; they had wreaths of white roses around their heads and long tulle veils that hung to the hem of their skirts. We, too, wanted to look like brides.

Holding each other's hands, we stared at ourselves in the mirror. "Gloria," I howled, "we don't look like brides at all in our short dresses, we look like horrid little ballerinas; you know, like the Degas picture that hangs in the drawing room." It wasn't a horrid picture, really, it was a very pretty picture, but it didn't look at all like a First Communion.

"Never mind, Thelma," Gloria said, as Mamma entered the room, "our wreaths are pretty."

When Mamma came into our room, she was all smiles. "Look at my twins," she said gaily, "they look like real angels." But when she saw our tears, her gaiety turned quickly to hostility. "Now, what's the matter with you? What are you crying about?" she shouted.

"Please, Mamma, don't be angry with us. It's these silly dresses," I said, between sobs. "We don't look like brides at all."

"Brides! Brides!" Mamma screamed. "What has that to do with it? Time enough for that. I have told you a thousand times money does not grow on trees. Why should I spend money on dresses you will never be able to wear again?"

"But, Mamma, this is our First Communion," Gloria said pleadingly.

"Don't interrupt me, you ungrateful girls." She rose from her chair and started pacing the floor, her hat bobbing up and down. Her long silk dress made a rustling noise like dried leaves gently blown by the wind, her fan constantly snapping like the crack of a toy gun. Trembling, we looked at her. Trembling, we looked at each other. We had never seen her so angry.

"Do you think," she said, pointing her fan at us, "that your father is perfect, that he will give us anything we ask for? Ha! You don't know what he's really like. How I suffer! How I have to beg for everything! How I save! How I have to penny-pinch! How I deprive myself, all for you ungrateful children!"

She sat down. Then she, too, started to cry. We looked at her in despair. We had seen Mamma angry before, but never in tears. "Oh, how I suffer!" she wailed.

We had never heard Papa refuse Mamma anything. It was all very confusing. All we could conclude was that our kind Papa was really not kind at all; he was a monster in disguise. We dashed into her arms. Our tears mingled with hers.

"Please, please, Mamma, don't cry," I said. "We don't really care about the dresses. Anyway, we will be different. We will tell the girls in school—I know what we'll say; we'll say that we're Americans and that is the way they wear them over there."

I was trying desperately to calm Mamma; I think I would have said anything that would have ended this storm of emotion. But unconsciously I had been an arch-diplomat; I had said exactly what Mamma wanted to hear. "That's right, darlings," she said, picking up my words, "always be different." Then, rising from her chair, all signs of tears now gone, she smiled. "Come, twins, we will now go down and show Papa how pretty you look."

Obviously, what Mamma had said made no sense at all; all her complaints were inconsistent with the facts as we knew them. But in the face of this overwhelming show of emotion we did not care; Mamma was happy again, and with this transformation we were properly bribed. We were totally dependent on her; and we interpreted this dependence as intense love. Meanwhile, Mamma had planted in us a distrust of Papa; it was only years later that we understood him as the sweet, generous man he always was.

Once Mamma left us in Barcelona while she went to America for a short visit. We were then eight, going on nine, and we had not yet seen our own country. We asked to be taken with her. Mamma did not approve, so we stayed home with Papa. But a week or so after Mamma left, we had a wonderful surprise. Dr. Mann, our family physician and friend, arrived at the house with four pigeons—a pair for each of us. Carlos, the butler—also our friend—built us a cage for them on the terrace. The pigeons seemed happy in their new home, and we promptly named them. They were Isabella and Ferdinand, Jeanne and Carlos. One day, when we got home from school, our friend Carlos met us at the door. "I have news for you, twins," he said, leading us to the pigeon cote. "Look, they have laid eggs and are sitting on them. Someday soon you will have baby pigeons."

"When? How soon?" we asked.

Carlos smiled. "You will have to wait," he said. "Nature takes its own time."

Naturally, we were excited. We had never had any pets of our own before, much less baby pigeons. Every day after school we would sit by the hour, watching the nesting birds. We sat in silence, afraid that any sound might disturb the delicate balance of nature. Then one day as we clambered up to the terrace we heard Carlos calling to us. "Look, twins," he said, "they are here —the little pigeons—six of them."

We ran to the nest, and we were horrified. We had expected soft, fluffy little things—like the baby chicks you see at Easter. Instead, we saw six wet, ugly little creatures with heads bigger than their bodies. We were ready to cry. But Carlos comforted us. "Wait and see," he said. "In a few days they will be beautiful." And they were.

Meanwhile, we racked our brains trying to find suitable names for them. Mamma returned from America. "Come, Mamma," I said. "Come outside and see what a beautiful sight we have to show you."

Mamma took one look at our baby pigeons; then, to our horror, she ordered them killed. From inside the house we heard her say to Carlos, "Let the parent pigeons loose, Carlos. Then kill the baby pigeons. We will have them for dinner."

"Oh, no, Mamma!" Gloria wailed; "please let them stay at least until they are old enough to fly away." Now, very near hysteria, we screamed in turn: "Don't kill them! Don't kill them! Why? Why? They're so little—they don't take up any room at all."

All our pleading left Mamma cold. Her mind was set.

"Why are you doing this?" I screamed, as she turned to leave. "Why?"

"Why?" Mamma looked at me with ice in her eyes; I had dared to question her orders. "Because," she said, "my dear grandmamma always told me that pigeons bring misfortune, bad luck, and poverty into a house—and my dear grandmamma was always right."

Gloria and I put our arms around each other and cried helplessly and in desperation; this was our first great grief. But whether we were brokenhearted or not, that night we were given squab for dinner. Carlos must have been crying, too, for as he served our baby pigeons we noticed that his eyes were red and swollen.

Heads down, out of the corners of our eyes we watched Mamma. "Eat your dinner," she commanded.

"Oh, no, no, Mamma," Gloria said pathetically. "We cannot eat our babies."

"Stop this nonsense," Mamma snapped. "Eat your dinner or leave the room."

The tears again started down our cheeks. Together we got up and left the room. Through the fog of our feelings we were conscious of her brittle voice announcing, "No dessert for a week."

We went to our room and sobbed until we were exhausted. "I don't care if we never have dessert again," Gloria wailed. "I only want to bring our baby pigeons back to life." And together we cursed this ogress of a grandmother, a woman we had never seen—and would never see—who seemed to stand for everything that didn't matter, and who seemed to destroy everything that did.

CHAPTER II

Hither and Yon

Thelma

In 1913 Papa was appointed Consul General at Hamburg. On hearing the news, Mamma exploded. We heard her say to Papa, stamping her foot, "This is final, Harry. I'm not going to take the children to that dreadful country. And that's that."

Papa shrugged his shoulders. "Have it your own way," he said. "You always do. But I'm going to miss you and the children." Apparently Papa had had all he could take of Mamma's whims and tantrums; he was now preparing to lead his own life in his own way.

Mamma had a phobia about Germans, as she had about money. I don't suppose it is possible to pinpoint the origin of phobias; their roots seem imbedded in some dark, disturbed area of the brain, and they are not necessarily related to actual events or experiences. But it seems clear that Mamma's hatred of Germans began early—probably under the tutelage and with the encouragement of her "dear" grandmamma who was so vehement against pigeons. Her father, General Kilpatrick, when American Minister to Chile, had been delegated to mediate the Tacna Arica, a border dispute between Chile and Peru; the territory included rich saltpeter mines claimed by the Germans, and at this time in Chile feeling ran high against the Germans.

At any rate, Mamma stood firm on her refusal to set foot in Germany; and Papa went alone to his post in Hamburg. Mamma meanwhile moved us all to a small apartment in Barcelona. And with this move Mamma began the penny-pinching which we were to know—unnecessarily, it seems—for many years to come. Gone was our terrace, our big playroom; gone was the warm and thoughtful Carlos—and most of the other servants. Mamma had decided to keep only Jeanne, our nurse, and Maria, who became the maid-of-all-work. We gave Maria, affectionately, a nickname; we called her "Maria the Horse"—because Mamma worked her like a horse. Originally, she had been Mamma's personal maid, but after Papa left she did everything.

Mamma's insidious innuendoes relating to Papa did not stop with his departure. One day she said bitterly, "Your father doesn't send me enough money to keep body and soul together. I suppose he's spending a fortune on some German woman. He doesn't care what becomes of us."

Even at this time Mamma's complaints did not make sense. Papa had always been kind to us, and when he was with us, we always had everything. But whenever we questioned what Mamma said, she would unleash her tears, saying pathetically, "You don't understand. You don't know your father." Then, with the gestures of a Bernhardt, she would declaim: "Oh, how I suffer! How can he treat his children so?"

But we were not yet wise enough to stand up to Mamma's distortions. Mamma dominated us. We needed her; disturbed and disturbing as she was, she was all we had to cling to. And when Mamma indulged herself in hysterics and mock-heroics, we suffered through contagion; our only world was threatened. We would rush to her and try to be comforting. "Please, Mamma," I would say, "don't cry. You have us and we have you. And we love you so much. We don't care if Papa is mean. We have each other—and we always will have each other."

She naturally attempted to make us consider ourselves indirect victims of Papa's self-indulgence. "You had both better marry rich men," she would say with Cassandra-like solemnity. "You're extravagant, you know. You never save. You give everything away. If you want to play at being Lady Bountiful, you had better marry someone who can give you what you need. When your father dies, you know, there won't be very much to divide among you children, and he probably has squandered even that little bit on his mistresses."

Yet for all this our life in our new home was, on the whole, a happy one. The darkest times were the days Mamma received letters from Germany. There was, for example, the time Papa described his meeting with the Kaiser:

"'Last night I dined on Albert Ballin's yacht.'" Mamma was reading aloud from Papa's letter. "'Herr Ballin is the president of the Hamburg-American Line. The Emperor was his guest.'" The letter went on to describe the dinner. We found the details exciting. Papa told of the Kaiser's valet who brought the Emperor a special knifelike fork which made it possible for him to cut his food adequately with his left hand; he gave us a graphic picture of the Emperor resting his deformed right arm on the dinner table. But to Mamma all this reporting was a veiled description of royal orgies. "That's your father for you. There he is, dining on yachts, cavorting with emperors and God knows whom, and all the while I sit here looking after you children."

None of us had courage enough to ask, "Why are we here? Why don't we join Papa?"

One day, a few months later, Dr. Mann joined us for lunch. Mamma sat at the head of the table. She seemed preoccupied. Suddenly turning to Dr. Mann, she said, "Doctor, I had a letter from Harry yesterday. He says the assassination of Austria's Grand Duke might have grave repercussions. It might even mean war."

Gloria and I glanced at each other. We could not understand. "War?" "Austria?" "Assassination?" What did these things have to do with us, happy in Spain? Why did Mamma look so worried? We looked at Dr. Mann for the answer, but he, too, sat in deep thought, his head lowered, his great white beard almost reaching the top of the table. Then, slowly raising his head, he turned to Mamma, and said, "Don't worry, Laura. Harry may be exaggerating the seriousness of the situation. It may pass over."

Mamma started to cry. Great tears rolled down her face. These were not the hysterical, tempestuous tears we knew so well. These went far deeper.

"Why don't you stay here in Barcelona for the time being? You will all be safe here." He took her hand. "Perhaps you are making things worse than they are, Laura," he said. "The situation may not be as serious as you think."

During the next few days a thick gloom settled over our lives. Our cramped apartment seemed like the House of Usher, waiting, in ominous calm, for the walls to crumble. Then the war came. The ominous calm gave way to hysteria. Through the open windows we heard frenzied shouting in the streets: *"Es la guerra! Es la guerra!"* Mamma dashed to our room and held us close to her. "I knew it! I knew it!" she shouted. "Those barbarians! Those assassins! We will never see Papa alive again! I know it! I know it!"

We stood there, her arms about us, clutching us in frenzy. Mamma's panic extended to us; we, too, were frozen with fear. At this moment Jeanne intervened tactfully. "Mrs. Morgan," she said in a calm voice, "don't you think it's time for the twins to take their walk?"

Mamma's panic turned instantly to rage. "Do what you like with them," she snapped, then stalked out of the room.

What had we done? "Oh, Mamma, Mamma," Gloria pleaded. "Come back to us. We love you. Don't leave us."

But now Jeanne was mad. "Stop this nonsense," she said. "Go wash your faces and get ready for your walk." Meekly we did as we were bidden.

Mamma's hysterics must have overbalanced her reason, for a few days later she announced she was taking us all to England.

Why? Barcelona was so safe and friendly. It had been our home for many years. And Spain was not at war. The obvious thing to do was to remain where we were; but Mamma never did the obvious thing.

Our sister Consuelo, Mamma, and we left Barcelona early in August of 1914. Jeanne was not coming with us; she wanted to return to her family in France. Poor "Maria the Horse" was also left behind.

The trip, as we remember it, was a nightmare. The train taking us to Bilboa was jammed. Mamma had not been able to secure sleepers; third class was the best she could manage. How we hated the confusion, the rush, the melee of that trip. We would take turns sitting; there were not enough places for all of us. If we thought the trip was a nightmare, it must have been agony for Mamma.

The voyage from Bilboa to England was not much better. The ship was small, hardly able to accommodate half the people that crowded her. We huddled together against the cold, damp night air and tried to sleep on the hard deck. I am sure Mamma never closed her eyes the whole night through. I vaguely remember her gently replacing a rug that must have slipped in our restless sleep, her hand placed tenderly on us, reassuringly. What a strange woman this mother of ours was! What a paradox! In one breath she was selfish, demanding, arrogant; in the next loving, kind, tender, indulgent. The contradiction confused us then, as in retrospect it still does.

We all breathed a sigh of relief when we sighted England. The Hyde Park Hotel was to be our first home in London, but not for long. Mamma had entered us in Strathalham House, a French boarding school conducted by Mademoiselle Dessin. As soon as we were settled, she reversed her anti-German stand and left for Hamburg.

This was our first experience away from home. We missed Mamma. We were homesick. We were miserable. Our few words of English were of no help to us. The English could not understand us, nor we them. We could talk only with a few French and Belgian girls who were as miserable as we were.

The autumn and winter of 1914 were frightfully cold in London. We missed the friendly, warm country we had left. We suffered from chilblains, from the boiled food, from those eternal Brussels sprouts, those awful blue serge uniforms, and those rough black cotton stockings. Nothing is more depressing than an English schoolgirl's outfit. But what we hated most of all were the daily walks we were forced to take, rain, fog, or shine. In our blue serge creations we were marched two by two to museums, to the Tower of London, and sometimes—this to our delight—to the gardens at Kew. There is nothing more beautiful than Kew in the spring.

The war at first did not affect us much, save for a night air raid every now and then. Then we would be rushed to the cellar. When the all-clear sounded we would return sleepily to our beds. We learned to roll bandages. We learned to knit.

Just after Christmas we got a letter from Mamma, announcing her return to London. She would be with us within the week. We jumped up and down. We hugged each other. We went wild. Mamma was coming back.

The great day arrived and we got permission to spend the weekend with her. As the chaperone looked up at the number of the address we had given her, she said, "Are you sure this is the right address?" We took out Mamma's letter. There was no mistake.

"H-m," we heard her mumble, "a boardinghouse."

We didn't care whether it was a boardinghouse or St. James's Palace. Mamma was inside waiting for us. When the door opened, we flew to her. Partly in English, but mostly in Spanish, we told her how we had missed her, how we loved her.

"Now, twins, you must speak English," she said, with her

strong Spanish accent. "You know you're little American girls. Speak English from now on."

"Yes, yes, of course," I said. At that moment we would have done anything to please her—to bribe her to keep us with her.

"But wait, *queridas*," she said, smiling, "you haven't heard the best news yet. We are all going to spend the summer holidays with your father in Germany."

That weekend passed all too soon. Being with Mamma again only brought to a focus all the loneliness we had suffered at boarding school. We felt free once more. Mamma's ways were irrational and often cruel, but at least they were familiar; there is a feeling of liberation whenever one comes back to what is warm and familiar, no matter how tyrannical it may really be. As I look back, I am sure that Mademoiselle Dessin did everything within her power to make us happy. But we were such little misfits at Strathalham House. Our earlier childhood had been so erratically directed, so lacking in sensible discipline, that we must have been more than she could cope with. And, on top of this, we were so alien—so proudly, professionally Spanish!

Just before we left Mamma to go back to school, the recollection of the thoughtless if not snobbish remark of the chaperone prompted me to ask Mamma about the boardinghouse. "Why are you staying in this awful place?" I asked, looking at the faded green curtains and the shabby plush upholstery. "The Hyde Park Hotel was so nice. We don't like to see you living here."

"Do you think I like this any more than you do?" she shouted. "I have told you a thousand times your father won't give me enough money to keep body and soul together. I just have to scrimp and save. If I don't, what is to become of all of us?"

We retreated at once. "Of course, Mamma," Gloria said soothingly, "we understand." The last thing we wanted, at that time, was to have Mamma angry with us. Of course we did not understand. But this was no moment for parliamentary debate.

The next few months were an agony. We were waiting for

liberation; and no two prisoners in Siberia could have waited more anxiously for the day of reprieve. June, it seemed, would never come. We did our school chores, wore our drab uniforms without complaint, and took our walks dutifully in the damp English air.

At last June arrived; we were to leave our prison and sally forth to high adventure—a new country, a new life, fun, Papa.

Our apartments at the Hotel Vier Jahreszeiten were large and comfortable; we were once again surrounded with all the luxuries we had always had when we were with Papa. No more was there the scrimping Mamma insisted on, with the explanation that Papa deliberately deprived her—and us—of the pleasant things of life. Gloria and I had a large bedroom overlooking a beautiful garden; we also had a large classroom in which we were to study with our governess. We were introduced to this governess, Frau Hoffmann, soon after we arrived. She was what the Germans call *hoch geboren*; and, like a noncommissioned officer, she made it a special point to assert her rank. We hated her from the moment she came into our lives; and her distaste for us seemed equally strong. She considered us undisciplined, self-willed brats, which we undoubtedly were; but she also considered it her duty, a German duty—which is a kind of perpetual self-flagellation— to teach us manners, German manners. The social graces, as she interpreted them, required us to kiss the hands of married women and to stand whenever she entered the room.

When Mamma learned of Frau Hoffmann's orders to us, all of her lifelong hatred of things German rose in her. "No, *Fräulein!*" she bellowed, in the process demoting Frau Hoffmann to the status of an unmarried woman. Then she intensified the insult: "My daughters will never be taught to kiss a woman's hand, nor to rise when a servant enters the room."

Frau Hoffmann shot Mamma a look of disdain, as if to say, "What can you expect from such a woman?" Then she spun stiffly on her heels and left the room. We expected Mamma at that moment either to go into her standard hysterics, or else give Frau Hoffmann her walking papers. She did neither. She merely turned to us and said, with supreme detachment, "You see, I always told you the Germans were barbarians. Think of *my* daughters kissing German women's hands! Never!" Nevertheless, we were left in the scarcely sympathetic care of this new governess. Meanwhile, Mamma, ever unpredictable, announced calmly that Papa was expecting us to have tea with him at the Consulate. "Come, twins," she added, "we must hurry."

We loved to go to the Consulate; there exciting things were always happening. Each day the war situation created new emergencies. Papa had organized a committee of American businessmen, who contributed funds to aid Americans stranded in Hamburg. The money from this emergency reservoir was doled out weekly. Many of the visitors to the Consulate were Americans who could no longer get money from home, nor enough money to pay their passage home; others were Germans who had become American citizens and now found themselves caught between the jaws of an international vise. Although Papa at that time had a large staff to help him, he saw personally as many callers as he could. His patience was unending; he not only took care of American consular affairs, but doubled for the now absent British and French consuls. He once described to us how in the middle of the night of August 3, 1914, Sir Walter Hearn, the British Consul General, had waked him from a sound sleep and asked his help to seal the archives and destroy the codes and confidential files in the British Consulate; the German government had given him only a few hours in which to pack and leave the country. Papa and Sir Walter worked through what remained of the night.

When we first arrived from England we had with us white middy blouses Mamma had bought for us at Selfridge's, in London. The pockets of those middy blouses were embroidered with American and British flags in bright colors. Not giving any thought to what we were doing, much less realizing the possible consequences, we sailed out into the streets of Hamburg one day gaily flaunting the Stars and Stripes and the Union Jack.

Frau Hoffmann was not a naturally observant woman. Walking a few steps in front of us, she found it hard to understand why a little boy, pointing his finger at us, shouted belligerently, "*Schweinehund Englisher! Schweinehund Englisher!*" She turned quickly and looked at us. Then she noticed the flags. "*Ach, mein Gott,*" she screamed, and made a grab for us. But by this time we were thoroughly scared. We ducked away from her and bolted down the street. I was in the lead; Gloria, panting behind me, shouted, "What's happened? What have we done now?"

"Don't be an idiot!" I screamed back over my shoulder. "This is no time to ask questions. Just run!"

We ran, but not fast enough. A woman caught up with us and started to tear off the offensive pockets. By this time we had a mob around us, everybody screaming, everybody shouting, everybody pulling at us. Frau Hoffmann finally managed to get through the mob. Grabbing us with a firm hold, she yelled at them, "Stop! Stop! These are the daughters of Mr. Morgan, the American Consul General."

I don't know whether it was the American Consul part or the General part, but the crowd slowly dispersed, glaring at us. Germans have always had great respect for rank and, after all, she had said "General."

"Wait till I get you home," Frau Hoffmann said threateningly as she dragged us back to the hotel.

"Wait till Mamma hears about this," I snapped back at her.

When Mamma saw us, our clothes torn and disheveled, and my nose bleeding, she was in a rage. Gloria, taking a page out of Mamma's book, screamed, "Look, Mamma, look what these Huns have done to us! Look at what they've done to Thelma—she's bleeding to death."

Mamma glowered at our governess. "What is the meaning of this, Frau Hoffmann?" she demanded. "What have you done to them?" Her tone was granite hard; and her cold, penetrating look would have frightened a woman even stronger than Frau Hoffmann.

The governess, backing toward the door, explained to Mamma about the middy blouses. "Surely," she said, justifying herself, "surely I can expect children of their age to dress themselves."

"Frau Hoffmann," Mamma answered scathingly—and she looked five inches taller at this moment—"I did not engage you to dress my children. I engaged you to see that they were properly dressed. You may leave the room."

This was not the Mamma of tantrums and hysterics; this was our Mamma—dignified, stately, calm; this was the way we wanted to think of her. This was the Mamma we loved.

For the most part we followed Papa's instructions obediently—we spoke only Spanish in public. But one day, going up in the hotel elevator to our rooms, we noticed next to us a German officer standing at attention—standing with the special Cleopatra's Needle stiffness that only German officers seem capable of assuming. His spiked helmet seemed glued to his head, his handle-bar mustache stood out in arrogant pride. The sight of so much pomp and pretense was too much for us; Gloria and I immediately started to chatter in English.

At once the mustache quivered. The officer glared at us ferociously. "How dare you speak English?" he bellowed at us in his rough Prussian English. "Shut up!"

With all the dignity we could muster, we turned to him and said, "We are not speaking English, we are speaking American. And we think it is you who should shut up."

"Stop this elevator at once," the officer roared at the elevator girl, who was thoroughly frightened.

"*Ja*, Herr General von Hindenburg," she said, her voice quavering, "*ja, mein General*." She brought the car to a sudden stop and threw open the doors. We flew. We were halfway up the stairs before we heard the great champion of *Kultur* yell, "Get out! Get out!"

A time came when Mamma was to be presented to the Kaiser. We wanted to be presented with her. By then we had learned who General von Hindenburg was; and as we had acquired a somewhat personal interest in his mustache, we had the kind of desire now to be found only among bobby-sox autograph hunters to appraise the Kaiser's famous mustache and compare it for length and curvature with the General's. To console us for not meeting the Kaiser, Mamma took us with her to Berlin and allowed us to have tea at the Embassy with Mrs. Gerard. The Ambassador's wife seemed a poor substitute for Emperor Wilhelm; she could not, under any circumstances, offer us a mustache to contemplate; but this was to be our first opportunity to attend a tea party for grownups, and we were thrilled. We were dressed in our prettiest white frocks. Facing us in the carriage on our way to the Embassy, Mamma gave us our last-minute instructions. "Now remember, twins," she said, "don't speak until you are spoken to—and behave yourselves."

The Embassy was large, ornate, and—to our eyes—beautiful. Mrs. Gerard had been an old friend of Mamma's. She rose from the tea table as we entered, and said, "Laura, how nice to see you!" Then, looking at us, she added, "So these are the twins I have been hearing so much about."

The last remark seemed cryptic. Had we been in so much trouble that word of us had been sent to the American Embassy in Berlin? Or had Papa merely been boasting? Apparently all was well, because Mrs. Gerard smiled at us warmly and said, "Come, twins. Do sit down and have some tea and cake."

We sat down timidly. We became worried, however, when we discovered that there was no table on which to rest the cup and saucer and the plate of cake that were handed us. It seemed to us that Mrs. Gerard was quite thoughtless. Gloria looked over to me to see how I was handling the acrobatics of the ceremony. I, who was served first, put the cake plate on my lap. With two hands I clutched the cup and saucer. I saw a determined look in Gloria's eye, and I knew she was saying to herself, "If Thelma can do it, so can I."

As I raised my teacup to my lips, I heard the crash. Gloria had not quite made it. I looked at her from the corner of my eye; she had definitely not quite made it. The cake and broken china were a mess on the floor; the spilt tea made a spreading stain on her lap. She tried to apologize—half in English, half in Spanish.

Mrs. Gerard cut her short. "That's quite all right, Gloria," she said. "The maid will bring you another cup." And to Mamma she added, with dubious diplomacy, "Please, Laura, don't worry. You know how children are."

I was furious at Mrs. Gerard—"You know how children are!" She "knew," indeed! This is the kind of diplomacy that creates wars; if she knew how and what children are, she should have known that their laps are not as big as grownups' and were never intended to balance a small buffet. But Mamma characteristically put all the blame on the German nation. "I knew it," she said angrily, on our way home. "Frau Hoffmann can't even teach children how to behave at a tea. All she can teach them is how to kiss women's hands. But what can you expect? These Germans!"

A month or so later Mamma decided to put us in school in Switzerland. One afternoon she went out to get the necessary exit permits and visas. We were at home with Papa, who entertained us by reading aloud from "The Lady of the Lake"—one of his favorite poems. Papa was always a romanticist; he belonged, by nature, to the world of Walter Scott. We were deeply engrossed in the poem when suddenly the door of Papa's study flew open and Mamma stormed into the room. "Harry," she shouted, "what is the meaning of this?"

Papa carefully closed the book. "The meaning of what, Laura?"

"What? What, indeed! These filthy Germans have just informed me that should I leave the country they will not allow me to return. When I asked why in heaven's name not, they politely told me that while they were delighted to have me remain in Germany, they would prefer I do not leave again till the end of the war. What do they mean, Harry?" she said, stamping her foot. "Answer me!"

Since Mamma had come to live with Papa in Hamburg, she had made many trips out of the country—including her visits to us in England. Papa tried patiently to explain to her how this travel might be regarded by a country at war. "Now look here, Laura," he said. "You must understand what all this means. A serious war is on. And you have insisted on making trips to England—an enemy country; to Switzerland, to Holland, to England again, and then each time come back to Germany. I have told you before, the authorities here consider your journeys highly suspicious."

This was too much for Mamma. Her breath had now come back to her. "What do you mean?" she screamed. "Do they think I am a spy?"

"Damn it all, Laura," Papa answered, for once losing his calm, "this is their country. And they are at war. And they have a perfect right to question any scatterbrained woman who decides, at the drop of a hat, to come and go as she pleases."

For once in her life Mamma was speechless. She simply stood in the middle of the room and glared at Papa. Gloria winked at me. "Papa," she whispered, "is really mad."

Papa must have overheard this whisper, because he slowly turned around, faced us, and said, "Twins, I think you had better leave the room."

Reluctantly we got up and moved toward the door. From the hall we heard Mamma's voice, now shifted to the tone she used for irrevocable decisions. "Very well, Harry," she said, "we are going to Switzerland."

HITHER AND YON

The next few days were not pleasant. Papa was angry with Mamma. Mamma was angry with Papa. The only one in the household who was pleased was Frau Hoffmann; she beamed; her face was radiant with a beatific glow. Frau Hoffmann, I am sure, was delighted with the prospect of saying good-by to the whole confusing Morgan family. Our own reactions were mixed. We were happy at the thought of leaving Germany and moving to a country where we could understand and be understood. On the other hand, we hated to leave Papa. We also felt we were abandoning our responsibilities; we had been visiting the wounded British soldiers in the military hospital in Hamburg; we believed they depended on us, and would miss us.

We were heartbroken when Papa said good-by to us on the train. "Don't cry, twins," he said gently. "I'll come to see you soon."

We reached the German-Swiss frontier late that night. The cold was intense; the mountain slopes were blanketed in snow. The passengers on our train were herded into another train, which was to take us into Switzerland. As we got up to follow them, a German in uniform approached Mamma and said, "Mrs. Morgan, will you follow me?"

"What next?" we heard Mamma say to herself.

We were taken into a wooden shack lighted only by kerosene lamps. An acrid, vile smell from an old-fashioned oil stove permeated the room. We all huddled together, partly for warmth but mostly from fright. It was long past midnight when a tough-looking woman, who could well have been a movie version of a hard-boiled prison matron, came into the room. Without a word she walked up to Mamma and roughly started taking down her hair. Mamma must have been in a state of shock for she meekly allowed her to continue.

Then, to our horror, we heard the woman tell her to undress. Mamma quietly and deliberately did as she was bidden. The woman then took the clothes and handed them to someone outside the door.

Out of a bowl of what looked like dirty water she took a sponge and proceeded to wash Mamma's back. We presume now she was in search of invisible writing. Then, turning to us, she said, "Now, *kinder*, it's your turn."

When our clothes were returned to us, we were taken to another room, where our trunks and suitcases were standing open, being gone through with a fine-tooth comb. All the hems and linings of our clothes had been ripped. All printed and written material had been set aside, including Mamma's little mother-of-pearl prayer book her grandmother had given her on the day of her First Communion. One of the guards picked it up and turned its pages. Then we heard Mamma say to him, in a tone like the rat-tat-tat of a machine gun: "Take it and read it! You need it!"

By the time the ordeal of our examinations was over, the train we were to have been on had long since departed. We stood for many freezing hours waiting for the next train that could take us into Switzerland. When we finally arrived in Montreux, we were convinced of the truth of Mamma's "dear, dear grandmamma's" opinion: The Boches *were* barbarians.

In Montreux we stayed in a charming residential hotel set in the center of a large park. Mamma was delighted to find several of her old friends there: Amelia Ortuza and her mother, who had been a Figueroa and was related to Mamma; and Mimi Pecchi, a niece of Pope Benedict. Also at the hotel was the Infanta Eulalia, who was my godmother.

Although Mamma remained at the hotel, Gloria and I were moved to a nearby boarding school. Our recollections of that school are vague; we were there only a short time. What I recall are the delightful weekends we spent with Mamma, and the pleasant days we had rowing on Lake Geneva, picknicking near the Château de Chillon, where the "prisoner" was held; and going up and down the funicular railway.

Papa arrived in Montreux on our birthday, making it a doubly significant occasion. We were all together again; and we were terribly happy. But that day was also important to us for the news we picked up through a half-opened door in Mamma's hotel suite. We heard Papa's voice saying, "The *New Amsterdam* sails for New York on the fourth of September. You will have to board her at Plymouth."

We pricked up our ears. This meant another move—this time to America. But could we go along? At eleven we had become veteran diplomats, depending largely on our own wits to keep ourselves from being shunted off to places where we were strange, unhappy, or alone. And the world of Papa and Mamma, with its secrets, its wars, and—to us—its irrational and unpredictable twists, was not easy to cope with.

Then we heard Papa's voice rise; once again, it seemed, he was losing his patience. "I'd loathe to ask for a transfer at a time like this," he said to Mamma, "a time when the world is in such chaos, and every conscientious diplomat is sticking to his post. You could have made it possible for me also to perform my duties properly, but no, Laura, oh, no, not you! Your arrogance, your instability, your wanton and utter disregard of my position and my wishes have forced me to make this trip."

He paused for a moment. Then, in a quieter tone, he continued: "No one knows how long this bloody war is going to last. And how can I remain in a country to which my wife is not allowed to return—where, in fact, she is even *persona non grata*? Don't you realize, damn it, that I want you and the children with me? Why, in heaven's name, did you have to enroll Consuelo and the twins in that school in Paris? Surely even you must realize that they would be safer here."

"Now, let's not argue about that any more, Harry," Mamma answered. "I've already told you that all the arrangements have been made. We leave for Paris Thursday. Besides, the twins have to improve their French; they're already speaking with a Swiss accent."

Gloria and I looked at each other; so this was it. We were being shipped to France. If we wanted to get to America, we had to do something—and do it quickly.

That night after dinner, when Papa was comfortably settled and smoking his cigar, we decided to attack. Together we threw our arms around him. "Oh, Papa," I said pleadingly, "can we go, too?"

"Go? Go where?"

"Why, to America, of course," Gloria said. "We heard you talking to Mamma about it this afternoon."

Papa smiled. "I see," he said. "My twins have long ears. But the answer is no—not at this time, darlings. The trip is much too dangerous." Then, noticing our look of disappointment, he pulled us close to him and tried to explain. "You know I'd love to take you two to America with us, but this is no time for children to be crossing the Atlantic. The ocean is heavily mined. Our ship might be blown up at any time."

"Well, if you and Mamma are going to be blown up," Gloria said, "we want to be blown up with you."

Hugging us, he said, "And what makes you think I could get accommodations for you? It's difficult in wartime, you know."

"Oh yes, you can; you can do anything."

"That's enough of this," Mamma interrupted. "The idea is preposterous. The answer is no, and that's final."

Looking up at Papa, we howled, "You promised, you promised us. Please!"

The hours passed and we got nowhere. The following night Papa returned to Hamburg. Even at the station we pleaded; but our last efforts were no more effective than our first. "No, darlings, not this time," Papa repeated firmly from the steps of his train; then he was gone.

HITHER AND YON

Early the next morning I woke with an idea burning my brain. I had the solution; I had a plan. Trembling with excitement, I rushed over to Gloria's bed and shook her. "Wake up, Gloria!" I shouted. "Wake up! I've got it! I've got it!"

"What's happened?" Gloria asked, still half asleep. "You've got what?"

"Gloria, wake up," I said, still shaking her. "We're going to America."

The magic word "America" waked her like a glass of cold water thrown in her face. "America? Oh, Thelma, how? When?"

"Listen to me," I said, getting quickly down to business. "We are supposed to leave for Paris tomorrow morning. Well, this afternoon we are going to send a telegram to the American Consulate at Rotterdam—and sign Papa's name to it."

Gloria was puzzled. She was delighted with my enthusiasm, but naturally I had not made very much sense.

"What," she asked reasonably, "are we going to say in the telegram?"

"Simply this," I said. "I've thought it all out: 'Secure accommodations for twin daughters of Consul General Harry Hays Morgan sailing on the *S.S. Amsterdam*, September 4. Harry Morgan.'" Then, with more confidence than I really felt, I added, "Papa won't hear about this until he gets to Rotterdam and gets on the ship, and we won't tell Mamma until we get to Paris."

Gloria was too excited to argue. All she said was, "Don't you think the telegram would sound more like Papa if we put a 'kindly' before the 'secure'?" I agreed.

At lunch Mamma asked us what we had planned for the afternoon. Gloria looked at me. I noticed she had her fingers crossed. Crossing mine, I said innocently, "We thought we might go for a walk by the lake."

"That will be nice." We breathed a sigh of relief. Suppose Mamma had made other plans for us?

As we approached the telegraph office, our knees were shaking. Suppose we were too young to send telegrams? Suppose we didn't have enough money? Suppose the clerk called Mamma to ask if it was all right? Realizing Gloria was thinking the same things, and more for courage than anything else, I grabbed Gloria's hand and rushed in. "After all, Gloria," I said, "the only thing Mamma can do to us is kill us."

The next thing we knew we were out again on the street and the telegram was on its way.

From the train windows, as we crossed into France, we saw the horrors of war for the first time. We saw whole villages and towns burned to the ground. The roads were thronged with homeless people. We passed factory after factory, now no more than tangled masses of girders and rubble. Trainloads of wounded rumbled past our car. On all sides we saw at firsthand the suffering, the tragedy, and the horrors an invading army can inflict on a country.

Paris was far from the gay city Mamma had told us so much about. We saw a somber Paris, gray, a city enshrouded in a heavy stillness. Everywhere women were in mourning. Old men shuffled about aimlessly; here and there were young men, crippled, staring vacantly into space, pain and helplessness etched in their faces—as in the faces of the men depicted by Goya in the "Horrors of War." Mamma had made reservations for us at the Hotel Regina, on the Rue de Rivoli. It was dark when we got to the hotel. We were all tired, depressed, hungry.

"After dinner and a hot bath we will all feel better," Mamma said cheerfully, as we were shown to our rooms. "Then we'll all go to bed early. There is so much to do in the morning. I haven't much time, and I have to get the two of you and Consuelo ready for school."

Gloria and I looked at each other, and our hearts sank. The

time had come to tell Mamma. But how? Would she believe us? Would she be furious? Would she even take us? Or would she skin us alive? When we had planned what we were going to tell her, it had all seemed so easy. Now, faced with it, it was not easy at all. We were scared. "Here goes, Gloria," I whispered, and I took the plunge.

"We're going to America, Mamma," I said gaily. "We're going to America, too. Surprise! Surprise!"

"What are you talking about?" Mamma snapped. "What is the meaning of all this nonsense? Who said you could go?"

"Papa did," Gloria said.

"Your father did? How? When?"

"Just before he left for Germany. It was to be a surprise for you and a birthday present for us. Isn't Papa wonderful?"

Mamma stood there dumfounded, glaring at us. "I don't believe one word of this. I don't believe your father would do such a preposterous thing without telling me. He must be mad. Oh, no; I just don't believe it."

Grabbing hold of us, she shook us both so violently we thought our heads would drop off. "Are you telling me the truth? Answer me."

I wished I had never thought of this idea. I wished I could back out, but I was far too scared to think of what to say. "Yes, yes; it's true," I blabbered. "Papa said we could."

Mamma let go of us abruptly. "I don't believe a word of it. You're lying to me. I'm going to wire the Holland American Line at once and ask if your father has made reservations for you, and I hope for your sakes the answer is yes." Little did she know how fervently we hoped so, too.

The next few days were agony for us. We lived in fear and terror of what the answer would be, and we managed to keep well out of Mamma's way.

When we returned to the hotel one afternoon the desk clerk handed her a telegram. To our surprise, she did not open it at once. Instead, she walked deliberately to the elevator. Following behind, we wondered anxiously what our fate was to be. On the way up, tapping the telegram slowly against her gloved hand, she said, "Now, I'll know the truth, or whether you have been lying to me."

We made a dash for our room. We didn't want to be in front of Mamma when the bomb exploded.

"Oh, no, twins; no, you don't," Mamma said. "I want you here when I open this telegram. Sit down."

She deliberately took off her hat, leisurely removed her gloves, took off her coat and carefully hung it in the cupboard. We squirmed in our chairs. Would she never open that telegram?

Finally we heard her say, "I am going to open this telegram in front of you and I'm going to read it aloud." We took a quick look at each other and held our breath. Then, as if from a distance, came the ominous words: "'This is to confirm accommodations for daughters of Consul Morgan, *S.S. New Amsterdam* sailing September 4 Holland American Line.' *Madre de Dios*," Mamma shrieked; "it's true!"

It was only then that we breathed again. At this point we even believed our own story.

When Mamma got over her shock, she began one of her standard tirades against Papa: "So he thinks I'm irresponsible and unstable? What does he think this madness is? At least I advise him of my plans, but not your father. He lets you tell me and calls it a surprise."

To our utter amazement she then added, almost gaily, "Ah well, perhaps it's all for the best anyway."

The only thing we remember in the hectic days that followed was the touch of remorse felt at leaving Consuelo alone in that terrible school Mamma had picked out for us. She looked so forlorn and frightened as she stood in the doorway waving good-by to us. Looking back on it now, we can't understand what possessed Mamma to leave Consuelo alone in Paris, with the German army pounding at the gates of the city. The rumbling of guns in the distance could be clearly heard the day we left. What was Mamma thinking about when she left a fourteen-year-old girl in a school she knew practically nothing about? We had no relatives in France; and Mamma's friends there had scattered at the outbreak of hostilities. We would like to think she did not realize the enormity of what she was doing.

Our trip to Plymouth was uneventful. We landed at five in the morning. Later that morning, when we were on the tender taking us to the *New Amsterdam*, Mamma looked at us strangely. "What's the matter with you two?" she asked. "You look green. Don't tell me you're going to be sick even before we get on the ship." Little did she know how sick we were—although not for the reasons she thought.

"Why don't you take a walk up and down the deck?" Mamma suggested. "You'll feel better."

When Gloria and I were alone, I suddenly knew what we should do: confess. "Gloria," I said, "we've got to tell Mamma everything before we see Papa. That's the only way we can save ourselves."

Gloria was skeptical. "Do you think Mamma will really help? Or will we just be getting ourselves double trouble?"

"I don't know," I answered. "You can never tell what Mamma will do. We can only hope."

We were nearly alongside the *New Amsterdam* when we got up enough courage to tell Mamma what we had done. "Papa didn't get the reservations," we said together, our words tumbling over one another. "Papa didn't do it. We did." We told her how we had sent the telegram; we told her how we had lied; we told her everything.

"Oh, twins, how could you?" Mamma said, when the story finally made sense to her. "Your father is going to be furious. How could you think of doing such a thing? He's sure to think I plotted all this with you."

We started crying. And then Mamma, whose ways could never be predicted, hugged us tight. "Don't be scared, *queridas*," she said, "I'll help you. Now stop crying."

Papa met us at the gangplank, glaring at us. "Follow me, Laura," he said curtly. "And you, too, twins." Meekly we traipsed behind Mamma; there was nothing else to do. He led us to his cabin. Then, turning to Mamma, he said in a low, gentle, but extremely austere voice, "Well, Laura, perhaps now you will kindly explain."

Before he could go on, Gloria and I indulged in an orgy of confession. We explained that we had engineered this trip all by ourselves. We told him the whole story—larded with details. He looked at us, first with disbelief, then with amazement. Finally he smiled. "Well, I'll be damned," was all that he could say. But after the shock wore off, he seemed actually pleased. "I really should send you packing back to school," he added, "but if going to America means this much to you, you deserve to go. Bully for you!"

CHAPTER III

America, Here We Are

Thelma

We had our first glimpse of our own country early on the morning of September 15, 1916, as the *New Amsterdam* sailed majestically into New York Harbor. We saw the Statue of Liberty and waved at it madly. A fog blanketed the lower part of the skyline, but we saw what were then the "tall" buildings, the giant of which was the Woolworth Building, jutting above the haze into puffy clouds just then turning pink in the refracted light of the rising sun. New York seemed to us to be a magical city, suspended in midair.

Gloria and I rushed to find Papa. When we reached his cabin, he was surrounded by reporters. "Mr. Morgan," one asked, "what are conditions like in Germany?" "What do the Germans think of Americans?" asked another. "Do they believe President Wilson is working for peace?"

Papa was evasive. But when we entered the cabin, his eyes brightened. "Here are my twins," he said to the reporters. "*There's* a story for you."

We went back on deck; there were too many interesting things for us to see to waste our time listening to Papa's interviews. One of the reporters followed us. "Are you the Morgan twins?" he asked pleasantly. We acknowledged that we were. "Would you like to have your picture taken?" We agreed that we would. He focused his camera, made several shots, then asked us many questions, which we were only too delighted to answer. Here was a reporter, an American; and he was interested in us! We were flattered no end; we chattered like little sparrows, telling him everything he wanted to know.

We went straight to the Knickerbocker Hotel. The next day Mr. Regan, the manager and an old friend of Papa's—going back to the days when Papa was Consul in Lucerne—joined us. "I'm sorry, Harry, I was not here to greet you," he said to Papa, "but I had a meeting and couldn't get away." He turned to Mamma. "Laura, you look wonderful." Then his eyes fell on us. "So these are your famous twins," he said. "They certainly have grown up, and in real life they look even prettier than in their picture."

Papa looked puzzled. "Their picture? What picture?"

"Haven't you seen this morning's *Herald*?" Mr. Regan asked.

"No," said Papa. "Why?"

Mr. Regan sent for the *Herald*. And when it was spread out on the table, there on the front page was a picture of the two of us. Above it, in bold headlines, was the statement: "Morgan Twins Outwit Their Parents and Come to the United States." We were thrilled; there was our picture—without any question. The story gave every detail—with a few melodramatic additions —of our escapade.

Mamma turned on us accusingly, her face darkening. "Twins," she said, "did you give the reporters this story?" We started to tremble; here was trouble coming up again. No matter what we did, we started trouble. Sooner or later, we were sure, everything would tumble on our heads; up to now we had simply been lucky.

But this time Papa came to our rescue. "Laura," he said, laughing, "don't blame the twins. I also talked to the reporters."

Our first days in New York were spent sight-seeing and gaping; we were really little European girls seeing the New World for the first time. Although by now we spoke three languages more or less fluently, we had never seen an Automat or an animated electric sign; and we had never tasted an ice-cream soda. We proceeded at once to make up for these deficiencies. We dashed in and out of the Automat, dropping our nickels and collecting sandwiches from their niches behind the glass windows; we hung for hours out of our hotel window staring at the signs that made Broadway the world-renowned "Great White Way." And we parked, like bar flies, at the soda fountain at Schrafft's, sampling the endless varieties of sundaes and milk shakes. But what we loved most of all was "Mr. Woolworth's Five-and-Dime Store." This was a bottomless maw into which we poured almost all of our pocket money.

We learned to keep abreast of the news by looking from our hotel window at the flashing signs which moved across the side of the old Times Building, in the center of Times Square. This was an election year; and the night the returns came in we stood excitedly in our window watching the returns as they were flashed on the board state by state. Papa and Mamma had gone to a dinner party. They returned, shortly after midnight, and we heard Papa say, in tones of profound satisfaction, "Thank God, Hughes is in." Gloria and I stayed up, secretly, getting more and more excited as we found ourselves in possession of news as soon as it was flashed. Around two in the morning a great shout went up from the streets below. We looked at the board. California had just been heard from. Mr. Wilson was re-elected. We chuckled to ourselves, thinking of Papa and Mamma. Gloria giggled to me, "We know something they don't know."

Soon after this Papa returned to Hamburg. And Mamma, true to form, once again deciding that we were poverty-stricken, moved with us from the Knickerbocker to a small and dingy hotel on the West Side.

Mamma intended to put us in a convent; we were to be enrolled in Manhattanville. Convent of the Sacred Heart. But the

United States had just declared war on Germany, and the war situation suddenly made all Mamma's planning indefinite; it also made Gloria and me acutely aware of the odd nature of our family. It was not merely that we were international gypsies, with no permanent home, no roots in any one city, or even a single country; we were an erratically scattered family. At this moment Harry was at school in Lausanne, Consuelo at school in Paris, Gloria and I were only temporarily in New York. No one knew exactly where Papa was; we had not heard from him in weeks. And Mamma was now making plans to gallivant off somewhere—neither we nor she knew exactly where. When more time passed, and no word came from Papa, Mamma got desperate. Always suspicious of the Germans, she confessed to us one day that she believed he was in a prison camp. She put the blame on herself; the Germans were punishing Papa because of her many trips across the frontier.

Leaving us alone in the hotel, Mamma went to Washington and badgered the already harassed State Department; where was Papa? The only thing she came back with was the frustrating information that the State Department had no knowledge of his whereabouts; all they could tell her was that Consul General Harry Hays Morgan was not with the Embassy staff which, by then, had been evacuated from Germany.

As the days passed, with no news of Papa arriving from any quarter, Mamma grew more and more worried, more and more indignant at the Germans, more and more desperate. Finally she decided she would go alone to Europe and do her own investigating. Again we were to be left alone; again the trip across the Atlantic was pronounced too dangerous for children. And again we begged to be taken along. We begged, we pleaded, we howled; we used every argument we could think of. This time it was Gloria who suddenly hit on a workable idea: she decided to attack Mamma's most vulnerable side—her sentimentality. Although Mamma was scarcely what anyone would call a responsible mother, she was more sensitive than a Chekhov character to the overwhelming appeal of "mother love."

"Remember, Mamma," Gloria said, slyly and tearfully, "if anything happens to you, we will be orphans."

That did it. Mamma was convinced. We all sailed together on a small Spanish ship, the S.S. *Alfonso XIII*.

Although we had a distinguished passenger list on the *Alfonso XIII*, including the beautiful and spectacular Mary Garden, and Nijinsky and other members of the Imperial Russian Ballet, the ship was a depressing contrast to the luxurious *New Amsterdam*. We shared a small cabin with Mamma, whose berth was under the porthole; Gloria and I were stacked in double-decker bunks. I had the top bunk, which was only a few feet from the ceiling. In the middle of the night I felt something crawling on my face. Switching on the light, I made a horrible discovery: it was cockroaches. I screamed.

Mamma's light immediately went on, then Gloria's. "What's the matter?" Gloria asked, in a panic. "Have we been torpedoed?"

"No," I yelled, "but I'm crawling with cockroaches."

Mamma, who had raised herself half out of her berth, now lay back on her pillow. "Is that all?" she said scornfully, as if to imply that I was trying to put on the airs of a princess. "Your father is probably rotting in a rat-infested prison, and you are complaining about a few harmless little bugs. Pull the sheet over your head and turn out the lights!"

When we docked at Vigo, in Spain, we found, to our amazement, that Papa was standing at the gangplank, waiting to meet us. It seems that he had left Germany, after many delays, then gone to Lausanne to pick up Harry. He had brought Harry with him to Spain, where he had made reservations to return to America on the very ship that had brought us over. In Madrid he had had a cable from the Secretary of State, informing him that we had already sailed—on the *Alfonso XIII*.

Mamma immediately went into one of her emotional turnabouts. All her pent-up anxieties were transformed into rage. She was furious at Papa; she bombarded him with insults; she stormed, she fumed, she turned purple; we thought she was even going to strike Papa. In his very quiet voice Papa countered with a simple fact: "Laura, come; Harry is waiting for us. We'll miss the train to Madrid."

I don't know how or when Papa explained to Mamma exactly what had happened to him. But we have this account, which he left in his unpublished memoirs:

Ambassador Gerard was handed his passport and left Berlin with his staff. The day before his departure he advised me at the Consulate in Hamburg that a special train would be passing through Stuttgart at a certain hour, and if I so chose, I could join him. But there were many consular offices in outlying districts left to shift for themselves, so I did not take advantage of this offer. Only after all the consuls had been accounted and arranged for did I feel warranted in leaving with my own staff. When I demanded safe conduct from the Hamburg Foreign Office, much to my stunned amazement it was denied me. They told me that if it were left to their discretion, they would send me out of the country with due honor, but they said they had received instructions from the Prussian Foreign Office that I was to be held. I was virtually held a prisoner there for ten days before being allowed to depart. When I arrived at Munich, my staff and I and the ten consuls were taken off the train and detained for another ten days. They gave no reason for the detention. When I was allowed to leave, I proceeded to Lausanne.

Once more we played our chaotic family game of transatlantic musical chairs. A few days after we arrived in Madrid, Papa and Harry returned to Vigo, to sail for America; Mamma, Gloria, and I went on to Paris. If any one in our family had any regard for safety, had even routine common sense, the fact was not reflected in our collective way of life. Paris had been under bombardment; the Germans had brought up their giant gun,

"Big Bertha," and had placed it within shelling distance of the city. Nôtre Dame had been shelled while it was filled with worshipers, on Good Friday. Food was scarce; coal and oil were commodities only dimly remembered. And yet, all the while, Consuelo had been left at school in the city—to perfect her French and survive any way she could. Mamma had been terrified when a few weeks passed with no letter from Papa, but she had given little thought to her daughter, who had been left directly in the range of enemy guns.

As soon as we had been settled at the Hôtel Regina, we all went to see Consuelo. Gloria and I were startled when she entered the room. Consuelo looked like one who had survived a siege and was still in a state of shock. She was a skeleton; her eyes seemed enormous in her thin, haggard, frightened face. The slightest noise would make her jump. And she seemed to move in a trance.

We have no idea what Mamma's thoughts were at that time, or whether she had the slightest feeling of guilt or remorse for having left Consuelo to suffer alone through those harrowing months. But at least she was moved to some sensible action: she took Consuelo out of school, and brought her back to the hotel with us. Meanwhile, Mamma put us all in day school in Paris. Now that Papa was safe, it seemed quite proper to Mamma that we should stay in the danger zone.

A few months later Papa wrote that the State Department was sending him to Cuba (as a special agent representing the Food and Fuel Administration and the War Trade and Shipping Boards) to make a report on the unsettled conditions there. He urged Mamma to bring us all back to America. Mamma was irritated. "Doesn't your father realize," she said, "that it takes time to pack three children and travel miles—yes, miles—and cross the Atlantic, in wartime?" Eventually, however, we found ourselves on the *Rochambeau*, one of the smaller ships of the French Line. The other passengers, some twenty-five in all, consisted of French fliers who were to be instructors at American army aviation centers and a handful of Red Cross nurses going home on leave.

Once more we slept on deck, using our life belts for pillows, and assuming that the ship would zigzag sufficiently to by-pass mines and dodge torpedoes. Two days before we were due to arrive in New York we went below to our cabin to dress for breakfast. Suddenly there was a loud explosion. The ship keeled. Mamma, Consuelo, Gloria, and I found ourselves piled in a heap on the floor. We all grabbed our life belts and one another, then made a dash for the deck. We found the other passengers assembled around the lifeboats, and the captain making a reassuring speech. A smoke cloud was settling around the ship. "We have been sideswiped by a torpedo," the captain explained. "There has been no great damage done, and with God's help and a little luck we'll get to New York under our own steam."

When we limped into New York Harbor and up the Hudson River, we found that dozens of reporters were scurrying over the ship. One reporter spotted us. "My God," he said, "it's the Morgan twins! Now we have a real story."

I don't remember what we told him, but by then we were seasoned chatterers. The next day our pictures were again on the front page; at twelve we had become standbys for the press. We were "news."

There was no Papa waiting for us when we got off the ship. We looked for him at the gangplank; we looked for him on the dock; we looked for him under the letter "M" in the baggage area—but Papa was missing. "So like your father," Mamma sniffed. "He's gone to Cuba and left us here in New York alone."

We all went in a cab to the old Waldorf-Astoria where Papa, although absent, had engaged rooms for us. The hotel was on Fifth Avenue, where the Empire State Building now stands. As I look back these many years, I remember it as an enormous brownstone building surviving from the late eighteen hundreds.

The foyer and the many rooms which led off from it, decorated in Early Victorian, were overcrowded, overpowering. There were sofas and chairs resplendent in red plush velvet; tapestries hung on the walls; wherever you looked you saw classical statues holding electric-light fixtures. Every available niche was filled with a potted plant. Every column was of marble, and from each radiated the eternal four gilt brocaded chairs. The old Waldorf must have been magnificent in its day; but in the summer of 1917 it had the quality of a flower pressed too long between the pages of a book; it was crumbling, faded, tired. Even we felt a little sad at the sight. Could it have spoken to us, I am sure it would have said, "Youth, be wary; don't look at me with such disdain; I, too, have had my day."

No sooner were we comfortable in the Waldorf than Mamma decided to join Papa in Cuba. She sent Consuelo to her old friend, Mrs. George Jay Gould, in the Catskills, and she announced to us that we were to go to Manhattanville. We pleaded with her to take us to Cuba with her. Why couldn't we go? Why did we have to go to school in the middle of summer, when all other children were on vacation? But this time nothing we could say or do would change her mind; she had made all the arrangements. We were to go to Manhattanville, the Convent of the Sacred Heart, and that was that.

The fateful day arrived. On the way up in the taxi Mamma told us all about Manhattanville—how nice it was, what a beautiful place it was, how happy she had been there when she was a girl. We were skeptical. And as we neared Convent Avenue, our spirits sank lower and lower. "Please God," I said inwardly, "don't let it be another Strathalham House." When we turned into the driveway, however, we considered ourselves doomed: we saw an enormous, somber, brick building that looked more like a prison than a school.

A sweet-faced nun answered our ring. "Why," she said

sweetly, "these must be the twins. Please come in; I'll tell Reverend Mother Dammen you're here."

As she led us to what I think they called "the parlor," we noticed the stone floors, the statues of saints in niches, red night lights glowing at their feet. All of it had a strong, aesthetic appeal; all was so silent, so cool, so peaceful.

We had not waited long before the door swung open. Reverend Mother Dammen rushed into the room, her black habit and her rosary beads extended behind her like the tail of a comet. It was only later that we learned about Mother Dammen's way of locomotion: she never really walked—she was always partially in flight, always in a hurry.

"Mrs. Morgan," she said, greeting Mamma, "how nice to see you. You don't have to tell me—these are the twins. I have never seen anything like it; they are actually identical!"

Mother Dammen was middle-aged, a little on the plump side; she had bright, shiny eyes, red cheeks, and an endearing smile. And she was indescribably warm, sympathetic, understanding. We loved her from the moment she came into the room; and many were the times we were to return to her, in happiness or sorrow—or for advice—even long after we were married women.

Sitting down, Mother Dammen took our hands in hers; hers were soft to our touch, and cool. Then she played the "twin" game with us. "Now let me see," she said. "Which is Gloria and which is Thelma?"

We both curtsied. "I'm Thelma," I said meekly. And Gloria added, "I'm Gloria."

Mother Dammen smiled. "That's all very well," she said, "but how am I going to tell you apart later?" Then she laughed. "Let's try something. Both of you run out of the room. Then come back one at a time. Let's see if I can tell you apart."

We dashed out together. "Isn't she wonderful?" Gloria whispered to me. We had been in so many schools, lived in so many places, and been in charge of so many women. But until now we had never known any woman who seemed really to love us; with Mother Dammen we knew this instinctively; she did.

Gloria was the first to go back. I left the door open and watched; I was dying to see whether Mother Dammen would guess right. Gloria walked sedately across the long room and stood quietly in front of Mother Dammen. Then I heard Mother Dammen say, "It's Thelma."

"No, it's not, it's not!" I shouted, running in and throwing my arms around her.

Mother Dammen gently disentangled herself from my clutches. "Mrs. Morgan," she asked, very much amused, "how do *you* tell them apart?"

"I don't often make mistakes," Mamma answered proudly, "but their father has a terrible time with them. He always makes a point of looking under their chins; that's the final test. Thelma has a scar she got roller-skating—when she was small. They knew I did not approve of these rough sports and had forbidden them, but Thelma disobeyed me." She looked at me with a forced smile. "You see, Mamma was right."

Mother Dammen, I observed, looked at Mamma with surprise and only faintly disguised disapproval.

"Reverend Mother," Mamma said, as she stood up, "I leave my twins in your hands." Then she was gone.

Mother Dammen took us to meet some of our schoolmates. To our joy, we found that most of them were South Americans from Peru, Chile, and the Argentine. Because of the war—and the distance of their homes—they were in the same plight as we. "These are the Morgan twins," Reverend Mother said, introducing us. "They speak Spanish as well as you do." In no time we were all chattering together in high excitement; Gloria and I didn't even see Mother Dammen leave the room.

We spent that Christmas with Margaret Power, one of our schoolmates. Margaret lived with her aunt, Mrs. Peter Larson, in a magnificent house on Fifth Avenue, facing the Metropolitan

Museum. This house was fascinating to us; we found treasures in every part of it. There was a grand ballroom whose walls were covered with rare tapestries. There was a Louis XIV drawing room whose floor was covered with an exquisite Savonnerie carpet; we imagined Madame de Maintenon holding her salon in a room like this. Aunt Nana, as Margaret called Mrs. Larson, was tall, her gestures were brisk, and her voice was loud. She loved jewelry, and she decked herself with it at the slightest excuse. But her heart was big. Having no children of her own, she spoiled Margaret, and there was nothing she—and Margaret—did not do to make us feel wanted and at home. It was well that they had the Anaconda copper millions behind them, for there were never two more generous and extravagant people.

When the holidays were over, we returned to school to find a letter from Mamma saying Papa wanted us in Cuba for the summer. We ran down the hall to announce the news to Mother Dammen. She smiled as we entered her room. She knew in advance what we intended to say; we had forgotten that at the Convent all mail is opened and read before it is delivered.

The years at Manhattanville passed quickly; we were happy. We spent the first summer with Papa and Mamma in Havana. This was our first visit to a tropical country, and we were fascinated by all that we saw—the palm trees, the bougainvillea that crawled up the walls of the pink stucco houses. El Morro Castle, and jai alai. We feasted on platanitos—the bananas no bigger than your little finger—and on mangoes, which would be thrown to us as we swam in the clear, warm water. And Gloria, at the age of fourteen, fell madly in love with Regino Truffin, a handsome boy not much older than herself. The romance was nipped in the bud when we returned to school.

Shortly after the Armistice, Papa was appointed American Consul General at Brussels. This entitled us to a summer in Belgium. We didn't see much of Papa that summer; when we arrived in Belgium he had taken over the work of the Inter-Allied

Commission on Industrial and Agricultural Reconstruction of Belgium, and was busy organizing relief measures and administering funds appropriated to rebuild devastated areas. In spite of this, we had an eventful time. We lived in a lovely house that belonged to the Countess Lidekerque, and had been used during the war as the headquarters of General von Bissing, German Occupation governor. Very often we drove with Albert, Papa's chauffeur, over the famous battlefields of Flanders. And we spent much time with Pierre, the old butler who had been with the Countess for more than thirty years, and who came with the house. He told us endless stories about the Occupation: how the Germans had removed from the house all the beautiful doorknobs and ironwork, all the copper cooking utensils—everything they could melt and use for the war effort. He also told us of the tiny newspaper, *La Libre Belgique*, which had been published by the underground; every morning, religiously, a copy was slipped under Von Bissing's door.

We returned to Manhattanville that fall; this was to be our last year at the Convent.

In May 1920 we had a letter from Mamma telling us that Consuelo was to be married the following month to Count Jean de Maupas, and that Margaret Power had been asked to be one of the bridesmaids. Mamma wanted us to sail with Margaret and Mrs. Larson. Naturally, we were excited; but what we didn't know at this time was that the marriage was not a love match; it was something Mamma had arranged. Poor Consuelo scarcely knew her future husband.

Our crossing on the S.S. *France* was gala; all the gloom and tensions of our earlier trips seemed to be balanced by the excitement we found in this. The world was in holiday mood. Thousands who had never before thought of going to Europe now were headed for Paris. And the rich, whose extravagances had been curtailed by the war, were once again Paris bound: at last they could seek out their beloved Worth, Lanvin, and Poiret for clothes; Reboux and Maggy Rouff for hats; Révillon for furs. On the *France* every available berth was taken. Concerts, fancy-dress parties, dances were nightly entertainments; the ship's pool, which reached astronomical figures, was auctioned each evening to the highest bidder. The dining salons, glittering with lights and crowded with beautiful women, beautifully gowned, and with carefree, spendthrift men in black formality, reflected an era which is now long past, and whose glamour will perhaps not be seen again.

Mamma's apartment at the Ritz, in Paris, was a madhouse when we arrived. Worth and his fitters were at work on Consuelo's bridal gown. Lady Duff Gordon and her fitters were at work on the bridesmaids' dresses. There were salesmen from the Maison de Blanc solicitously discussing their wares. And in the center of this bustle, which could well have been staged in the market place of Marrakesh, Consuelo, being fitted to shoes, sat passively, staring into space.

The night before the wedding Gloria and I were left very much to ourselves, and told to keep out of the way. Papa, Mamma, Consuelo, and Harry had dinner together in the apartment upstairs. We were told to have ours alone in the restaurant on the Cambon side of the Ritz. With no one to hold us back, we ordered everything we liked best—iced melon, cold lobster with mayonnaise, and, as a topper, strawberries with sour cream. A few hours later we felt violently ill.

The following morning, when Mamma came to our room, I announced that we were not going to the wedding. "We're too sick," I explained. "We'll be sick all over the church."

Mamma, in cold fury, had the maid pour bismuth down our throats. Then we were marched off to the ceremonies.

Our first visit was to Consuelo. When we saw her, she was standing in the middle of the room, like a Christmas tree waiting for the final decorations. Her simple white satin gown was deftly draped and held at the hip by a pinned sheaf of calla lilies.

From her head a Chantilly lace veil, over yards of tulle, hung loosely to the ground—the same veil that "dear grandmamma" had worn. Indifferently, like a well-coached Trilby, Consuelo allowed the fitters to put the finishing touches to her gown. Her face was pale and drawn. Her eyes listless, but quite dry, smiled at us as we hugged her and said formally, "Darling, you look beautiful."

We then went to the church—the Roman Catholic Church of St. Pierre de Chaillot, one of the oldest and, to our minds, the loveliest in Paris. The High Mass, it seemed to us, would never end; and the smell of incense made us feel sick again. As we prayed, we inwardly added our regrets for the glut of strawberries and cream. We had, however, two confederates at the ceremony: Ivor O'Conner, who later married our brother, Harry, and Margaret Power, Consuelo's other bridesmaid, knew of the delicate balance in our stomach. They looked at us sympathetically.

The priest's sermon droned on interminably. The lecture was too much for a tall young man who rose and quietly slipped out of the church; this was Benjamin Thaw, then First Secretary of the American Embassy in Paris. He had been sent to represent Ambassador Herrick, who was then out of the city. How we wished we could have joined Benny Thaw!

At sixteen we were living with Mamma and Papa in Brussels, and we were bored. Life in Belgium was dull by comparison with what we had come to know in America; and Gloria and I were anxious to get back. We were reasonably grown by now; at seventeen Consuelo had been married. We felt quite capable of taking care of ourselves. The question was: how to get Mamma and Papa to agree. We confided in Mamma and, to our surprise, Mamma, who always did the reverse of what was expected, connived with us to win Papa over.

Soon after this Mamma went to Paris with Papa, and while

there she managed to persuade him to do as we wanted. The success was announced to us by a legalistic letter which was sent to us by Papa; the letter seemed to be a cross between a contract and a sermon:

I'm surprised to hear you should wish to leave us and go to America. I am reluctant to let you go alone. However, your mother has persuaded me. She tells me that you have made arrangements to stay with the Horters in Nutley. Providing you do this, I am willing to allow you two hundred dollars a month, which will have to suffice. I have arranged passage for you on the S.S. *Zeeland*. I am afraid, my dear twins, that new pastures are not always greener and it is likely Nutley may not come up to your expectations, so I won't be too surprised to see you back soon.

Then followed a lot more fatherly advice.

Agnes Horter had been one of our most intimate friends at the Convent. She was a couple of years older than we, dark, thin, tall, striking. She was quite moody, however—at times moody to the point of melancholia. Her temperament was poles away from ours, but the difference seemed to establish an emotional balance; we loved her. We had kept up a steady correspondence with her after we moved to Brussels, and she had been urging us to come over and visit her in New Jersey.

As soon as we had digested Papa's letter, we rushed to the Consulate to see that our passports were in order and to get funds and tickets. Then, after hasty packing, we were off. Mamma and Papa were still in Paris when we boarded the S.S. *Zeeland*.

Mrs. Horter and Agnes met us at the pier. We were overjoyed at seeing them, and on the long drive to Nutley we talked over all the things we wanted to do; Gloria and I were overflowing with plans. Our spirits sank, however, when the car drew up to the Horter home. It was a dreary, gray wooden house, more or less, we soon observed, like every other house in Nutley—and it symbolized for us a monotonous, funless, rigid life. Inside, however, the house was warm and friendly; it had the quality of a place where there was much love. Mrs. Horter was the mother of twelve children; Agnes was the youngest. She took us gracefully under her wing; to a woman with a brood this large, two children more or less made very little difference. Agnes' father, on the other hand, was a taciturn, unbending man, then nearing eighty. His one redeeming grace, in our eyes, was his love for poetry; ensconced in a rocking chair on the porch, for hours at a time he would read aloud to us from Shakespeare and Milton. Our fondness for poetry, we noticed, was shared by no other member of the Horter family.

In a way, our emigration to Nutley was a rebuff to our fantasies. Whatever else we were, we were not typical little American girls, enured to the routines of a typical American small town. We were little sophisticates. The Horters' family life was as foreign to us as we were to it. Nutley, too, was alien: in cities where we had lived, people had their apéritifs at sidewalk cafés, but in Nutley the social set gathered each afternoon for ice-cream sodas at the corner drugstore. We had graduated from the stage of our lives in which ice-cream sodas were treats; and the atmosphere of the corner drugstore seemed to us as hostile as it was dull. The first time Agnes took us with her to this Nutley institution we found ourselves, with our French clothes, our French-Spanish accents, and our European manners, regarded as the sensation of the town. But this was not the sensation for which we had planned; we wanted to be belles, not oddities.

We had many friends in New York, but in Nutley we were in isolation. Although we had been invited to a number of parties in the city we had to decline most of them because the trek was too long and too inconvenient; and young men who might have taken us dining and dancing rebelled at the idea of escorting us back to Nutley in the dead of night. Gloria and I quickly concluded that the hinterland of Jersey was not for us. We put our heads together, resumed our Machiavellian roles, and decided to intrigue our way to an apartment of our own in the city.

One morning we took the train to New York, had a leisurely lunch at the Brevoort Hotel on lower Fifth Avenue, then began hatching our plans. We had been told that apartments in this area were more reasonable than uptown, and we assumed that sooner or later we should find one that we could afford. As we left the hotel, after lunch, we were undecided whether to turn right or left. The psychological pulls simultaneously in opposite directions caused us to look straight ahead. We were in the position of Buridan's ass who, finding himself midway between two bales of hay, remained motionless and starved. Our fate, however, was much happier. Directly facing us was a well-kept, brownstone-front house, No. 40 Fifth Avenue; and on it was the sign, "Apartment for Rent."

Gloria put her hand on my arm. "Could this be it?"

"If it is," I said, "it's a miracle."

We rang the bell. An elderly, gray-haired lady opened the door for us. We explained that we were interested in the apartment. "I am Mrs. Travell," she said, taking us into the drawing room. "Are you young ladies looking for an apartment for yourselves?" Her voice was kind.

We introduced ourselves; then we unburdened ourselves. "Mrs. Travell," I said, "our big problem is to find an apartment in a private home. Our parents would never let us stay alone in New York otherwise."

On the way upstairs Mrs. Travell told us she had a daughter only a little older than we were; she also told us that this was the first time she had planned to rent part of her house. She then showed us two charmingly furnished rooms on the top floor; with the rooms was a kitchenette. We were taken with the place at once. "Oh, please, Mrs. Travell," I said, "can't we have it?" Then as a sober afterthought I asked, "How much is it?"

Mrs. Travell was amused by our mixed enthusiasm and fear. "One hundred and twenty-five dollars a month," she said.

Gloria nodded at me approvingly. "Oh," I said, now too numb to think, "we'll take it."

"Not so fast, please," Mrs. Travell said, trying to hold our enthusiasm in check. "I will write to your parents, if you want me to, and see, first, if this is all right with them." And then she added warmly, "I'll tell them that I will keep an eye on you." As we left, she told us she would hold the apartment until she received an answer from our family.

That night, back in Nutley, we composed a masterpiece of a letter to Mamma. We painted the apartment in glowing terms, we eulogized Mrs. Travell, we begged her to persuade Papa to answer "Yes"—and at once.

Mamma's favorable letter and Mrs. Travell's confirming note came simultaneously. We packed. And with fond good-bys and hugs and kisses to the Horters, we said our farewell to Nutley, New Jersey.

On our way to our new home—"Chez Nous," we called it—we had our taxi driver stop at a florist's. We arrived at 40 Fifth Avenue armed with masses of varicolored flowers. We put the flowers in vases, rearranged the furniture, then sat down, exhausted, to contemplate our holdings. For the first time, in our lives we were our own masters.

CHAPTER IV

We Become Two

Gloria

In many ways the hectic life of the Roaring Twenties seems to have passed us by. Thelma and I tasted no bathtub gin. We found speakeasies and petting parties slightly distasteful. It amazed us when, even at the most fastidious debutante parties, we saw apparently demure girls retire to the powder room, remove their corsets, roll down their stockings, then rejoin their partners in the ballroom. On the other hand, we were extremely young; and while we were quite sophisticated in many ways, we were naïve in others. We knew a great deal about places, very little about people.

To us, now, it seems rather shocking that two girls of sixteen should have been permitted to live in New York alone. But then, either because of our naïveté, or because of sheer dumbness, nothing about it seemed odd or unusual. We could have been highly criticized. But at the time such ideas never occurred to us; and, as far as we knew, they seem not to have occurred to others. Mamma probably by accident, and the nuns by plan, had instilled in us a strong sense of propriety. Affairs were to us unthinkable. We were extremely conventional "unconventional" girls; we wanted love, romance, marriage, children. We were highly romantic; but our conception of romance was strictly in accord with the standards that would bear the stamp of approval of any woman's magazine.

WE BECOME TWO

Every Sunday we went to St. Ignatius of Loyola, the Catholic church on Park Avenue in the Eighties. We chose this particular church for two reasons: first, after church we could go to Margaret Hennessy's across the street at 905 Park Avenue; Margaret gave charming Sunday buffet lunches for the younger set. Second, we were sure it would please Mamma; she had told us St. Ignatius was also an ancestor of ours.

Margaret was one of our best friends. We loved going to her place because she made us feel so at home and always had such a gay young crowd. We usually found there other friends, such as Peggy Stout, who married dashing Lawrence Copley Thaw and later divorced him; Jimmy and Dorothy Fargo, whose name is associated with Pony Express fame; the two daughters of Mrs. Richard T. Wilson, Marion and Louise; Juan Trippe, now president of Pan-American Airways; the two Jimmys, Leary and O'Gorman; and Margaret Power, who had introduced us to Margaret Hennessy. They were both from Montana; their families at one time jointly owned the Anaconda copper mines. After divorcing Jimmy Drumm, Margaret Power became the Countess of Carrick; we saw a lot of each other in London when Thelma was married to Viscount Furness.

Our first fancy-dress party was given by the fabulous Cobina Wright at her home in New York. Society, the music world, the theater, were well represented. This party was not as grand and magnificent as her later and now famous "Circus Parties," but we all had a wonderful time. Thelma and I wore identical medieval page-boy costumes, our long hair tucked under black wigs. Ever since that night I have had a fondness for fancy-dress parties. My very first ball in Newport, after I married Reginald Vanderbilt, was fancy dress.

We made a good friend at this party, Maury Paul, the original and unsurpassed "Cholly Knickerbocker" of the New York *American*. He was the social arbiter par excellence. He knew all and everything about anybody who was anybody, and printed it; he took us under his wing and dubbed us "The Magical Morgans."

It was not long after Cobina's party, where we had enjoyed ourselves so much, that Thelma and I recognized we preferred mature men to the boys of our own set. We had been by far the youngest at the party, but we seemed to fit in that adult picture. We felt more at home there than with our own teen-age group. In some strange way we seemed to have stepped from childhood into womanhood. We had no time—or taste—for adolescence.

At a party given by the Chauncy Olcotts I met George Brokaw; he was very attractive—tall, thin, and wiry. He looked older than his forty-odd years, perhaps because he took himself so seriously. He was an interesting companion and I enjoyed going out with him. I was surprised, however, when he asked me to the Bachelors' Ball. Invitations to this event usually were sent out by a "bachelor" only to his best girl.

"What's going on?" Thelma asked. "Can this be serious?"

"I'm just curious," I said, with affected boredom. "I've never been to a Bachelors' Ball." Naturally I'd never been to a Bachelors' Ball.

After the ball, George became rather persistent. Hardly a day went by that he didn't ask me to go to this or that affair. It came to such a point that when the phone rang, Thelma would say, "Bet you a new hat that's George," and it usually was. As time went on I realized that he was falling in love with me. Then came the night he asked me to marry him. I must admit I was flattered, for this would have been what Mamma's generation called a "brilliant marriage." But I had to tell him I was sorry; I liked him very much, but I was not in love with him.

One of our pleasantest memories is of Mrs. William Randolph Hearst's corraling of debutantes to help her raise money for her then recently founded Milk Fund. Millicent Hearst, wife of the late owner and publisher of the many Hearst newspapers and magazines, has a charm which is a special form of beauty. She is petite—and a dynamo. Her conversation is punctuated by a fascinating little giggle which is all her own. Only the other day we ran into her at Le Pavillon in New York; it seemed unbelievable that so many years had passed, so little had she changed.

I remember well the first Milk Fund committee meeting in her apartment on Riverside Drive, overlooking the Hudson. I don't know how she managed it—she must have charmed the city fathers—but when we afterward went out to collect donations, we had at our service an entire squad of motorcycle police. In those days the police vehicles were equipped with sidecars; each of us was driven in a sidecar to her destination. We were thrilled. We considered this a novel and effective way of calling attention to our work—and ultimately collecting donations.

The nuns had taught us needlework and we were deft at it. Our limited funds pressed that talent into use. The rent for our little "Chez Nous" took a good slice of our income, leaving only $75.00 for food, clothes, and luxuries. We had, however, ideas and ingenuity; when we wanted new dresses, we bought some pretty but reasonable materials and whipped them up in our own inimitable style. Our creations, we maintain, were chic and attractive as well as practical. A bit of chiffon, for example, artfully wrapped into a turban, would turn into a smart hat. We had quite a wardrobe, for pennies.

At Christmastime we made personal gifts for our friends. We made embroidered sachets and pincushions and those monstrous overdressed DuBarry dolls to place over the telephone—dolls which we then thought too, too beautiful. Our gifts, completed and spread out on the table, looked extremely professional to us; we would stand back and admire our handiwork.

Thelma

Just after Christmas I was getting dressed to go to dinner and thinking to myself what a pity it was that Gloria wasn't coming with me; parties were always more fun for me when we were together. But she had promised to dine with George Brokaw.

My partner at dinner was a good-looking, dark young man in his late twenties or early thirties. A small, narrow mustache gave him a rakish look. His dark brown eyes were bright and merry. I had noticed just before we sat down that he was not especially tall—a pity, I thought; two or three inches more would have made him a moving-picture scout's dream. When he had been introduced to me I had not heard his name. I took a quick glance at the place card in front of him; it read James Vail Converse. Across the table, they called to him as "Junior."

We seemed to hit it off from the start. His stories were fantastic; I didn't know whether to believe them or not. At one moment he was telling me he had just got back from hunting bear in the Northwest; the next, how he had walked out on one of the biggest brokerage firms in Wall Street, just because his many absences were questioned. I had a sneaking feeling that it was not he who had engineered the separation. Junior Converse's utter lack of responsibility, his flights of ideas, his want of honesty and uprightness were later to cause me many a heartache, but at this point my heart was doing flip-flops. I thought this man sitting next to me was charming, amusing, witty. I was still only sixteen, and enormously flattered by what I then considered an older man's attention. He was so different from the rah-rah, raccoon-skin boys I had been dancing with at debutante parties. He monopolized me through the entire dinner, and by the time coffee was served I was purring like a kitten.

When he drove me home that night, he asked me to dinner and the theater the following night. If I liked, he added, we could go later to the Montmartre for supper.

"I've got the most wonderful thing to tell you," I said breathlessly to Gloria, as soon as I got home—and I had bounded up the stairs. "I've met *the* man." In jerky, incoherent sentences I told her about Junior Converse. "And just think, darling," I added, "he asked me to dinner and theater tomorrow, and to go on to the Montmartre."

Gloria seemed worried. "But darling," she asked seriously, "who is this Junior Converse?"

"I don't know," I said, "and I don't care."

Gloria was scarcely overjoyed. For some reason my exuberance only stirred in her what I then considered unnecessary caution. "Do you think you should go alone to a night club?"

"Oh, piffle!" I said. "Don't be a killjoy, Gloria." I was terribly disappointed to find that she was not sharing my excitement; but I wished, later, that I had listened to her; I would have saved myself a lot of grief.

I had never seen any place as glamorous as was the Montmartre the next night. I was enchanted by the effect of the dim lights, the lavish *décor*, and the seductive waltzes played by Emil Coleman's orchestra as Junior and I danced. I didn't know exactly what was happening to me, but something most certainly was happening. For the first time I had the feeling of identity with a man—the strange sensation of being dual and being one. Whether or not this is the basis of love is a matter for psychologists; but in the language of a sixteen-year-old I simply said to myself that my heart was not mine any longer. I remembered Longfellow's lines: "How beautiful is youth, how bright it gleams / With its illusions, aspirations, dreams." I soon was to go beyond Longfellow and to learn that youth is also easily deceived.

As we sat at the table that night, Junior told me a little about himself: how he had married and divorced when young; how Nadine, his wife, had never understood or loved him; how he adored his little seven-year-old son, Petey. He told me all about the big deal he was about to put over. How many, many times I was to hear about those big deals that he was just about to "put over." I was also to find out that Nadine had loved him very much and had done everything in her power to help him. Junior went on to explain to me how he had lost most of his inheritance from his grandfather, Theodore N. Vail, on some oil deal he had been sure would make him a millionaire.

All the inflated stories of deals, of repeated failures, semi-failures, semi-demi-failures, of a lost inheritance, of the classical wife "who never understood," should have warned me that I was facing a man of pathological fantasy. But at this instant, as the music played on softly and my eyes, half-closed, peered wistfully through a romantic haze, I could see only a dashing, adventurous, brilliant young man who was making my heart do queer things.

From this time on we saw each other almost every day, and I begrudged the hours Junior's "big deals" kept him away from me. He fascinated me; and this fascination made me proof against the unfavorable things my friends reported to me about him. They told me he was unreliable, that he was temperamentally incapable of sticking to anything, that he drank to excess, that he flirted with every woman he met; but the more they said against him, the more I thought I loved him.

One day Agnes Horter, who had stage aspirations, rushed up to our apartment and told us that Cosmopolitan Studios were casting for extras in a picture called *The Young Diana;* Marion Davies was the star. Here was a chance, we thought, to bolster our slim income: we would be actresses. We were worried, however, about what Papa and Mamma might say—if they learned we had plunged into that unholy profession, the movies. On our way to the studios we decided to hide ourselves behind a stage name; we hit on the name "Rachel." Where that name came from we still do not know, although it was probably an unconscious revival in our minds of the name of the great French tragedienne.

At the studio we found some hundred and fifty other would-be actresses lined up in front of the casting director's office. The director was brusque; he glanced disapprovingly at the girl who stood at the head of the line, and barked, "too fat."

"Thank goodness," Agnes whispered to us encouragingly, "we're all thin."

When our turns came, he looked us up and down critically, then said crisply, "Go to wardrobe."

We were horrified when the wardrobe mistress handed us a pair of tights and a wisp of chiffon. "What are we supposed to be?" I asked.

"Northern Lights," she said. "Next."

With much tugging, and a professional sacrifice of modesty, we got into our costumes. There was still the problem of shoes. We made another visit to the wardrobe woman. "No shoes," she said.

Gingerly picking our way in bare feet through a tangle of electric wires, nails, and splinters, we reached the set. If we thought the trip to the set was hard on our feet, we were still innocents. The enormous stage was ankle deep in rough salt, representing snow. At the far end they had erected an enormously high platform upon which was a golden throne. Staircases led to it from either side. In the space under this structure we were to remain concealed until the director shouted "Action!" then we were to flit in and out, up and down the stairs, rush around the set, and return to base. To make matters worse, wind makers, intended to ripple our chiffon costumes, only managed to blow salt and dust over us—and into our eyes.

After hours of rehearsing we were ready to drop. The salt bit into our bleeding feet, got into our hair; the klieg lights hurt our eyes; every muscle in our bodies ached. We were grateful to hear the director say, "Okay, girls, we'll make the next one a take."

At this point an apparition appeared: Marion Davies. Her costume was snow white, laden with pearls and diamonds. At the shoulders was attached a long, wide maribou train. Her enormous headdress was also made of maribou, and studded with jewels. She looked like a jewel-sprinkled powder puff. As she took her place on the throne, we thought we had never seen such a beautiful and glamorous woman. "All right, girls, back to the beginning. This will be a take," the director shouted, and we wearily pitter-pattered back to what we by then called "The Black Hole of Calcutta." Waiting for our cue, we wondered how we could seem to be scintillating, flitting Northern Lights even one more time. But the sound of music, the burst of lights, and the electrifying shouts, "Camera!" "Action!" catapulted us from our lair.

When we opened our pay envelopes, we each had the magnificent sum of twelve dollars and fifty cents.

We got home just in time to dress for dinner; Hannibal de Mesa had asked us and Junior to dine with him at Sherry's. I was stiff when I got into the tub. My muscles ached and my eyes hurt.

Gloria, Junior, Hannibal, and I hadn't been at Sherry's long when suddenly my eyes shut tight. I couldn't open them. I pressed the palms of my hands to the lids trying to ease the pressure and the pain.

"What's wrong?" asked Junior.

"I don't know," I said. "I can't open my eyes. They hurt horribly."

By this time Gloria, too, was concerned. She led me to the powder room and helped me bathe my eyes with cold water. I still couldn't open them. "Come, darling," she said, "we'll take you home."

I was terrified. Total blindness blacked out everything. I was glad when we got to our "Chez Nous" and heard Junior call his doctor. When the doctor finally arrived, he took one look at my eyes and said "Miss Morgan, are you in pictures? You have 'klieg eyes.'"

"Nonsense," I heard Junior say, "of course she's not in pictures. You must be mistaken, doctor." Gloria corrected him. Until then, we had kept our "careers" secret.

The cure that was prescribed for me was almost worse than the malady. Every hour my eyelids were agonizingly pried open, and castor oil was dropped on the eyeballs. Junior came every day to hold my hand. He was kind and gentle, and extremely worried; I couldn't understand how people could have said such terrible things about him.

It was only after the third day that I could see anything at all. Junior was with me when my sight came back. "Oh, Junior," I cried, half-hysterical from shock and fear, and overjoyed to discover that I could see again, "hold me tight, darling. I've been so scared."

Junior lovingly put his arms around me. "This is where you belong always, darling, always," he said, with excusable exaggeration. And then he took aim with his heaviest artillery: "Will you marry me, Thelma?"

The combination of happenings had created in me an emotional state that left little doubt what the answer would be. "Yes," I said, and tears streamed down my cheeks.

Soon after this we began to make wedding plans. "The first thing," Junior said sagely, "is to cable your parents for their consent and blessing." My heart skipped a beat. "Consent?" "Blessing?" In my excitement I had forgotten all about Papa and Mamma. Oh, God, I thought, they will never give their consent, much less blessing. I could already hear Mamma raging, "My daughter marry a divorced man? Never!"

I got hysterical. I threw myself at Junior, who, I suddenly realized, actually knew very little about me. Between convulsive sobs I told him about Mamma; I told him about the Convent, and about Mamma's obsessive concern for the world and preachments of "dear grandmamma." "Mamma," I said, "would never, never give her consent. Never!"

"Don't cry so," Junior said, practically. "The solution is

simple. We'll elope, and after it's all over, they won't be able to do a damn thing about it."

Junior's scheme at the time seemed both romantic and simple. Later it was apparent that, romantic as it might be, it was anything but simple. I was under age and needed my parents' consent if I was to be married in New York State. Meanwhile, we made our wedding plans as enthusiastically as if no obstacle were in our way. We let Margaret Power into our secret, and she, darling that she was, lent me enough money to buy my wedding gown, and the few other things I would need for the honeymoon. The dress I was to be married in—a periwinkle blue frock—was made by Peggy Hoyt, as was the large picture hat that went with it.

Meanwhile, Junior was doing frenetic research to locate a state where a sixteen-year-old girl had a legal right to give herself in marriage. Then one day he rushed in with his happy news. He had found the state—Maryland. Looking back, it occurs to me that any competent lawyer could have given him this information in five minutes, but for Junior the search was a production.

Gloria, unable to see Junior through the rose-colored glasses I was wearing, was not overjoyed by Junior's solution to our problem. "Are you sure, dear," she asked, "that this is what you want? Why don't you wait a little—get to know Junior better?" But I was not to be dissuaded; this was my moment, my great adventure, and I intended to make the most of it.

One cold morning—it was February—Gloria, Agnes Horter, and I took the train to Washington. It had been arranged that we were to meet Junior and his best man, Ballard Moore, at the Shoreham Hotel. Ballard Moore and Eugene West, another friend of his, were to be Junior's witnesses; Gloria and Agnes were to be mine. We arrived at the hotel around noon. Junior had reserved a suite for us. I changed into my wedding gown, and we all set out for a little Baptist parsonage in Rockville, Maryland, a town not far from Washington.

The parsonage was not exactly what I had dreamed of as a

child, when I pictured myself walking down a church aisle in a beautiful white wedding gown, with yards and yards of billowing tulle flowing behind me. But I consoled myself by thinking of Consuelo's wedding; I saw in my mind her beautiful wedding and her sad, haggard face. And I said to myself that a wedding is more than protocol and stage settings. At least, I concluded, I am marrying the man I want to marry—the man I love.

But as I stood in front of the minister, the Reverend Rowland Wagner, I suddenly had doubts, and my knees began to shake. For the first time since I believed myself in love with Junior, I was frightened. After all, I asked myself, what did I really know about this man standing next to me—this man I was solemnly promising to "love till death do you part"? What did I know of life? What did I know of anything? Then, before my fears had time to get the better of me, I heard the voice of the minister, as from a great distance, say solemnly, "I pronounce you man and wife." I was a married woman, and there was a reception waiting for us at the Chevy Chase Country Club.

The next morning, as I stood on the observation platform of the Florida Special, waving good-by to Gloria, my sense of loneliness was overwhelming. For the first time since our birth Gloria and I were to be separated. And here was I, at sixteen, on my way to Palm Beach with a husband I scarcely knew, to begin a life I had as yet not stopped to imagine.

CHAPTER V

We Become Four

Gloria

There were gaiety and laughter all about me as the merry little group waved good-by to Thelma and Junior when their train pulled out of the station, but there was no gaiety in my heart. I felt only a dull, detached sensation of bewilderment as I saw, through tear-filled eyes, Thelma waving me a kiss. It was not until Agnes and I were in our drawing room on the way back to New York that I felt the full impact of my separation from Thelma; its meaning then hit me like a tidal wave, and my tears fell unrestrained. We had always been together. We had shared our thoughts, our dreams. Our lives, which until now had seemed to be a single life, were for the first time divided; and each would acquire an identity and a history of its own. I felt, then, that I would never recover from the feeling that swept upon me —the feeling of utter aloneness. I had realized, of course, that this separation was one day bound to come, but now that I was facing it, the fact was overwhelming.

During the next few days I often wondered what Mamma and Papa would think of Thelma's elopement. I did not have long to wait to find out. I also learned, to my dismay, that Papa had made reservations for me on the S.S. *Finland*, and that I was to be aboard her at the appointed day, or else! With a heavy heart I closed "Chez Nous," said a tearful good-by to dear, kind, sweet Mrs. Travell, and sailed to Belgium.

WE BECOME FOUR

Brussels, the gay "little Paris" of Europe, as its inhabitants fondly call it, was anything but gay to me that lovely early spring. I was miserable without my twin. The familiar streets and places only reminded me the more of her. Shortly after my arrival I wrote Thelma, telling her I was going to ask Papa to let me come back to America if I could stay with her. "If I could?" How strange the words seemed to me as I wrote them! We who had never dreamed of using such words as "If it's convenient," "May I?" or "I hope you can," between us, now had to resort to such terms. But, young as I was, I realized that from now on we were two separate identities, and that it was not only our wishes and inclinations that mattered. From now on others would have to be considered in the pattern of our lives.

Thelma

The first two or three weeks of our honeymoon at the Everglades Club in Palm Beach were golden. Junior and I were wined, dined, feted. I felt thoroughly possessed; and I enjoyed the possession. I would coo like a pouter pigeon whenever I heard Junior say, with such pride, to his friends, "This is my wife." I was not what today I would consider a woman in love, but I was all that is implied by the cliché: a girl in love with love. To be wanted, to be loved, pampered, admired—this was enough. That between us there was no deep understanding, no basic rapport, was not then important; a pleasant way of life sometimes passes as a reasonable facsimile for love.

But as the weeks passed, my misgivings about the marriage took more definite form. Junior was drinking much more heavily. Our friends began to raise their eyebrows when we entered a room together, with Junior obviously not quite steady on his feet. But with the naïve confidence of youth, I assumed that this drinking was no more than a honeymoon trait—at most a part of the holiday mood. To myself I said, "He'll stop when we get back to New York." Youth is really the season of blind credulity. I went on believing blissfully that I would always be as happy as I imagined myself at that moment.

In the latter part of April, Junior and I returned to New York and took an apartment on East Fifty-first Street. But his drinking got worse, not better; and in his drunken moments he was abusive. I was thoroughly frightened; this was to me a new kind of danger, one I had not come up against in the world I knew with Mamma and Papa. I did not know how to cope with it, and I was too proud to seek advice.

Mamma's long-delayed letter, which I got on my arrival in New York, didn't help matters any. It was a short, peremptory note, stating that since I had made my own decision, and had not considered it necessary to advise her of my intended marriage, the only thing she could say was that she hoped we would be happy. I knew the moment I opened the envelope just what the tone of the letter would be. When Mamma was happy or pleased, her writing was careless. Words would run into one another. But when she was angry or displeased, her writing was a model of calligraphy; every word would be carefully, almost painstakingly written, and all the significant words would be underlined. This was such a letter. I could almost hear her say, "Thelma has made her bed, now let her lie in it."

Junior and I rarely dined at home. Life for us seemed to be a continuous, mad social whirl: Tuxedo Park, Saratoga, Belmont, Southampton. Junior set the pace, and I followed—blindly. Occasionally, however, I would protest. I would beg him to let up a little, to stay home—above all, to stop drinking so much. Then he would snap at me. "After all, damn it," he would say, "my job as a broker demands that I see people. I have to circulate." And I would try to hint, tactfully, that the people he liked to "circulate" with were not always the kind I liked to be with, or the kind I would like to have in my house. Some were a little shady. All were very rich. All were the kind that carried enormous quantities of bills in their wallets. I began to hear, moreover, that Junior was borrowing money from these "friends." The picture was not pleasant.

In no accepted sense of the word was Junior "stable." He would change jobs at the drop of a hat. At one moment he would be wildly enthusiastic about one of his "big deals," the next moment he would be maudlin drunk. As a consequence we were —on paper, at least—either very rich or very poor; and it would have required a genius of an accountant to establish our credit rating on any given day. But whether we were rich or poor, Junior never believed in paying a bill. At times I would be afraid to open the mail. I still recall with horror those interminable bills on which were the red-printed words, heavily underlined: "Please—Long Past Due." When I would approach him tearfully, and ask him to pay what he owed, he would take me in his arms and, like Cary Grant in one of his scoundrel roles, assure me that he was doing all this for me—he wanted me to have everything in the world that was beautiful. At these moments I would tend to forget the heartaches and the worries of the past months; I appreciated his desire for me to have everything that was beautiful in the world—I only wanted him to have, in addition, the desire and ability to pay for it.

One day it became clear that I was going to have a baby. I was overjoyed; I believed then, as most young girls do, that having a baby is tantamount to owning Aladdin's lamp. A baby is by nature magical; it is the culmination of love; it fulfills all the hopes and longings of a lifetime; its mere existence is a guarantee of happiness. I was certain, now, that Junior would change. But when I told him about the baby, expecting him to become radiant, as I was, with pride and excitement, I found, instead, that his face dropped. He was not looking for competition; he was not looking for responsibility; he didn't want the baby. I covered my face with my hands, to hide the agony in my eyes.

"Oh, come now, dear," he said, lying politely, "of course I

want the baby." But it was obvious that his words were intended, if not as gallantry, at best as a device to prevent my making a scene. I went to my room and cried.

A few days later I got a letter from Gloria saying she was coming to visit me. This was wonderful news; I had missed her enormously during the months of my marriage. And there was no one in the world whom I needed at this time more than Gloria. But now that I knew she was coming, I was a little frightened. How could I tell her what was going on in my mind? I was supposedly mature, now, with divided loyalties. How could I tell her about Junior's extraordinary behavior towards me? My foolish pride made it hard for me to tell her that her suspicions had been well founded, that, after a few short months, my marriage was a failure.

But all my fears in this connection were as foolish as my imagined pride. Gloria and I have always had a kind of psychic rapport; our thoughts seemed to move from one to the other with telepathic certainty. When I met Gloria at the dock, I didn't have to tell her anything: she knew.

Gloria had gone away for the weekend, Junior was out, Elise, Gloria's maid, had gone out shopping. I was alone in the house that hot August day. I found it difficult to breathe and decided to go out for a short walk on the Avenue. I felt miserable and depressed as I put my hat on and started for the door. As I got out on the stoop, I don't know whether I was dazzled by the bright sunlight after the dark room with its shades down, but I missed a step and fell headlong into the street. A crowd soon gathered. Somebody said, "Get an ambulance."

"Please, please, don't get an ambulance!" I heard myself say. "If somebody will just carry me into the house, I'll be all right. I live here."

A policeman had arrived by this time. He carried me upstairs and placed me on the sofa in the drawing room. "I'd better call for a doctor," he said, realizing my condition.

"Yes, yes, of course; Dr. MacPherson," I said, giving him the telephone number. I hope I thanked that policeman. I don't remember now. The only thing I remember is that I was in great pain and that he, sitting next to me, was saying gently every now and then, "There, there; the doctor will be here soon."

I don't know how long it took Dr. MacPherson to arrive, but it seemed an eternity to me. After he had examined me, he told me I would have to go to the hospital at once. He was afraid I was going to lose my baby.

Dr. MacPherson did all he could, but I lost the baby early the next morning. Junior had come to the Flower Hospital the previous night, but I had refused to see him. In some ridiculous way I blamed him for my accident. Of course he had nothing to do with it, but in my sorrow and agony I thought his not wanting the baby was the cause, directly or indirectly, of my miscarriage. I was terribly ill. Gloria sat at my bedside hour after hour, holding my hand. If it hadn't been for not wanting to leave her behind, I would not have cared if then and there I had died.

My husband came into my room the second day. I noticed he was a little drunk. He had a silly, inane look on his face.

"Well, darling, you look fine," he said jovially. "It won't be long before you're up and about again." With a sheepish smile, he informed me he was going to Saratoga that afternoon for a few days' racing, but would be back in time to take me home. I lay there facing him quietly, and all of a sudden I felt a complete indifference to him; I didn't care where he went, why he went, or if he went at all. He had become a complete stranger to me. Nothing is deader than a dead love.

When I got back from the hospital, my married life with Junior was over. We went out together. I was polite to him, but distant; he was distant but not always polite. The newspaper columns started to hint at a rift between the "young, beautiful Mrs. Converse and her husband, Junior."

One day Junior asked me to arrange a dinner dance at the Beaux Arts on West Fortieth Street; he had some important customers he wanted to entertain.

Gloria

It was the night of Junior's dinner dance that I saw Thelma really angry with me for the first time. She was anxious to have everything perfect and had gone to infinite trouble about it. "Everything must be just right, Gloria," she told me the day before the party. "It's not a big party, I know, but I do want it to be a success. This morning I saw the maître d'hôtel, the chef, and the florist, and they promised me that everything would be perfect. Now it's up to Junior to get the liquid refreshments. I hope he picks out a good bootlegger. It would be terrible if anything went wrong in that direction."

The afternoon of Thelma's party I had promised to go to a *thé dansant* at the Plaza Hotel with Jack Addams.

"Please, Gloria, be in good time to dress for dinner," Thelma said. "Promise me you won't be late."

The Plaza was crowded that day. We saw friends at tables on all sides of us. And time passed quickly. Jack and I danced, we talked, we table-hopped. Suddenly I looked at my watch. It was almost seven, and Thelma, who was already on edge because of Junior, was waiting for me; I had promised to be at her dinner on time.

When we got outside, we discovered—to my horror—that there was a small blizzard blowing. No taxis were to be had; we had to walk to Thelma's, no matter how long it would take us. The snow was falling in heavy whirlings; the wind on Fifty-ninth Street lashed around our legs; it was difficult even to stand.

I reached home freezing. Thelma, ready to leave, was mad.

"Darling, I'm so sorry!" I said lamely, "but it's snowing; we couldn't get here earlier."

Thelma's thoughts, I knew, were on Junior, not me; she was tense because of him; she was understandably worried about the party. Anything might go wrong; Junior, for example, might get insulting, or dead drunk, or both. But for the moment her resentment was turned on me. "I have noticed it's snowing," she said curtly. "Now please don't waste time. As soon as the car drops us, I'll send it back for you."

I hoped Thelma would quickly get over being angry with me; I didn't want to add to her worries. Junior, even in my presence, had been unmanageable. Only a few afternoons before, when I was in the apartment, he had come home reeling drunk. Thelma, in despair, had blurted, "Oh Junior, not again!—not so early in the afternoon!"

Junior had staggered to the side of the door, glared at the two of us through bleary eyes, then rubbed his eyes, no doubt to make sure he was not seeing double. "Thelma," he mumbled, almost incoherently, "what are you doing sitting there in the middle of the night?" If a stranger had wandered in at that moment, he might have assumed that we were rehearsing some twins-and-a-drunk routine for a skit.

When Thelma pointed out to Junior that this was the middle of the afternoon—not the night—his only comment was, "Aw, the hell with you!—you're always nagging." Then he staggered out of the apartment. Thelma had cried bitterly after that, and asked me what I thought she should do. And I had suggested that she visit Papa and Mamma in Brussels for a while. "Things might be different when you get back."

Perhaps I did not know my twin as well as I thought I did, for as I entered the room at the Beaux Arts she came up to me and put her arm around my waist. "Darling, you look ravishing, and believe it or not, you are not the last to arrive. The storm must be getting worse." Then pointing across the room, she added, "You see that table over there, the one Angie Duke is sitting at? That's your table. I think you know most of the people there. If you don't, just introduce yourself."

As I walked over, I saw Angie Duke talking to a pretty girl whose name I don't remember. She was a typical product of the Twenties. She affected the thin, flat-chested look then in style. The "flat look"—which was exciting only to teachers of plane geometry—was achieved with a band of silk pulled tightly across the bosom and hooked in back. As far as the effect was concerned, the band might just as well have been a tight strip of adhesive tape.

This girl, like the others, also displayed what was then called the "debutante slouch." Her tummy was thrown forward, her back well arched, one hand perched on her hip, while the other manipulated an almost foot-long cigarette holder. I believe Irene Castle was responsible for this composite slouch-and-plane style, but somehow it was becoming to her. Irene Castle was always glamorous and graceful, but the style made most debutantes look ridiculous. Thelma and I let our bosoms and waists remain where God placed them.

As I approached the table, a man I had never seen before got up. Turning to Angie, he said, "Don't tell me, Angie. This beautiful girl must be Thelma's twin sister. I've never seen two people so much alike." Then he introduced himself. "I'm Reggie Vanderbilt," he said.

I sat down, pleased with the compliment. Reggie talked easily and warmly in a low voice. I liked him at once. He complimented me on my dress, which was green, but which to him in the dim light of the room looked gray, and he took it as an auspicious sign that at our first meeting I should be wearing his horse-show colors—gray and white. I was soon to learn that horses were an essential part of his life; and although every horse was Greek to me, I pretended to be enormously interested. I listened politely while he told me about his champion stallion, Fortitude, and despite my total unconcern for horses his talk fascinated me. Perhaps the truth is that he fascinated me, not the talk; but the one was a function of the other.

Reggie had a high, arched nose which was set off by thin, small, sensitive nostrils; I thought it a perfect nose. His blue-gray eyes were set far apart; they were gay eyes which fixed themselves on you, and made you, by identification, feel gay. His mouth was his only bad feature: it tended, in repose, to droop at the corners. Reggie was a good deal older than I, but to me that was part of his attraction.

After we had talked a long while, he asked me to dance. "Would you mind very much if we don't just yet?" I said. "I've been dashing all day, and I'm starved." I felt instinctively that he was only asking out of politeness, that he would much rather not.

I could almost hear his sigh of relief. It was only later that I learned that he abhorred dancing; he only got up on the floor when there was no way to avoid it. We were getting along famously.

"What a bore you must think I am," Reggie said later. "I've been talking your ear off, and I haven't given you a chance to say a word. But promise me you'll let me take you out to see Fortitude one day, then you'll see why I'm so proud."

I told him I'd love to see Fortitude with him; and to my delight he answered with the quaint exclamation I had associated only with Papa: "Bully," he said.

I glanced back and saw Thelma. She also seemed to be having a good time. She was laughing with a group of friends—Mrs. Richard Wilson, who had been so kind to us when we first came to America; Hannibal de Mesa; Margaret Power of our Convent days; Will Stewart; Peggy Watson, who later married the Duc de Nemours; and a few others. I looked for Junior. He caught my eye and waved. "Thank God," I thought, "he's sober."

Hannibal de Mesa left Thelma and came over to ask me to

dance. As we tangoed, he said teasingly, "Well, Gloria, I see you have charmed the most eligible bachelor in town."

The party broke up just a little before dawn. For Thelma it had been a success; for me a great success. The last stragglers: Jimmy O'Gorman, Angie Duke, Peggy Watson, Reggie, Junior, Thelma, and I went downstairs, joking, chattering, laughing, to ours cars. Someone suggested driving over to Childs for an early breakfast, but Thelma and I begged off.

As we reached the street, we found that my baby blizzard had turned into a real, honest-to-goodness blizzard. There must have been at least seven inches of snow on the ground. Waiting for our cars, I heard the sound of jingle bells. I turned around and, sure enough, coming down the street was a sleigh. The clip-clop of the horses' hoofs, the tinkle of the harness bells, the pure white snow made such an entrancing picture that, like a child, I clapped my hands. Turning to the man standing next to me I said, "Oh, look, a troika! We are in Russia," and found myself looking into the laughing eyes of Reggie Vanderbilt.

I felt like such a fool. All night I had, or thought I had, behaved like a woman of the world, and here I was in front of, of all people, Reggie Vanderbilt, clapping my hands like a schoolgirl.

With a little squeeze of my arm as he helped me into the car, he asked, "If the snow holds out, will you go for a sleigh ride in my troika?"

"Any time," I said.

Thelma had finally left Junior, and was staying at the Waldorf. The following day she was to sail to join Papa and Mamma in Brussels. Her room was in confusion; suitcases were on the floor, on the chairs, on the bed, and I was doing my best to help her get them closed. Suddenly the phone rang. I answered. "Is Gloria there?" I heard an unfamiliar voice ask. "This is Helen." Helen who?

Our father, Harry Hays Morgan

Mamma

Left to right, front: Our grandmother; our grandfather, General Judson Kilpatrick; Great Grandmamma; our great uncle, General Vickers; and his wife. *Back:* Aunt Rosa Blanca, Aunt Blanca Rosa, and Aunt Amelia. Taken at Santiago, Chile.

Double exposure

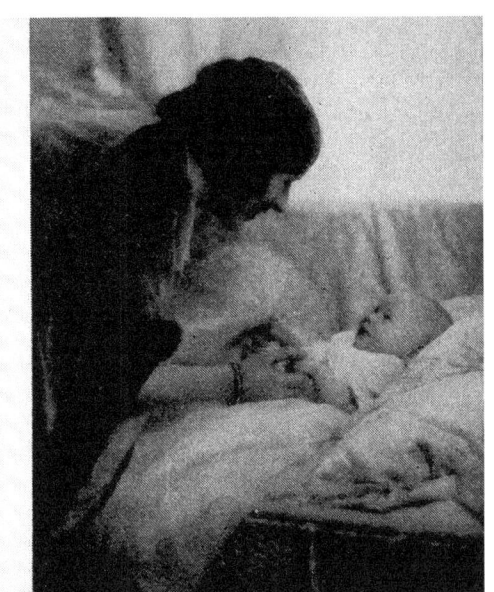

Little Gloria and her mother

Little Gloria and her father

Gloria

Hugh Cecil

Presented at court

Thelma

Thelma, Tony, and Duke

Burrough Court

Averill and the zebra and Andrew Rattray

Friedel Hohenlohe

Margarita and Friedel with their first son

Entrance to Schloss Langenburg, the ancestral castle of the Hohenlohes

Phyfe

Young Gloria at sixteen

Look Magazine Photo

Young Gloria's wedding to Pat De Cicco. Her mother is wearing her own wedding dress.

Gloria with Elizabeth Wann, a faithful friend

Thelma and Edmund Lowe

Tony

Photograph by Walter Bird

Dick

Photograph by Vandyk

Our sister, Consuelo, painted by Clemente del Camino

Phyfe

Gloria in the forties

Thelma in the forties

Dorothy Wilding

WE BECOME FOUR

It turned out that the call was from Helen Beadleson, whom I had met several times but certainly did not know well. I was surprised that she had called me, and I was doubly surprised when she asked me if I could dine with her that night and go to the theater. "There will be only four of us," she said, and then added what I assume she felt was necessary encouragement, "It's a big first night."

I hesitated. I was torn between a desire to go and the feeling that I should stay with Thelma during her last night here. I decided to go.

As I entered her drawing room, Helen, looking very chic, as though she had just stepped out of *Vogue*, in a simple black velvet dress, was talking animatedly with two attractive men: Reggie Vanderbilt and his best friend, Julian Little. Reggie looked up. "Oh, the troika girl," he said teasingly. "Hello, Gloria."

Surprised, Helen said, "Oh, so you two have met before."

During dinner Reggie directed most of his talk to me. He sat next to me at the theater. And, putting two and two together, I decided that Reggie had taken a liking to me. I hoped this was so, for this second meeting confirmed the impression I had of him at Thelma's dinner. I liked him; I liked his worldliness; I liked his combination of charm and relaxed ease. My feeling about him was largely intuitive; it seems absurd, now, to say that I was taken with his seriousness, when so much of his conversation hinged around his horses and the social trivia which made up the day-to-day world Thelma and I then knew; yet my reaction was emotionally sound. Reggie was a mature, thoughtful, thoroughly civilized man; I had not known his kind before, and he fascinated me.

At intermission time he drew me aside. "Gloria," he said, "after the show let's chuck the others and go night-clubbing." The suggestion was tempting; if my conscience had not already been burdened by my desertion of Thelma, there would have been nothing that would have pleased me more. I explained that Thelma was sailing the next morning on the *Lapland* and that I really should get back. Reggie was understanding. "I'll be down to see her off, too," he said.

Thelma's cabin, the next day, was crowded with friends. Her sailing had developed into an impromptu party. Thelma was depressed, but she hid her feelings with the skill of an actress. I looked around for Reggie. Although the cabin and the passageway leading to it were thronged with our friends, Reggie was not to be seen. Absently I picked a grape from a large, luscious steamer basket that had been set on Thelma's berth. Picking up the card, I read, *"Bon Voyage*—Reggie." He had sent a gift, but had not come himself. I was disappointed.

When the first call of "All visitors ashore" was heard, I quickly kissed Thelma and whispered that I was taking French leave. I was not up to the strain of maintaining appearances in front of kind friends; parting from Thelma was always like losing part of myself. Even now, when Thelma is away, I find myself stopping in the middle of a sentence, expecting her to finish it—or at least to supply the precise words for what I have only partially framed in my mind.

At that moment I felt very sorry for myself. I felt lost without Thelma, and it seemed ridiculous to me that I had not sailed with her. I decided that a change of scene would do me good; I had been invited by the Figueroas to visit them in Cuba, and all of a sudden I was eagerly looking forward to the trip.

At loose ends, I went back to my room in the Waldorf. There, to my surprise, was a huge box of flowers. I started to open it. Just then the telephone rang. "Gloria, this is Reggie. I'm so sorry." Reggie spluttered a long, disjointed explanation for his not appearing that morning—something about Norton, his valet, not calling him in time, and about getting down to the ship only to find me gone. Finally he said, "Darling, just to show me I'm forgiven, please have lunch with me. I don't care how many engagements you have to break—break them all. I'll pick you up in ten minutes." Then he slammed down the receiver.

"Well!" I said aloud. "When this Reggie Vanderbilt wants something, there's no doubt about it, he wants it; and, what's more, he probably gets it."

We had lunch at the Ritz Grill. I told him all about Thelma's reasons for her trip to Europe. He was sorry about the breakup, he said; he liked both Thelma and Junior so much. I then told him I was leaving the following week to visit the Figueroas in Cuba. And I was startled when he interrupted, saying, "Must you go? Can't you put it off?"

My face must have revealed my astonishment. Reggie answered his own question. Somewhat glumly he said, "No, I guess not."

The next few days were packed with excitement. Reggie gave me what in those days was called a "rush"; we lunched together each day; we dined together each night; we went together to parties, to the theater. Naturally I was thrilled and flattered, and the world seemed full and beautiful. But then, in the rare moments when I was alone, disturbing thoughts began creeping into my mind. I realized I was falling in love with Reggie, and the banal, but nevertheless significant question posed itself to me: To what was all this leading?

The morning of the fourth day Reggie called and suggested we drive up the Hudson to lunch at a roadside inn he knew about. I was delighted. The pace Reggie had been setting for me was wearing, and the prospect of a quiet drive to the country sounded like heaven. He picked me up around eleven in his car, which I observed was finished in gray and white, his horse-show colors. It was a crisp February day; I snuggled into the seat, and Reggie solicitously tucked a warm opossum rug around me.

For a long time neither of us said much; we both, for some reason, were in a reflective mood. There was a bright sun shining, the Hudson sparkled, and the brisk, clear air was to me as heady as champagne. I was happy, sitting next to Reggie, and I realized that I enjoyed just being close to him. I tried to analyze my thoughts. I was certain now that I was in love--deeply in love. Reggie must have sensed my thoughts, for suddenly he broke into my reveries, saying, "I hope the items in the gossip columns are not upsetting you too much. Those idiots with their meddling can surely ruin things."

The enchanting day passed, and Reggie had me back at the hotel in time to change for dinner and the theater. I chose one of my prettiest dresses and dressed quickly in happy anticipation of seeing the current hit *The Music Box Revue*.

In this fabulous period the theater was at its peak of popularity and glamour. There were many, many openings in a season and each was a glittering occasion. Everyone dressed. The few who were not in evening clothes looked out of place in the dazzling assemblage. Even before the curtain went up, you were aware of the excitement that pulsed in the audience, of the atmosphere of exhilaration. The audiences were a mélange of artists, the demimonde, intelligentsia, westerners who had struck it rich, gamblers, politicians, and "society"—all enjoying enjoyment. It seems rather a pity to me that today there are so few occasions like these—when women dressed and looked their prettiest, and their escorts dressed and looked their handsomest.

Those were the days of extravaganzas and spectacles, and in these areas the *Ziegfeld Follies* and *George White's Scandals* have never been surpassed. The productions provided a combination of lavish, extravagant costumes; superb sets; the lilting music of Irving Berlin and Jerome Kern; and outstanding talent, as well as ravishingly beautiful show girls such as Peggy Hopkins Joyce, Lilyan Tashman, and Olive Thomas. Dolores, who was known only by this single name, was to my mind the queen of all the beauties; she had an exquisite face and a perfect body. I still remember a fabulous costume she wore in one of the *Follies*, when the *Follies* were still staged on the Ziegfeld roof; it was patterned after a white peacock, and was heavily embroidered in pearls and rhinestones; the costume was said to have cost a fortune. The peacock symbolism was directly in line with Dolores' personality; she herself strutted like a peacock. At the end of the tableau, with a grand flourish and fanfare accenting her movements, she would turn majestically, and the bejeweled tail would rise and spread out behind her as a spectacular and breathtaking finale.

The theatrical productions reflected the luxury, indulgence, elegance, and profligate spending of those postwar, speakeasy days. Pleasure and entertainment were never more prized, nor sought after with less restraint. And it was against this feverish background that, in a few short days, my romance with Reggie bloomed.

It seemed altogether in keeping with the pace, the excitement, and the mood of the time that at the Colony restaurant, after the theater, Reggie asked me to marry him.

We decided to ask Maury Paul to dine with us the following night. He would be the best person to advise us how to handle the press, which we knew would descend on us like an avalanche. Ever since his divorce a few years before Reggie had been the target of every columnist and gossip writer in town. You could scarcely pick up a newspaper without reading, "Reggie Vanderbilt, the gay, debonair bachelor, was seen doing such-and-such." We were sure that unless it was handled by someone experienced in these matters, the news of our engagement would give the papers a field day.

After dinner in Reggie's house, the following evening, we all retired to the "den" for liqueurs and coffee. This was quite a large room, facing what had once been the back yard but had been transformed into a miniature garden. Reggie had patterned the den after one of the rooms in the famous Inn Guillaume le Conquérant, near Deauville. I was fascinated by Reggie's den; beautiful old dark-oak paneling gave it a warm, friendly feeling;

the banquettes, upholstered in *toile de Jouy*, and the little tables around the room with their bright red-and-white checkered tablecloths were gay, cozy, and inviting. At the far end of the room, facing the garden, was a bar, the first one I had ever seen in a private house.

Over our drinks I noticed that Reggie seemed preoccupied as we sat down facing Maury. "Maury," he said, "you know both Gloria and I value your friendship. What I am about to tell you Gloria has already heard from me."

"Please, darling," I tried to interrupt, knowing what was coming.

"No, dearest," he went on, "I want Maury to know that you are entering this marriage with your eyes wide open—and what you may be letting yourself in for."

Turning to Maury, he went on, "Most of the inheritance left to me outright by my father has long since gone. I now derive my income from a five-million-dollar trust, which, after my death, must go to Cathleen and any other children I might have." He paused. "And there may well not be other children," he said thoughtfully.

I could not stand this morbid talk any longer. Putting my arms about him, I said, "Darling, all this is not necessary. I told you last night I love you. I want to marry you, and I will not hear another depressing word out of you."

With a smile he turned to Maury. "I'm the proudest and happiest man in the world. What this angel sees in me I will never know." Then, shaking his head, he added, "But I still don't believe Gloria realizes what she might be up against. Good Lord, a Mrs. Vanderbilt without any money!"

Maury and I laughed. Reggie, now smiling, got up. "I haven't talked this seriously in years," he said. "I need a drink."

Over our drinks we told Maury we planned to be married February 17 with as little publicity as possible. Maury roared. "Wishful thinking won't make it so, old boy; but seriously,

WE BECOME FOUR

Reggie," he went on, "the best and only way is to have Gloria's parents make a formal announcement through the Associated Press. This will prevent any wild speculations my confreres might come up with."

As I was getting into bed that night Reggie's words came back to me: "I want Maury to know that you are entering this marriage with your eyes wide open." Reggie's concern regarding my financial position did not worry me at all. Money had never played a big part in my life. What did worry me was meeting his mother. Would she like me? What was she like? Would she think me too young? Would I like her? Would I be capable of running a big house? We had lived mostly in hotels, and on the rare occasions when we did have our own home, Mamma did not think it necessary to teach us this complex art. The very thought of hiring, worse, of firing servants sent shivers through me. Would the chef laugh at me behind my back at my obvious lack of knowledge of the mysteries of his kitchen? My thoughts tumbled about like Mexican jumping beans on a hot stove.

That night I cabled Mamma and Papa: "Divinely happy. Regino has asked me to marry him. Leaving for Europe immediately after wedding February 17. Love. Gloria."

There was an amusing mixup over this cable. My reason for using the Spanish translation of Reginald was that I was afraid the press would catch on and print the news before a formal announcement could be made. This little trick confused my whole family. They thought I meant Regino Truffin. Only Thelma, who must have remembered my disappointment when Reggie didn't show up at the time of her sailing, guessed the truth. The two shortest cables ever exchanged between us were Thelma's "Vanderbilt?" and my answer, "Yes."

When the mystery was unraveled, I received a long cable from Papa and Mamma, wishing me all the happiness in the world, and saying that Mamma would be over on the next ship, and that I would have to postpone the wedding as she would not have time to make all the necessary preparations. This horrified me, as a big wedding was the last thing Reggie and I wanted. I cabled and explained to her as tactfully as I could that I loved her very much, but that it was unnecessary for her to come, as it meant changing all our plans. Much as I loved her and hated hurting her, I couldn't bear the thought of the chaos she would create if she were there. To this cable she answered she understood and was sending Consuelo.

I chuckled to myself, thinking how poor, dear Mamma must have hated sending these lengthy, costly cables.

The day came when I was to meet Mrs. Vanderbilt; I was scared. I suppose every young girl must have some sort of qualms when she is about to meet her future mother-in-law for the first time, and I was no exception. Adding to this natural apprehension was the knowledge that I was going to meet not only Reggie's mother, but the head of the Vanderbilt family as well. The Vanderbilts had fired the imagination of both the public and press ever since the days of old Commodore Vanderbilt of "The Public Be Damned" fame. And they symbolized the romantic "Rags to Riches" story the public loves so well. The name Vanderbilt had also become synonymous with fabulous wealth—vast estates in Newport, France, England, and almost any other part of the world you might care to mention. They owned "palaces" up and down Fifth Avenue; their marriages were brilliant alliances whose branches spread across two continents. With the constant repetition in the newspapers of the family's name, holdings, endowments, and activities, a legend had been born, and there were many who had come to believe that the Vanderbilts were a race apart. It was not the legend, however, that worried me at this time; nor was it the Vanderbilt money. My family and my upbringing had equipped me well to meet "prestige" situations. What frightened me was the possibility that Mrs. Vanderbilt might think me too young for this son she so adored, and might not give her approval to the marriage.

After the tragic death of her son Alfred on the *Lusitania*, torpedoed by the Germans in 1915, Mrs. Vanderbilt had given Reggie all the love she had formerly lavished on Alfred.

As we drove to his mother's house, I held on tight to Reggie's hand. "Don't worry, dearest, she'll love you as much as I do," he assured me.

"I'm petrified," I whispered, almost in tears. "If she doesn't like me, I will never marry you, Reggie. I really mean it." He tried to reassure me by putting his arms around me.

Mrs. Vanderbilt's house occupied the block from Fifty-seventh to Fifty-eighth Streets on Fifth Avenue (the site of the present Bergdorf-Goodman and the Tailored Woman stores). It had enormous black, wrought-iron gates on the park side, facing the Plaza. I never saw those gates opened. In the past Mrs. Vanderbilt had entertained in the "grand manner" and large balls were a yearly occasion. But now that she was in her eighties, she had decided to close the gates and use the less imposing entrance on Fifty-seventh Street. It was through this that we entered.

Mrs. Vanderbilt received us in one of the smaller downstairs drawing rooms. My first impression was of a tiny woman with snow-white hair, standing very erect. Her long, black dress, simple to austerity, was relieved only by a *sautoir* of magnificent pearls. Around her throat was a dog collar of pearls and diamonds. This small woman stood tall in dignity, dominating her surroundings. She led the conversation into many channels: my life abroad, the diplomatic service, interesting things I must have seen, Mamma, and my sisters. But not a single word was said on the subject then closest to my heart.

As soon as we were in the car I said to Reggie, "Darling, did you tell your mother? I can't understand. She never mentioned our engagement."

He took my hands in his. "Gloria, my mother is a very undemonstrative woman and will not permit herself any show of emotion. But you will find out that this reserve covers a sincere nature and a warm heart."

A few years later I was to remember these words. Had she lived longer, the infamous Vanderbilt-Whitney case would never have developed.

"But, Reggie," I said, "I don't know where I stand."

"Don't worry," Reggie said confidently. "You'll be hearing from her."

We were sitting in the den on Seventy-seventh Street, waiting for James Deering, Reggie's intimate friend and lawyer. He was to bring the necessary papers and marriage license for our signatures. Jim finally arrived, explaining that it was "snowing like hell outside. Quite a storm." Reggie got him a drink, after which Jim the friend became James the lawyer. Spreading the numerous legal documents all over the table, he got down to business. "I have just come from the license bureau. I told them that, to avoid publicity, we would sign the license here. This, of course, I arranged through the proper channels. I have yours all made out, Reggie. Now, Gloria, first, what is your full name? Where were you born? What date and year?"

I answered, "August 23, 1905."

Reggie said, "Good God, you're only seventeen!"

I don't know why he had never asked me my age before, or why I had never told him.

Jim then explained that our plans would have to be changed. The laws of the state of New York require the written consent of parents if a minor is to be given a marriage license. It was necessary for me to cable my father for his written consent. Since there was then no air mail across the Atlantic, it would take several days to get an answer. We had to postpone our marriage until the sixth of March.

In a few days I had a note from Mrs. Vanderbilt:

Dear Gloria:

You will be at my house tomorrow afternoon at four o'clock to meet your future relatives.

Affectionately,

ALICE VANDERBILT

Promptly at four, Reggie and I arrived at the Vanderbilt mansion. We were ushered into what I later called the Bird Room. Gilt panels, on which were painted brightly colored birds and fruits, adorned the walls. I use the term lightly, as they did anything but adorn this large drawing room.

Mrs. Vanderbilt came to me, took my hand, and led me into the room. I heard her say, "Florence, I want you to meet my future daughter-in-law, Gloria." Florence was Mrs. McKay Twombley, née Vanderbilt. Of the many persons I met that afternoon, those that remain sharpest in my memory are Brigadier General Cornelius Vanderbilt and his wife, Grace; Mrs. John Shepard, Mrs. Vanderbilt's sister; and Mrs. Henry White, née Emily Vanderbilt.

I was greatly relieved that Reggie never left my side, for the Vanderbilts, en masse, are a distant and restrained group, formal to a fault. I was to find out that individually they were warm and charming and, in time, most of them became my friends; but in that room, at that moment, they seemed frighteningly aloof.

The one bright spot was when someone suddenly put friendly arms around me and said, "I'm your Aunt Lulu. Welcome into the family." Looking around, I recognized Mrs. Fred Vanderbilt, who had known Papa and Mamma in Lucerne. I heaved a sigh of relief and in my heart thanked her for this gesture.

The days that followed were crowded. Parties in our honor came one after the other. The press was really snapping at our heels now, and I was bustling around, trying simultaneously to by-pass reporters and to get my trousseau together.

For my wedding gown I had decided upon a pearl-gray taffeta, as I knew this would please Reggie. Jacqueline Stewart, wife of Glen Stewart, a friend of Reggie's, suggested a small but very good dressmaker, Sonia Rosenberg. I was delighted with my final fitting. The gown was lovely.

In the meantime, Reggie begrudged every moment I spent away from him at what he called "unnecessary nonsense."

"But, Reggie," I'd say, "I have to have a trousseau. Don't you want me to look pretty?"

"There'll be plenty of time for that," he would answer. "I'll buy you the whole of Paris."

Consuelo arrived a few days before the wedding and I moved from Margaret Power's home to the Marguery, where Consuelo was staying. I was happy to see her and have her with me.

The plans had been that the small wedding would be held in Consuelo's apartment at the Marguery, but by now the press was turning our wedding into a circus. It was unbearable. Reggie told me his great friends, Mr. and Mrs. Van der Koch, had offered their house on East Ninety-second Street for the ceremony and if Consuelo and I didn't mind, he thought it would assure us more privacy. I couldn't have been more grateful.

The night before my marriage Consuelo and I dined quietly in our apartment. I was glad to stay home. The past few days of bustle and excitement had left me exhausted.

I awoke the next morning with a very sore throat. My cheeks were burning; I felt terrible.

Elise, my maid, came in, set the breakfast tray on my bed, and went to the window to open the blinds. I could see it was still snowing and the storm was raging. I shut my eyes, as the light hurt them.

"Come, Mademoiselle," said Elise, "don't go back to sleep. This is your wedding day. Drink your coffee while it's hot."

As I sipped the hot coffee, I began to feel a little better. Finishing it, I got out of bed. The minute I stood up I was dizzy and lightheaded.

WE BECOME FOUR

"What on earth is the matter with me?" I thought. "What could I have?" I'd never felt this way before.

As I dressed, I felt myself getting progressively hotter and hotter, then suddenly was cold. I noticed Elise watching me carefully. I must have shown the way I felt more than I thought. Deciding I'd better take my temperature, I went into the bathroom. When I took the thermometer from my mouth, I saw, to my consternation, that the mercury had shot past the danger mark. It read 104°.

I didn't believe it. I couldn't believe it. This just couldn't happen to me.

My first thought was, "I'm not going to tell Consuelo—or anybody." I knew what would happen—another postponement of my wedding.

I defied whatever it was. Nothing was going to prevent my marrying Reggie that day.

Consuelo came into the room as Elise was helping me into my gray taffeta wedding gown. In her hand was the velvet Tiffany box that Reggie had entrusted to her, to give to me this day. "Darling," she said, "this is Reggie's wedding gift."

I opened the box and gasped. Resting on black velvet was a diamond chain, attached to which was the most enormous, beautiful, pear-shaped diamond I had ever seen.

As I took it out of its box, Elise exclaimed, *"Mon Dieu,* Mademoiselle, is it really real?"

My hands trembled as I put the necklace around my neck. How exquisite it was! What a wonderful symbol of Reggie's love!

I was pleased to see only a few of the press outside as Consuelo and I left for the Edward Van der Kochs' house, but my pleasure was short-lived, for nearing the house we saw that they were all there. Mrs. Van der Koch received us at the door and said, "Thank goodness you're in time, Gloria. Reggie has been here for hours, shaking like a leaf."

Soon I heard the strains of "Here Comes the Bride" and on the arm of Glen Stewart I walked across the green-and-yellow drawing room, which was banked with yellow and white flowers.

Reggie and Julian Little, his best man, Consuelo, my matron of honor, and Jacqueline Stewart were waiting at the improvised altar. As I approached them I became lightheaded again, and the scene began swimming.

I went through the ceremony like an automaton; the figures before my eyes merged and separated in blurred patterns. I remember certain details only as they might have been seen by a being who was not quite myself, a part of me which was detached and which attended the ceremony merely as a dreamy onlooker. I can recall Reggie's kiss; and I can recall Mrs. Vanderbilt, as she put her arms around me and kissed me, in continental fashion, on both cheeks.

When champagne was served at the wedding breakfast, I took a timid sip, then found that it was not possible for me to swallow it. Mrs. Vanderbilt noticed my difficulty. "Why don't you and Reggie slip out?" she said understandingly. "It will be all right."

Vaguely I recall driving, with Reggie's arm around me, to Grand Central Station; and I recall being whisked through a special entrance to the Vanderbilts' private car. The drawing room of the car was peaceful. And I was grateful that at last we were alone. But as I sank into the big armchair and rested my head against the soft pillow, everything was blurred. The walls, the furniture, the many baskets of flowers—all receded into a phantasmagoric backdrop, then came forward again, clear and large, to press against my eyes with a force that seemed unbearable. My skin was as dry as a crust of stale bread. It seemed impossible to swallow.

The last thing I wanted at this time was to have Reggie know that I was ill. What could be more devastating to a bride, more unromantic and more anticlimactic, than to be ill on her wedding night? But when dinner was served, the cumulative effect of fever, chills, pain, and nausea was too much; nothing I could do could conceal the way I felt.

"Darling," Reggie said, "you look really ill. Are you?"

It was then that I collapsed. "Oh, Reggie dear," I said, abandoning all pretense of appearing brave, "I didn't want you to know, but I really think I'm going to die." Reggie helped me to our stateroom and got me to bed.

The next morning when we left the private car, which had been sidetracked from Providence to Bristol Ferry, we saw enormous drifts of snow banking the tracks. We got into a waiting automobile, and began the trip to Reggie's Sandy Point Farm. A storm was raging; the wind lashed at our car; snow and ice clung to the windshield.

We passed through the big stone gates of the farm, then drove to the small cottage; the big house had been closed for several years. Reggie carefully helped me out. Then I fainted. When the doctor arrived, his diagnosis was direct: diphtheria.

CHAPTER VI

New Horizons

Thelma

I was dismayed, in Paris, to learn that any divorce action sought there by an American, to be legal, must be brought on the grounds of the state in which the plaintiff resided. My attorney advised me to return to New York and apply for a divorce there. But this was easier said than done. The only ground for divorce in New York was adultery, and Junior, with his many faults, to my knowledge had given me no such basis. I was discouraged and miserable. I did not want to return to America so soon. I didn't want my friends to sympathize with me. I wanted to be near my family. I wanted to lick my wounds among those I loved.

A few days later I went to Brussels to stay with Papa and Mamma. I shall always be grateful to them. Never did they in any way censure or condemn me. Mamma never even once said, "I told you so."

Junior bombarded me with letters and cables, begging me to return, threatening to come over and get me. All this left me cold. So far as I was concerned, he didn't exist. This marriage of mine was a closed book. I now wanted to open and read a happier one.

Mamma was getting over a bad bout of the flu. I hated to see her so pale and quiet, so unlike herself. She was also suffering from what doctors called *tic douloureux*, a very painful type of facial neuralgia.

It was at this time that Papa got a cable from Reggie, saying that Gloria had diphtheria and was in a critical condition. Mamma, upon being told, had hysterics. "My baby, my darling Gloria, oh, my God, diphtheria! My baby is going to die and here I lie on a bed of pain. Get me up! Get reservations at once! I must go to her!" It was obvious that in her condition she could not have gone anywhere. As I stood by her bed, she kept up a constant moaning: "She's going to die, she's going to die."

So it was arranged that I sail on the next ship. Even if Mamma could have gone, wild horses couldn't have kept me from going.

I had to wait in Paris three days before my ship was to sail. On the day before the last I lunched with a friend at the Ritz. As the coffee was poured, I looked up from the table. To my horror, I spied Junior staggering in. I had no idea what I should do. If he came over to me, I was sure he would make a scene. Even if he didn't, it would be extremely hard for me to get away from him. I hoped he hadn't heard I was sailing the next day and decided, on his own, to sail with me. I turned my face away, hoping somehow that if I didn't see him, he, by some force of sympathetic magic, would not be able to see me. But my stratagem was useless; when next I looked up he was standing beside me, trying to put his arm around me, and babbling with a thick tongue, "Thelma, darling, oh, Thelma, darling!"

Suddenly I had one of my reliable inspirations. I looked up with a stony glare. "Really, Junior," I said, "you must be drunker than you look. Surely you should be able to tell the difference between your own wife and her sister. I'm Gloria."

For a moment he seemed stunned. Then, relying on that pseudo-dignity drunkards try to assume when they are caught in embarrassing situations, he drew himself up stiffly and said, with the greatest formality, "I'm sorry, Gloria. For a moment I thought you were my wife." He then carefully and slowly navigated his way out of the room.

"Whee! That was a close call," I said to my companion.

I stayed with Gloria and Reggie all that spring. Gloria gradually came back to health; she lost the terrible pallor that had so frightened me when I first saw her, and she began to talk with Reggie about plans for their delayed honeymoon. And it was wonderful to hear them talk, each competing to suggest places whose charm and excitement the other had not as yet known. Eventually the time came for them to leave. I hated to see them go, but I consoled myself with the thought of their happiness; and once again the Morgan twins took their opposite places on the transatlantic seesaw.

All these months I had done nothing about getting a divorce. But now that Gloria was no longer my chief concern, I discussed the necessary steps with a lawyer. He reminded me that a divorce in New York State required evidence of adultery, and since I did not have evidence of this kind, he suggested that I have Junior followed. I didn't want this for two reasons: for one, it seemed to me an underhanded way of going about a divorce; for another, it was costly. I managed, however, to overcome my distaste on both counts. I was determined to have this divorce; and my determination had a sufficiently realistic basis to outweigh both squeamishness and a realistic need for economy.

Not long after this I had a telephone call from one of the detectives who were trailing Junior. The detective informed me that Junior not only was seeing but spending many of his nights in the apartment of a well-known and much-talked-about beauty. All the necessary divorce evidence, the detective informed me, was theoretically available; all that now was required was the technicality of a raid. With my approval, the raid was made.

Junior's lawyer came to see me a few days after the raid. He begged me not to use the evidence I had. "Why not?" I asked.

NEW HORIZONS

The lawyer explained that Junior was already on probation at the brokerage firm where he now worked; the scandal would ruin him. Further, he said, the scandal would be hard on Junior's little boy, Petey, who had just been entered in a boarding school. I certainly didn't want to hurt little Petey; I had become very fond of him in the course of the few visits he had made to us during the months I lived with Junior. I asked the lawyer what alternative there was, and he, apparently prepared for this question, told me that Junior would agree not to contest any divorce action in a state where adultery was not the only ground for divorce. And so it was decided; when I was ready, I would file suit in California.

I was staying in New York, at the time, with Reba Owen, in a delightful apartment in the East Sixties which we together rented from Mrs. Lydig Hoyt. I, of course, got no money from Junior. Papa was still sending two hundred dollars a month as he had before I was married, which, since Gloria's marriage, was all mine. Gloria and Reggie gave me an additional three hundred. This meant that I was the happy recipient of five hundred dollars a month, and was able to keep my personal maid, Elise, who Gloria had insisted should accompany me to California.

One night at a dinner with Sam Goldwyn I met Allen Dwan, the famous director. I mentioned Gloria's and my hilarious and brief movie career as "Northern Lights." Since my comment was intended as a joke, and seemed to amuse the dinner company immensely, I was surprised, a few days later, to be called by Mr. Dwan and to be asked, seriously, if I would be interested in a movie part. He was in the process of shooting, in New York, a picture called *The Society Scandal*, starring Gloria Swanson.

"Mr. Dwan," I said, "I have never actually acted. I don't think I could do it."

"Of course you can," he said. "All you have to do is play yourself—a young society matron."

As I hung up, I was already picturing myself as a great star. In my imagination I saw my future swimming pools, ermine bathmats, and long, black Rolls-Royces. I also saw myself as a great tragedienne—the new Ethel Barrymore.

When I signed the contract, I was amazed to discover that I was to get a hundred and fifty dollars a week—a fortune, I thought—with a guarantee of three weeks. "By the way," he said, "you ride horseback, don't you?"

"Indeed I do," I lied. "I ride sidesaddle." The nearest I had been to a horse was when I once patted the nose of one of the horses that stand so passively in front of the Plaza Hotel.

"That's fine," Allen said. "Be in Central Park, under the bridge near the bridle path, ready and made up, next Monday morning at nine. I'm sure you'll like Miss Swanson—she's very easy to work with."

When Allen left, I began shaking. What had I let myself in for? I was certain Miss Swanson was easy to work with. The big question was: was I?

Eugenia Kelly Davis, a good friend of mine and an expert horsewoman, would help me, I was sure; she would certainly lend me a riding habit, and would advise me what to do to learn lightning horsemanship.

The next morning found me bright and early at Eugenia's apartment. Eugenia seemed as excited as I was about my new career, and she quickly outfitted me for my new role. There were two details, however, that bothered me. Her boots were too tight on me, they made me walk with little mincing steps; it was impossible for me to take the long strides she was showing me. My other problem was the hat: Eugenia's stiff bowler refused to stay perched on my head.

When Eugenia was at last satisfied that I was properly outfitted, she took me out for my first riding lesson. She tried to give me some pointers on the way to the riding school, located somewhere around West Fifty-ninth Street, but as far as I was concerned, she might as well have been talking Chinese. The riding instructor picked out for me a horse that was especially nice and quiet; and for a solid hour the horse and I walked in circles around the practice ring. I felt at last that I was getting the feel of the horse, and I prayed that this understanding might be reciprocated.

The following Monday morning I had Elise call me at the crack of dawn. Long before I was to report for work I was ready, in costume and made up. I had heard that "stars" always had their own maids on the set with them, and I wasn't going to be outdone. Elise had now become a "dresser."

As I went up to Allen Dwan, he was talking to Gloria Swanson. He introduced us. I noticed she was wearing a suit, which did not seem to me quite fair. Why did I have to be the one to ride? I was sure she knew how.

It took what seemed hours to get the cameras and reflectors in place. I didn't know what was expected of me so I just sat quietly on a large make-up box which I had borrowed from Agnes Horter. Then Allen came toward me, a handsome young man at his side. So this was to be my "husband," I thought. Allen introduced me and said, "Now, look, Thelma, the only thing you and Jack have to do is to ride under that small bridge at a walking pace. When you get about thirty feet beyond it, you will notice Gloria, who is taking a stroll, wave to you. You are to cut her dead."

"Why?" I asked.

Allen looked at me. I was sure he was thinking, "I hope she's not going to give me trouble." But he said, kindly enough, "She's been involved in a scandal and you, her best friend, won't talk to her." Nice friend, I thought.

The terrible moment had arrived. I was petrified; but to look at me you would have thought that taking a brisk canter around the Park before breakfast was for me an everyday occasion.

As I confronted my horse, my heart flew into my mouth. The horse looked enormous as he stood there, ears well back, sweating a little. The crowd had grown to nearly a hundred. Little boys were roller-skating over the bridge. It made my horse nervous, not to mention what he did to me.

I was just about to mount when I heard the groom say, "He's a bit frisky today. He didn't have much exercise during the weekend."

That did it. I was just about to turn and run, when I heard Allen shout, "All right, Thelma, we're waiting for you. Let's try and make it on one take."

I fervently hoped so.

At last I was mounted. I gently patted the horse's neck and said, "Whoa, boy, whoa, boy!" whatever that meant. It seemed to please the horse.

"Jack" and I started toward the bridge, making light conversation as we had been told to do. I noticed that he looked at me in a queer way. I prayed I didn't look as scared as I felt.

All went well till we got under the bridge and then hell broke loose. The noise and echo of the roller skates above frightened my horse and he shot off like a flash of lightning. I heard Elise hysterically shouting I had never been on a horse before—"Madame is going to kill herself." I wished she'd stop screaming, she was only frightening my horse all the more, to say nothing of myself. My hat was bobbing up and down. My hair had come loose and it was all over my face; I couldn't see.

Just then I remembered somebody had once told me that you could always stop a runaway horse if you could get him to go around in circles. I didn't know whether this was so or not, but I certainly was going to give it a good try. With my right hand I gave the rein a mighty pull. To my amazement I found myself going back the way I had come; and also to my amazement I noticed that my horse had settled down to a nice quiet canter. But what was more amazing than anything else was that I was still on him, my hat still on my head.

I don't think now that the horse was really trying to run away with me. I think he just needed the exercise.

CHAPTER VII

Heyday

Gloria

The day Papa and Mamma arrived in Paris, Reggie was in a dither. If I thought I had been nervous at meeting his mother, he seemed to me to be doubly nervous at the prospect of meeting my parents. But he needn't have been; he and Papa hit it off from the moment they set eyes on each other, and he was charmed with Mamma. That night we all dined together at Ciro's, and later went to Le Perroquet; I was happy to find that those I loved liked each other so much.

A few days later Mamma and Papa left for Brussels. But first they made us promise that we would arrive in good time for Consuelo's second marriage. Having divorced her first husband, Consuelo was now to be married, in Brussels, to Benjamin Thaw, then First Secretary to the American Embassy in Brussels.

After a glorious honeymoon in Europe, Reggie and I came back to New York. Thelma met us at the dock, and I whispered to her the wonderful news: I was going to have a baby. Reggie and I stayed for a few days at the Ritz so that I could be with Thelma. We had planned to go on to Sandy Point, which was in the process of being redecorated. Mrs. Vanderbilt called us from Newport; our rooms at Sandy Point, she said, would not be ready for another week. Would we stay with her at The Breakers until our place was finished?

The only other guests at The Breakers when we arrived were

Mrs. Raymond T. Baker and her sons by Alfred Vanderbilt, George and Alfred. Later, however, I met for the first time my sister-in-law, Gladys Szechenyi, wife of Count Szechenyi, then Hungarian Minister to Washington. She was a small, slender woman, extremely shy. Laszlo, her husband, on the other hand, was a tall, dashing, good-looking extrovert—a storybook Hungarian nobleman.

The Breakers, a massive white stone château facing the sea, was imposingly and magnificently Vanderbilt. The enormous entrance hall was medieval in its vastness. From this rose a lofty semicircular marble staircase. There were many and confusing drawing rooms on this lower floor; the dining room could easily seat a hundred and fifty people. It was at The Breakers that I was presented by Mrs. Vanderbilt to what was known as the "Newport Set."

Sandy Point Farm was a large estate, consisting of about two hundred and eighty acres. The Big House and several little cottages dotted the grounds. The largest was the one we were occupying. Reggie had moved into it after his divorce from his first wife, Cathleen Nielson, several years before. Two smaller cottages were used for guests when needed, the other quarters for the grooms and farmhands.

When we saw our newly-decorated rooms at Sandy Point we were delighted. Reggie's room, reflecting his tastes, was furnished in Empire. The drapes were of Burgundy-red damask. The whole effect, I thought, was traditional and masculine. And my room was a special delight—Louis XVI furniture, which was set against shell-pink walls and delphinium-blue glazed chintz curtains. The rest of this previously unloved house still required care, refurnishing, and redecorating, and we looked forward to a succession of exciting home-making projects.

The remainder of that season we did very little entertaining. Thelma was our only house guest. She came up for our birthday late in August and we went to the Clambake Dinner at the "oh, so exclusive" and pompous Clambake Club, of which Reggie was the president. Our only other entertaining was with a few luncheons and dinners before the opening of the horse show.

After Labor Day we installed ourselves in the house at 12 East Seventy-seventh Street in New York. This was a white stone house. The entrance hall was large and simple, the floor checkered in black-and-white marble. An eighteenth-century curved staircase led to the main floor. At the top was a life-sized portrait of Reggie's father, Cornelius Vanderbilt. The drawing room was well proportioned and furnished with a mixture of eighteenth-century French and English furniture. There was a beautiful Aubusson on the floor. In one corner stood a grand piano; from the center of the ceiling hung a magnificent crystal chandelier. The dining room overlooked the garden. The windows were leaded in the English style, with the Vanderbilt coat of arms in the center. The walls were paneled in a rich red cut velvet; the furniture was Georgian. On the sideboard stood three of Reggie's large silver trophies, the center one always filled with flowers. On the next floor were the library and our private apartments. The floor above was to be transformed into a nursery.

One of the first things I did, after we were settled, was to see Dr. MacPherson, who had looked after Thelma when she was married to Junior. I was shocked when he told me I would have to have a Caesarean operation. I asked him how serious this was. He told me that although it was a major operation, there was nothing to be afraid of; he had performed as many as eight such operations on one woman. The thought of a Caesarean worried me a little, but I was so happy I really didn't care; I made up my mind, however, that I was not going to tell Reggie until the last moment.

Reggie's friends and mine of the "Chez Nous" days all got on very well together. We gave cocktail parties in the den and small luncheon and dinner parties.

Among Reggie's numerous friends, those I saw most of were

Laura Andrews and Laura Biddle (we called them Laura A. and Laura B.). Laura B.'s daughter was William Rhinelander Stewart's first wife. Also, James and Violet Deering, Preston Gibson, Paul Andrews, Angie Duke and Leonora and Sailing Baruch, Sr., Barney Baruch's brother, and the Lucius Boomers.

I spent many afternoons in Leonora Baruch's charming house on Riverside Drive, as well as in Georgine Boomer's apartment, playing mah-jongg. Georgine was a very sympathetic and understanding person and we were great friends.

One day Reggie's sister, Gertrude Whitney, phoned to ask if she and Harry, her husband, could come over that afternoon. I had not met either of them before. She had been away most of that winter and could not be at my wedding, as she had sailed for Paris a few days before to attend the wedding of her son, Cornelius V. Whitney.

It was not surprising to me that Reggie was so fond of Gertrude. In many ways they were much alike. Both disliked any form of ostentation, any kind of show or ceremony. Each went his merry way, disregarding formalities, ignoring the pressure of convention and the snipings of gossip; each was a strong, highly individualistic, self-contained person. Gertrude was tall and very thin; she had a great deal of charm, a keen mind, and a quick wit. Harry Payne Whitney was a good complement to her. He was also tall; he was good-looking and impetuous. He formed his judgments of people quickly; once they were formed, he never changed them. I must have been especially favored that afternoon, because Harry apparently made up his mind to like me; he was to be one of my truest and most steadfast friends.

Time came for the arrival of my baby. As I was wheeled into the operating room, the last thing I was aware of was Thelma's pale, strained face. The next thing I knew, I had my baby in my arms.

Not even the lashing fury of the storm hurling itself against our windows could, I thought, ever touch or mar the utter peace and contentment I felt at this moment. Little did I dream then that a storm far more violent was to engulf my baby and me.

Reggie's look of pride and joy as he held the baby in his arms for the first time is a picture I shall never forget. As he handed her back to me, he whispered to her, "Don't forget Mummy's present." He had hidden a diamond and emerald bracelet in her blanket.

Little Gloria weighed seven and three-quarter pounds at birth and was a normal, healthy child, but Mamma insisted she was a delicate one—why, I shall never know. I had never before seen a newborn baby, and I was not equipped to dispute Mamma's dictum. Contrary to the reassurance the doctor gave me, Mamma insisted that Gloria was delicate and required special care; and I was either too innocent or too foolish to dispute her.

The first time Mrs. Vanderbilt saw little Gloria, she turned to Reggie and said, "Oh, she looks exactly like you, dear. Of all my grandchildren, she has the most pronounced Vanderbilt eyes." I have often wondered how the Vanderbilts came by those almond-shaped, almost Mongolian eyes.

I had asked Dr. Denning, little Gloria's pediatrician, if he could suggest a good baby nurse. He recommended one who came to me with excellent references. Her name was Emma Sullivan Keislich and she was never to leave Gloria from the hour I engaged her until the day she was dismissed by a judge of the Supreme Court of New York.

I stayed in the hospital for three weeks, a week longer than was expected, because I had developed phlebitis. I wanted to be home with Reggie, and I persuaded the doctor to let me go home in an ambulance with Nurse McBride. Nurse Keislich took over the baby's care after Miss McBride left.

Reggie asked me to have the baby baptized in the Episcopalian faith; I consented. The ceremony was performed by Bishop Herbert Shipman in our drawing room. James Deering was the baby's godfather; Gertrude Whitney and Jacqueline Stewart were the godmothers.

Circumstances prevented Gertrude from being present, but she had asked her mother to be her proxy. Mrs. Vanderbilt, with her soft, blue-veined hands and a radiant look in her eyes, held our baby while she was christened "Gloria Laura." I wanted to call her Regina, but Reggie insisted on "Gloria." "Laura" was in honor of Mamma.

Reggie beamed on everybody and everything.

Reggie's daughter by his first marriage, Cathleen Cushing, had her first child, Harry Cushing IV, in April; thus Reggie became a father and a grandfather at almost the same time.

Mamma decided not to go to Buenos Aires to join Papa at his new post there until I was up and around. She moved into the house with us. I was delighted at this, and was grateful for her help while I was confined to my bed. Reggie was as pleased as I, because he liked Mamma. She petted, pampered, and hovered over the baby.

I was laid up until late April, when the doctor suggested that after such a siege it might be a good idea to take me away for a change of scene.

I thought this might be wise for both of us; I had noticed Reggie himself was not looking well. I asked him if he had consulted a doctor; he said he had, and that his symptoms were nothing to worry about. Then he told me, for the first time, that he had had sclerosis since he was a young man at Yale. The doctor had advised him that if he curtailed his drinking for a while—and confined himself to light wines and champagne—he would be perfectly all right. Since I had never seen Reggie drink to excess, what he said did not worry me as much as it should have. I did not realize that his steady, consistent, although moderate drinking—particularly brandy milk punches—was seriously undermining his health.

I was sure a short holiday would do us both good. The only thing to prevent this trip was my unwillingness to leave the baby with just a nurse, as Mamma was planning to join Papa in Buenos Aires. But Mamma, sensing my feelings, suggested she stay until we returned. "Go with your husband, darling," she said, "have fun, enjoy yourself. You don't have to worry about a thing. I'll take care of the little one as long as you like."

At the end of May, after installing Mamma, the nurse, and the baby at Sandy Point, Reggie and I sailed for Paris.

We were back in Newport the first week in July.

To my surprise, Reggie suggested giving a ball. I was in a dither of excitement at the thought of being hostess at my first big party. I held out for fancy dress, remembering what fun Thelma and I had had at Cobina's, and I won.

The house became a beehive. Guest lists were made up, caterers hired, orchestras engaged. But the most important problem to me was, what was I going to wear? I took hours planning my costume, and how I wished Thelma, who had gone to California, were with me to share the fun and excitement!

I finally chose a regal costume of white-and-gold brocade and a cloak of royal purple chiffon bordered in ermine. I planned to wear a jewel-encrusted diadem on my white powdered wig.

Finally the invitations were on the way and we had a breathing spell.

Meanwhile, Mrs. Vanderbilt introduced me, for the first time, to Bailey's Beach, which was quite unlike the European seaside resorts I had known. I found to my astonishment that black stockings and below-the-knee skirted bathing suits were still *de rigueur*, and that there were more "do" and "don't" edicts than grains of sand on this chaste beach.

The sensation of that season was made by Rose Nano, a great beauty and wife of the First Secretary of the Romanian Legation in Washington. Poor Rose, unaware of the taboos, appeared in what was then called an "Annette Kellerman." The shocked hush could have been heard to the far end of staid Bellevue Avenue. Even the waves seemed to hang at the crest before crashing onto the beach. I met her later that night at Mrs. John Aspegren's dinner. She told me she could still feel the chill of the dowagers' lorgnettes sliding up and down her spine.

Newport of 1924 was especially gay. Not in years had there been such a brilliant season. The tennis tourney, the horse show, swimming, luncheons, and teas filled the days with an endless round of entertainments. Reggie by-passed the teas, spending that time in the Reading Room. For most husbands this exclusive men's club was a haven from what they referred to as the "cackling dowagers"; moreover, the Reading Room offered something stronger than tea.

While I was busy with my ball, Reggie was busier with his horse show. He had just succeeded the late Henry F. Eldridge as president. That year the feature of the show was Reggie's presentation of the Memorial Cup to perpetuate the name of his champion, Lady Dilham, the finest American-bred hackney of her size and type in the country. I was very proud that Reggie made this the most successful horse show in many years. Every box was taken. Among the boxholders were Mr. and Mrs. Moses Taylor, Mr. and Mrs. Forsythe Wickes, Mrs. Hamilton McK. Twombly, Commodore and Mrs. Arthur Curtis James, Mr. Edward J. Berwind, Mr. and Mrs. William Woodward, and Mr. and Mrs. T. Suffern Tailer.

That afternoon at Mrs. William Post's, after the show, the main topic of conversation seemed to be my ball, and there was great curiosity as to what everybody planned to wear. They pumped me also, but I wouldn't tell.

The big night arrived.

The entrance to the estate and the driveway were outlined in colored electric lights, with an occasional large cluster of bright Japanese lanterns. The whole house was a bower of flowers and ferns.

The ballroom was beautiful, with great baskets of flowers in every corner. An enormous sunburst of American Beauty roses formed a frame for the Meyer Davis Orchestra, which was placed on a raised platform at the end of the big room. To the left of the terrace, facing the Seaconnet River, a tent had been erected for supper.

I was pleased that Mrs. Vanderbilt had paid me the compliment of offering to receive with me. Although Mrs. Vanderbilt was not in costume, she looked magnificent in her simple black dress, diamond tiara, and rows of perfectly matched pearls. Mamma's only concession to costume was an exquisite old white Spanish lace mantilla draped over a large tortoise-shell comb.

The best I could do with Reggie was to get him to wear his Yale reunion jacket of the Class of 1902.

The guests started arriving and the rooms quickly filled with queens, kings, princes, harlequins, Indian potentates, *bergères*, Cossacks, mandarins, princesses, harem girls, Gay Nineties beauties, and clowns. The superb and lavish costumes, the fabulous and brilliant jewels, the handsome and colorful regalia of the men, made a picture reminiscent of the Arabian Nights. The beautiful Fernanda Goelet came as a Polish princess. Roly-poly Hannibal de Mesa chose to be a matador. Princess Miguel de Braganza looked charming in a panniered *bergère* costume of the court of Marie Antoinette. Everyone applauded when Hamilton Fish, as Louis XVI, danced a minuet with her to the strains of "Jardinier du Roi," said to have been written by Marie Antoinette for Louis XVI.

This performance started an impromptu pairing off—every Pierrot went looking for his Pierrette, every Anthony for his Cleopatra. Will Stewart, as Donnelly, in kilts, found his Mary Queen of Scots in Millicent Hearst. Townsend Burden, as Nelson, discovered his Emma Hamilton in Mrs. Raymond Baker. Fal de Saint Phalle, as Paris, spied beautiful Mrs. Drexel Biddle, Jr., his Helen of Troy.

Supper was served to the strains of a gypsy stringed orchestra; and it was not until after supper that Mrs. Vanderbilt left.

Reggie whispered to me, "Mother must have enjoyed herself. I haven't seen her up this late in years."

As we saw her to her car, Mrs. Vanderbilt said, patting my hand, "Gloria, it's been a beautiful party, a triumph for you, my dear. *Everybody* was here."

We danced and sang until morning. Dawn was coming up as the last guests left; and as we wearily went up to bed Reggie had to acknowledge that he had really enjoyed his own party.

We moved back to the New York house shortly after Labor Day.

Mamma by now had become a member of the household. She talked vaguely about rejoining Papa in Buenos Aires, but would drop the subject when either Reggie or I suggested her staying a little longer. We both liked having her. Reggie enjoyed her vivacious charm and gaiety. She never bored him.

Mamma, when she wanted to, could be a very clever and amusing conversationalist. I remember Aunt Lulu, Mrs. Fred Vanderbilt, who had known Mamma for years, telling me that Mamma was one of the most fascinating women she had ever met. She laughingly added, "I do believe she could charm the birds off the trees; and if she put her mind to it, she could make you believe that black was white."

The fall and winter of 1924 were spent mostly attending large and small dinner parties in our honor, given by various members of the family. The Vanderbilts are not a close-knit family; each branch holds forth in its own way, seeing little of the other branches except at weddings, gatherings to introduce a new member to "The Clan," or at funerals.

Reggie and I were often bored with these duty dinners but put up with them because we knew it would please Mrs. Vanderbilt. One was more formal than another. The butlers and footmen, standing like sentinels around the dining rooms, made any kind of intimate conversation impossible. The protracted ten courses of rich food, which Reggie disliked so much; the custom which required that, after dining, the ladies retire to the drawing room, leaving the men to themselves and their port—all of this poor Reggie found hard to stomach. Reggie was not just a rich man's son, but a very rich man's son. By virtue of his inheritance, he should have taken a conventional place both in society and in finance. But at heart he was a Bohemian. He was easily bored by people of small wit; and business activity which had no end other than activity itself did not appeal to him. He preferred to live his life solely to please himself. In a man without wealth, this temperament would be called one of philosophical detachment; in a rich man it is called sybaritic.

Gertrude Whitney in many ways manifested the temperament of Reggie; her sculpture, however, was a tangible creative activity, which provided a cloak for her Bohemianism. This unusual woman was a paradox. She lived two distinct lives, one always well insulated from the other. In her home on Fifth Avenue she was the highly proper society matron, the stereotype of all the Vanderbilt women. But in her studio in Greenwich Village she was, like Reggie, the unabashed Bohemian. Her studio was a meeting place for artists and their models, for writers, actors, musicians, raconteurs, geniuses, and characters. Anyone who had talent, or the earmarks of talent, was welcome.

Mrs. Vanderbilt, though proud of her talented daughter, did not fully approve of her life. I remember a time in Paris when she asked me to go with her to Gertrude's studio in Passy. She looked with distaste at a heroic figure Gertrude was working on, then shuddered, almost imperceptibly. On our way back to the hotel she turned to me and said sadly, "I do wish Gertrude didn't have to work at those horrible nudes."

There were many paradoxes in the Vanderbilt family. Another was Reggie's financial situation. Although he was born to excessive wealth, his early spending and the structure of the trust fund on which we lived left him with an income too small to continue living with the lavishness which was expected of him. One day we were lunching with Mrs. Vanderbilt at the Ambassador. Mrs. Vanderbilt suddenly turned to Reggie and asked, "Why hasn't Gloria any pearls? Doesn't she like pearls?"

"Indeed she does, Mother," Reggie said. "But the ones I'd like to give her I can't afford just now."

Mrs. Vanderbilt was wearing a sautoir of pearls, wrapped several times around her neck. She beckoned to the maître d'hôtel. "Bring me a pair of scissors," she requested.

She proceeded with great deliberation to untwine the long strand and place it on the table in front of her. When the scissors arrived, she calmly snipped off half of the strand. Handing me more than fifty thousand dollars' worth of pearls, she said sweetly, "There you are, Gloria. All Vanderbilt women wear pearls." Then, as if nothing out of the way had happened, and without further reference to the subject, she placed the remaining pearls in her gold mesh bag and resumed her conversation.

CHAPTER VIII

Movies and Moving

Thelma

When Gloria and her baby returned home from the hospital, I announced my intention of going to California to establish my residence there. None of my family was pleased at my decision. Mamma said she had heard Hollywood was a "den of iniquity" and no place for a nineteen-year-old girl. Gloria thought it was too far away and anyway she knew I would never be a good actress. What did she mean—a good actress? I was going to be a great actress! She had more sense than I, for it took me some time to find out that great actresses are born; no amount of wishful thinking can make one.

Late in March 1924 Elise and I set off for California. The Super Chief of today, with its air-conditioning, luxurious dining room, bars, radio in every drawing room, and soft music playing at the touch of a button, is a far cry from the train Elise and I took. But I was young and, comfort or discomfort, it all spelled adventure to me.

The attorney who was to handle my divorce met us at the Santa Fe Station in Los Angeles and drove us to the Ambassador Hotel. And there, as I was signing the register, I heard a man exclaim, "Thelma! What brings you to Hollywood?"

There stood Sam Goldwyn. Here, at least, was a friend in this strange new part of the world. I explained that my stay was indefinite, and gave the reasons. "I must give a little party for you," he said.

Sam Goldwyn's "little party" for me turned out to be a magnificent ball at his home. The formal garden was in bloom—with colored lights. The sapphire-blue pool, illuminated from below, was decorated with fresh-cut flowers—hundreds of them—floating on the water. Men and women, more glamorous even than my romantic imagination had led me to expect, danced on the terrace. Beneath a striped marquise tent caterers served delicious food; champagne gushed from magnums like water from a fountain—a singular sight in those prohibition times.

I made many friends that night, among them Louella Parsons and Anita Stewart. Dear Louella! She never ceases to amaze me; when you are talking to her, she doesn't appear to be listening, but the next day you invariably find that your every word is printed verbatim in her columns. She has never been seen with a pencil in her hand; her "news" is recorded with astonishing accuracy somewhere in the recesses of her mind. Anita Stewart, one of the great stars of silent pictures, subsequently married George Converse, a distant relative of the man I was divorcing.

I also met John Gilbert, the silent film's great lover, as debonair in life as in his romantic roles on the screen.

As I was dancing, I noticed a grave-faced, intelligent man with unruly gray hair watching me. When I was told that this was Charlie Chaplin, I could hardly believe it—he seemed so different from the pathetic little baggy-pants clown I had laughed at so many times. This man with the sorrowful, melancholy face must surely be a tragedian, I thought, not a clown. Later that evening Sam introduced us. Charlie's voice was low, and in it was the faintest trace of cockney. It was only when he smiled that bewitching, impish little smile of his that I saw any resemblance at all to the clown the world knew and loved. He drove me home that night and asked me to dine the following evening.

Charlie and I became good friends. I used to love to hear him tell me of his childhood in England, of his poverty; how, at times, he'd even had to forage in garbage cans for food; how, after years of struggle, he had finally been recognized in Hollywood. But what he didn't realize was that he had also been recognized by the world as one of the great artists of our time. He told me that on his first trip East after his success in Hollywood, at every stop, however big or little, crowds would be standing on the platform, shouting "We want Charlie! We want Charlie!" And when he reached New York, banners were stretched across Broadway:—"Welcome, Charlie!" He was so grateful and humble in the telling of this story that I had a hard time keeping back the tears. It is a pity he lost both gratefulness and humbleness in his success.

We saw a great deal of each other in the days that followed, and, as might be expected, the newspapers came out with headlines announcing that Charlie and I were to be married. This, of course, was nonsense; we liked each other, I enjoyed his intelligence, and responded to his charm—but we were friends and nothing more. Gloria and Mamma read the startling news back in New York and believed it. They immediately bombarded me with telegrams and letters. Gloria wired, "Are you out of your mind?" Mamma was more imperious. Her wired command was, "Come home at once." Yielding to pressure, I stopped seeing Charlie as often. A few months later he married Lita Gray.

I was getting impatient. I had been in Hollywood nearly two months with no sign of a part, when once again Sam Goldwyn was to open the door for me.

His casting director called up one day and asked if I would care to take a part in a picture called *Cytherea*. This was one of the first color films ever made—a pallid forerunner of the beautiful Technicolor films of today. I was to play the role of a

Spanish señorita. As he was talking to me I thought, well, here's one role Mamma won't object to.

"Now mind you," the director said, "it's not a big part."

I didn't mind if it was big or not; it was a start.

When I got to the studio the next day, the wardrobe department gave me a most beautiful Spanish costume to wear.

The director told me I was to stand under an arch. As the leading man passed, I was to flirt with him. The property man handed me a fan; I took my place. The action started; and as the leading man passed me, I heard the director shout at me, "Wink, Thelma! For God's sake, wink!" I winked. My big moment had come and gone.

Soon after this I met Laurette Taylor and her husband, Hartley Manners. Laurette was filming *Peg o' My Heart*, playing the role she had created and made so famous on the stage. She and Hartley were staying in a bungalow at the Beverly Hills Hotel, which in those days was practically in the country. Every Sunday they would have friends over for lunch. Later, we would play tennis, or drive over to Pickfair, Mary Pickford and Douglas Fairbanks' house, for a swim. Later, back at the bungalow, we would have supper and play charades.

These parties were rather special, and those included had to have something special, too. Laurette demanded intellect, talent, wit, beauty, separate or, preferably, combined. The only thing she was a snob about was mediocrity.

Ernst Lubitsch, King Vidor, both well-known directors; dear Marie Dressler; Eleanor Boardman; Norma Shearer; Charlie Chaplin, are some that I remember in her home.

When Melba Meredith was there, we would have music. She was then married to Charles Meredith, a handsome young leading man, and was the mother of a beautiful little baby girl, Diane. Melba was born in California and sang all the old Mexican songs like a native. She must have inherited her lovely voice from her grandmother, Anna MacKenzie, the well-known opera star of the Eighties. Her great-grandfather had been the first military governor of San Francisco.

It was at Laurette's, on one of these Sundays, that I met Richard Bennett, the father of Constance, Barbara, and Joan, and the great matinee idol of the day. At this time I had only one serious concern—what I grandly called "my career." My life was uncomplicated by attachments; my work—as yet undemonstrated—was my life. Thus I was totally unprepared for the forceful and immediate attraction he had for me. Yet he was not handsome in the conventional sense; his features were irregular, his face was square, and he was not a great deal taller than I. His appeal seemed to lie in his eyes, which were large, blue, questioning, and which focused intently on you; and in his personality, which was dramatic but sympathetic, and which was projected with great force.

The following day he called me and asked if I would like to lunch with him and friends at Malibu Beach. Obviously, I would. When we arrived at the beach, Dick had completed his personality spade work; I had passed the point of being attracted to him; I was fascinated by him. On the other hand, at my age, I was easy game for a man around whose head hung all the glamor of the theater and who was practiced in all the arts which are the province of a great actor. I was sophisticated in my own way, not Dick's. I knew places and parties; I was at home with titles and rank; but in the world where talent and imagination ruled, where complex humans wove personal patterns of great intricacy, I was incredibly naïve. Dick talked with spirit and charm, unrolling a wealth of opinion and fantasy; he talked of books, of poetry, of the theater—of the thousand small things that make up the variegated mosaic of a star's life. And it followed, altogether naturally, it seemed to me, that I found myself in love with him one day after we had met.

I teased Dick about his daughters. Connie, who was more or less my age, and a good friend of mine, was in Hollywood at this time, making *Sally, Irene and Mary*. I told him I was going to take Connie to task; I intended to ask her how she could consider herself a friend yet all the while keep such a fascinating father from me. I also told him, almost timidly, of my ambitions. "All I want," I said glibly, "is to be an actress—a good actress."

As we lay on the beach after lunch, we talked about the theater, about the plays he had starred in. I asked him which of the many plays he had starred in he preferred. He told me that there had been many, but the most gratifying to him had been *Damaged Goods*. This had been a highly controversial play, shocking to many, as it dealt with syphilis and its tragic consequences. Dick believed that if people could be made to face the facts concerning this scourge, something could be done about it; and he was pleased when his theory was subsequently proven correct. However, he told me that at the time he was sharply criticized for daring to utter the abhorred word "syphilis" in the theater. "You'd think," he said wryly, "they were afraid they'd catch it from the sound!"

From this time on we were inseparable. Was it infatuation, or could it be possible that I was actually falling in love with a man fifty-one, a man old enough to be my father, I asked myself? He was brilliant, famous, sophisticated, romantic, and poetic. And he loved me.

There were beauty, excitement, tenderness, and high emotion in him. Or was it his fame—and the accompanying applause and adulation that went everywhere with him—which created the aura surrounding us?

Even though I saw Dick nearly every day, between times he would send me little poetic notes. One touched me deeply. I copied it in my *Memory Book:*

Oh, graceless God of that thing we call love, bear with me, please. I do not call on powers above to guide me in my utterances—To her, my loved, who is my right hand, You know, my heart. Out of her inspiration all creation flows. Tell her this subconsciously and make her know. She knows only that she is a pet of mine. Make her know the truth, Dear God, Of that thing we call Love—And thus prove yourself a God—And me a man for her eyes to see.

Part of the magic must have been that he made me feel like such an attractive woman. He was the artist—in love as well as in his work, and I was in a dream world woven of poetry, romance, and adoration.

When we discussed my "career," Dick was kind and patient with me; but I soon realized that he was only humoring me. It was obvious to him that I was not prepared to make the personal sacrifices that a career demanded. In his oblique way he tried to explain that only the end product of acting involved bright lights, glamor, and applause. What the public did not see, and what I certainly seemed to him to be unaware of, were the years of grind, of sacrifice, of humiliations, conflicts, failures. But the more he reasoned with me, the more stubborn I became. I resented his subtle hints about my dubious determination. What made him think I could not take hard work? How dare he insinuate that I couldn't act? He had never seen me.

Yet this inward protest made even me laugh. Of course he hadn't. Apart from *The Society Scandal* picture, the only one he could possibly have seen me in was *Cytherea*, and had he blinked, he would have missed me in that. But I didn't think of that at the time. If I had to storm every studio, I was going to prove to him I could act. Of course he was right. I didn't have the slightest talent. All I had was youth and a certain amount of good looks. Some people and most newspapers at that time described Gloria and me as beautiful. As far as we were concerned, that was a lot of nonsense. We certainly didn't have the classical beauty of a Greta Garbo or a Lady Diana Manners, the great English beauty who portrayed the Madonna in Max Reinhardt's *The Miracle*. Perhaps we had a talent for creating an illusion of beauty. We didn't conform to type. We had a style of our own. Cecil Beaton's description of us in a book he wrote titled *The Book of Beauty* describes us better than I dare:

> The Morgan sisters, Lady Furness and Mrs. Vanderbilt, are alike as two magnolias and with their marble complexions, raven tresses and flowing dresses, with their slight lisps and foreign accents, they diffuse, like Lady Howe, an Ouida atmosphere of hothouse elegance and lacy femininity. They are of infinite delicacy and refinement, and with slender necks and wrists, and long coiled, silky hair, they are gracefully statuesque. Their noses are like begonias, with full-blown nostrils, their lips richly carved, and they should have been painted by Sargent, with arrogant heads and affected hands, in white satin with a bowl of white peonies near by.

While I was still eager to prove my ability to Dick, I met Henry King, the famous director, at a party Mary Pickford and Douglas Fairbanks gave at Pickfair. Mary was, as she is today, "queen" of the moving-picture colony, and will always be America's Sweetheart.

Henry King was about to make a picture called *Any Woman*, and that night he offered me a small part. Henry King was known for the interest and trouble he'd take with newcomers; many a star has been helped on the way up by this great director. Alice Terry was starred, and, as I remember, Ramon Navarro was her leading man in this picture. At the end of each day we would see the "rushes" that had been made the day before. That first day, when the lights went up in the projection room, I heard Henry King, not knowing I was there, say, "Who said Thelma Morgan was hard to photograph?"

I must say, whoever said it was right, but then I was also told everybody thinks the same way when he sees himself on the screen. But this time that dear cameraman, whoever he was, had made me look glamorous.

Henry King enlarged my part and I worked through the entire picture. I was never happier than when working in that film.

Henry King and Alice Terry couldn't have been kinder and more helpful. But I am afraid the part never gave me a chance to show my acting ability, if any. As usual, I was cast as a young society matron. I was getting discouraged.

After I finished *Any Woman* I moved into a small, charming house on Hawthorne Avenue in Hollywood. Elise and I loved it. We had our own little garden in the back with an orange tree and a lemon tree. And at last I could have all the flowers I wanted. To me a room without flowers is like a sky without sun.

Though I was happy in my new home, I was also terribly mixed up. Was I falling in love with Dick? This I knew in my heart of hearts I shouldn't do. Our worlds were far too far apart. It would be an intolerable situation. I would be a misfit in his world—he in mine. How could there be this strong attraction between two whose life patterns were so diverse? My emotions were whirling like a top. Yet surely, by now, I could tell the difference between love and infatuation! At one moment I longed for Gloria to be with me—I wanted to tell her all about it, ask her advice. The next, I didn't want her. How could she understand? How could she ever untangle for me this topsy-turvy world I all of a sudden found myself in, when it was more than I could do myself? I, and I alone, would have to find the answer.

Eventually the time arrived that I had anticipated with dread, the time Dick was to leave for a road tour. He was to open in Denver in the play *They Knew What They Wanted*.

I was depressed and he was quiet and thoughtful as we lay on deck chairs in my garden after dinner the night before his departure. You could almost hear the stillness, so quiet was the night. The stars seemed to wink at us as they twinkled in the sky. With a sigh I closed my eyes. I thought of Eunice Tietjens' lovely lines: "And nothing aches in all this beauty—Except my heart."

I felt Dick take my hand in his and place a ring on my engagement finger. I leapt to my feet. I hoped he wouldn't say anything, for I knew I didn't have the answer—not then.

"Darling, I want you to be mine always," he said. "I can't let you go out of my life."

As I looked at him, his eyes filled with tears. Did he know, had he guessed the turmoil I had been in for the last few weeks?

Before I could say anything, he took me in his arms. "No, my dearest, don't answer just yet. I know the way you feel now. Take a little time to think about it, then come to me and give me the answer I pray to hear. Please, my beloved, don't make it too long." With a gentle kiss on both my tear-stained eyes, he left me.

I threw myself into the deck chair and cried.

Those next few days I spent trying to analyze my feelings for Dick. I knew I loved the glamor and excitement that went with him. But—and it was a very big but—did I love him enough to marry him, and share the rest of my life with him?

One morning it came upon me suddenly: I could not marry him. It was just not in the cards. It had taken me nearly twelve out-of-this-world months to look clearly at the chasm between his world and mine.

Dear Dick! I dreaded to have to tell him, but I thought it only fair to do it at once.

Elise and I arrived in Denver and went straight to Brown's Hotel, where Dick had made a reservation for us. He had not been able to meet me; our train arrived after his evening performance began. My suite was filled with flowers. A note from Dick told me how sorry he was not to be able to be at the station, and asked if I would meet him in his dressing room at the theater.

The theater manager showed me to Dick's dressing room, and from it I could hear Dick's voice onstage. I could picture him there, playing to Pauline Lord, his leading lady. I saw the half-filled jars of cold cream; I saw the boxes of powder and rouge, the tubes of grease paint, the soiled towels thrown haphazardly on the table below the naked electric bulb. And suddenly all the glamor disappeared. It is difficult, after these many years, to account for the psychological subtleties of this moment. But it was clear to me then that, no matter what I had felt or believed before, I was no longer deeply in love with Richard Bennett. I realized I would never be either an actress or an actor's wife.

Reggie, Gloria, Mamma, and little Gloria sailed for France late in April, attended by Nurse Keislich, a maid, and a valet. A month later I got my interlocutory decree—cutting my legal ties to Junior Converse—and I joined them in Paris. Gloria and Reggie met me at the Gare du Nord. It had been more than a year since I had seen Gloria, and the feeling of belonging that came over me when we were together again made my decision to leave Hollywood—and all that went with it—seem emotionally right. This was the world in which I belonged; this was the world I knew.

Of course the first thing we did upon arriving at the hotel was to go up and see the baby. Little Gloria was not what one would call a "pretty, pretty baby." She had the slanting, heavy eyelids of her father and his rather sullen mouth. It was only when she smiled that her face lit up.

"My, she looks like you, Reggie," I said.

Reggie beamed.

Gloria had little hair for a baby a year old, a sort of silky soft light brown fuzz, but we all thought her beautiful. How Reggie would have loved to see her grow up into the truly beautiful young woman she is today!

Gloria and Reggie had planned a dinner party for me. Among the guests invited was Beth Leary. She used to spend the winters in New York and the summers mostly in Paris and Biarritz. She enjoys life so much; she is a good companion, and, more, a good friend.

The day of the dinner party Beth telephoned Gloria and told

her Lord Furness, a friend of hers from London, was in Paris for a few days. Could she bring him along? Gloria said she would be delighted, but as she hung up I noticed she didn't seem too pleased.

"Bother!" she said, "this means reseating my table."

Gloria decided to sit me at Lord Furness's right. I was glad she did, for he turned out to be a charming dinner companion. I learned that his mother had saddled him with the good, old-fashioned, romantic English name of Marmaduke. It was a good thing, I was to think years later, she had only this one child. Heaven only knows what she would have named the others! When my son Tony was born on Easter Sunday, she had the brilliant idea that we should name him Easter.

I liked Duke Furness from the moment I sat next to him. He was slender, of medium height, his red hair parted in the middle, his dinner clothes tailored as only the English can tailor them. He wore a silk handkerchief tucked in the sleeve of his jacket. It's strange how a mannerism like tucking a handkerchief in a sleeve can endear a person to you; I was fascinated by this act—which he performed so naturally and so gracefully. His eyes were keen, pale blue. I wasn't surprised to learn later that he was considered one of the most acute and brilliant businessmen in England. His word in the City was almost legal tender. I believe the sale of the Furness-Withy Line for some nine million pounds was concluded virtually on the back of a menu.

As we chatted that night at dinner, I noticed he had a slight North Country Yorkshire accent. His vocabulary, however, shocked me; it was more characteristic of the stables than the drawing room. But as I got to know Duke better, I realized that his strong language was more a mask for shyness than a sign of vulgarity. As an only child he had been terribly spoiled by his doting mother. When he decided not to return to Eton, he was allowed to remain out of school. I think it was at this time that his father, Sir Christopher Furness, M.P. for Hartlepool and founder of the Furness Line, a self-made man, decided that his son would never amount to anything in business.

When Duke married Daisy Hogg, his first wife, who died in 1921, his father gave him a place called Nid-Hall in Yorkshire and told him to get on with his fox hunting. To Sir Christopher, hunting and horses seemed to be the only things Duke knew—or cared to know.

When Sir Christopher died, he left his vast business interests in the care of Sir John Furness, a cousin of his, thinking that Duke could not or would not attend to them. He was to be proven very wrong. When Sir John died in an accident, in 1914, Duke took over complete control of all his father's enterprises.

When the dinner party broke up that evening, Duke whisked me off dancing. We made the rounds, it seemed to me, of all the night clubs in Paris—ending, almost at dawn, at the Casanova—the Russian *boîte* so popular in the Twenties, where champagne and caviar were served to an accompaniment of violins, balalaikas, and a Cossack choir.

It was not till the early hours, when the sun was turning pink over Montmartre, that we stopped at the flower market near the Madeleine and arrived at the Ritz laden with flowers.

As I finally got into bed, I thought, what a happy, wonderful evening it had been. Too bad he had to leave for London the next day. I wondered if I would see him again.

Late the following morning with my breakfast Elise brought me an enormous box of flowers. The card read: "I'm sure you were too tired to put your flowers in water this morning. I hope these roses will keep fresh till I see you again. Duke." They did, for he was back in Paris two days later.

CHAPTER IX

Duke

Gloria

The night of the dinner, Thelma's beauty and charm had, it seemed, completely captivated Duke Furness. It appeared that Reggie and I had become unwitting matchmakers.

The days passed, and we saw more and more of Duke. He found an inordinate amount of unfinished business to attend to in Paris, especially over weekends.

Thelma and I spent our days shopping at Fairyland, the Dior of babyland—where they had such wonderful children's clothes—at Vionet's, Chanel's, Lanvin, and Reboux, replenishing my Sonia Rosenberg wardrobe. Since the day when Sonia made my wedding dress I had gone to her for all the clothes I had made in New York. In between my shopping sprees, Reggie insisted that I sit for my portrait by Dana Pond, the American artist. This I did in our apartment at the Ritz.

Duke, Thelma, Reggie, and I made a happy, congenial foursome. We lunched together most days at the Pré-Catalan or Armenonville in the Bois de Boulogne. Thelma and I became infected with Duke and Reggie's enthusiasm for racing, and almost every afternoon we would end up at Longchamp. Our evenings were spent at the gay night spots, such as Le Jardin de Ma Sœur, Le Perroquet, and Chez Fisher.

It was at Chez Fisher one night that Cora Madoux was singing a humorous French song. Duke and Reggie, understanding little

French, and not able to get the point of the lines, became frustrated. Duke exploded in a way that I was later to find characteristic of him: "Why the bloody hell don't these people speak English?" At the time we thought Duke's outburst much funnier than Cora Madoux' song.

Toward the end of June Duke returned to London; Thelma, Mamma, Reggie, and I went on to the Hotel Normandy in Deauville, where we had planned to stay until time to sail for home. Reggie and I found Deauville a delightful, peaceful change from the Paris pace. The official season had opened, but the holiday crowds had not yet arrived. Deauville only begins to seethe on the great national holiday, the Fourteenth of July, when fireworks and a day and night of street dancing announce officially that fun making is a democratic right.

It was a joy to see little Gloria, brown as a pecan, gleefully splashing around in the ocean. She loved the water from the moment of her first dip, and she was fearless. The only protest to come from her was a loud howl when I took her out.

Mamma, however, would complain to me that the splashing was too much excitement for this "delicate child." So much exertion would be sure to give Gloria nightmares. Mamma would never, no never, have allowed *her* children, who were strong and healthy—"Thank God!"—any such folly. I really didn't see how she figured that out, as she'd always told me I was the puny one of the family, being born without nails and weighing under four pounds.

This was the only time I saw Reggie really angry at Mamma. "Laura," he shouted, "you are being perfectly ridiculous! There is nothing the matter with my baby. She's a perfectly healthy, happy little girl. What are you trying to do, scare your daughter half out of her wits?"

His tone must have startled Mamma, for she quickly said, "Of course not." It was only that she loved the baby more than life—that she'd kill herself if anything happened to "the little one."

DUKE

At this ridiculous remark, Reggie lost his temper completely. "Don't be a fool, Mrs. Morgan," he said. "We are perfectly capable of knowing what is good or not for our baby."

Mamma realized she had gone too far. "It's only because I love you all so much," she said, almost pathetically.

She never again breathed this "love motif" in Reggie's presence, but I, unaware of its insidious far-reaching, was to hear it daily for many years to come.

At luncheon one day Thelma, with an innocent air, announced that Duke Furness possibly would be joining us for the weekend. Knowing that since the day they met he had rarely been out of her sight, Reggie and I were amused by her attempt at nonchalance.

We dined at the Deauville Casino, eight of us, the night Duke arrived. Reggie and I had invited the Baron and Baroness de Rothschild and the Gaikwar of Baroda and his wife. The Gaikwar was such a short and unassuming man that it was difficult for me to believe that he controlled lands equal in area to most European countries, and that his wealth could make the combined Vanderbilt fortunes appear, by comparison, no more than the savings in a thrift account.

After dinner we all went to the gambling rooms. These rooms did not have the glitter or the impressive *décor* of Monte Carlo, but what they lacked in this respect was more than made up for by the extravagance of the women's gowns and the patrons' almost wanton disregard of money. It would seem that during these mad postwar years the sole idea of most players was to get rid of the "filthy stuff" as fast as they could—it was only "paper," after all. No one turned a hair when Hannibal de Mesa, the Selfridges, or the Dolly sisters would calmly lose or win two or three million francs on the turn of a card.

Thelma and I, who had never played chemin de fer or baccarat, were scared to death until we found a modest table to try our luck, and were thrilled when we both won.

"Beginner's luck," Duke and Reggie scoffed as we had supper.

"Sour grapes," we answered. They had both lost.

The following morning I went to Reggie's room to find out what the plans were for the day. As I came in I was horrified to see him with a bloodstained handkerchief to his mouth. "It's only a nosebleed, dearest," he said. But I knew this was not true; obviously the blood was coming from his mouth.

"Now, Gloria, dearest, don't get yourself all upset," Reggie went on. "I assure you this is absolutely nothing. My doctor's not worried about it, so why should you be?"

I was sure he was only saying this to calm me, and I insisted we go to Paris at once to see a specialist. Reggie argued that this bleeding had been going on for years; and anyway, he said, we would be sailing in a few days, and he would rather see his own doctor in New York.

I was hysterical. "What kind of a monster is this doctor of yours to let you go on this way, not doing anything about it, not even telling me?"

Reggie finally gave in. "All right," he said, "we'll go to Paris. If we leave today, we can still make the *Majestic* on the sixth of July."

When we reached Paris, I immediately called Ambassador Herrick's secretary and asked if he would give me the name of the Ambassador's doctor. A few minutes later, when I reached Dr. Giroux on the telephone, I learned he could not speak a word of English. This made matters easier for me. Now Reggie would have to let me go with him as interpreter.

After examining Reggie, Dr. Giroux told him that his state of health was far from good, and in his opinion could be serious if he did not take care of himself at once. Observing that I was on the verge of tears, he added, "I'm sure, Mrs. Vanderbilt, that if Mr. Vanderbilt will consent to take the cure at Vichy these minor hemorrhages will stop altogether."

On the way back to the hotel I repeated to Reggie all that Dr. Giroux had said. Reggie refused point-black to take the cure. How could he? He had to be back in Newport in time for the horse show. I tried to coax him, but he was adamant. It was not until I refused flatly to go back to America with him that he gave in.

I telephoned Mamma at once and told her the change in plans, and that we thought it best for little Gloria to stay on in Deauville during the three weeks Reggie would be taking the cure at Vichy. She was greatly concerned, but told me not to worry about anything. "Your place," she said, "is with your husband."

Poor Reggie religiously swilled gallons of the waters, which he said were "only fit to rot your boots," and he classified the diet as "foul." All in all, he hated every moment of Vichy, but while there he never had a drink. I didn't mind his grousing; I saw him improving daily.

The day before we left Vichy, Dr. Binet, the attending physician, asked to see me alone. He told me, underlining every word, that Reggie did not seem to understand the seriousness of his illness. He said he could carry on his normal life with the exception that he must positively give up any kind of hard liquor.

"Can't he drink anything?" I asked him.

"A little champagne or any of the light wines with his meals. I have explained all this to your husband, chère Madame, but he only laughs at me. I feel it my duty to tell you that I fear the consequences if he does not carry out my orders."

On my way back to the hotel, I was both relieved and worried. It was all very well for the doctor to say "Stop." How could he understand a country wallowing in the throes of a puritanical prohibition? How could I get Reggie to stop this habit of years?

How could I keep tabs on Reggie? How would I know what he ordered at the Reading Room, Brook, Yale, Metropolitan, or his other clubs? I longed to be able to keep him in Europe for another year. But this was only wishful thinking; I knew he would never agree.

We sailed on the *Leviathan* on August 6.

Thelma

When Gloria and Reggie sailed for Newport, taking little Gloria and Mamma with them, I decided to stay on in Paris. The reason was Duke, to whom by now I was deeply attached. Duke was a startling change from Junior and Dick, the only other men I had loved. Here was a man who combined boldness, strength, frankness, and imagination with another element—one that I had not yet been close to—power. There seemed to be nothing he could not do.

At dinner one night in the little apartment I had taken near the Etoile I happened to mention I liked plover eggs. The next evening Duke arrived with a basketful. He had had them flown over from Holland for me.

Duke came over to Paris as often as business would allow, and most weekends. On fine days we would motor to Versailles or Fontainebleau for lunch, or we would discover little out-of-the-way restaurants on the Left Bank. We dined, usually, at Ciro's, Le Château de Madrid, or the Café de Paris.

It was exciting going out with Duke. Wherever we went, "Milord" was always bowed, by the maître d'hôtel, to the best table. I'm afraid I was somewhat smug and pleased when women would look up with what I thought a little envy as we entered a restaurant. Traveling with him was almost like traveling with royalty. We would be met by tophatted stationmasters and escorted to our compartments; we would be followed by secretaries and two valets. I once asked him if one valet valeted the other. "You know, dear," he answered, "I think you're nearly bloody well right at that."

When Duke wasn't in Paris, he would bombard me with telephone calls, telegrams, urging me not to stay up too late, or to take care of myself. By this time I didn't really want to see or go out with anybody else. At twenty-one what girl would not be flattered or impressed by such attention—particularly when it was showered on her by one of England's most eligible peers?

Duke often talked to me about his two children, Averill and Dick, whom at the time I had not met. He gave me the impression that Averill, his daughter, then seventeen, was his favorite. This surprised me, as most Englishmen dote on their son and heir. Dick (he had been christened Christopher) was then fourteen, and at school at Eton.

Duke invited me to stay at Glen Affric, a shooting lodge he had in the north of Scotland not far from Inverness, for the "Glorious Twelfth," as the British call the day the season for grouse and duck shooting opens.

Elise and I arrived in London the morning of the day we were to go up north. Duke was away on business and was not to pick me up until later that evening, to take us to the train for Scotland. I was glad of the rest, as our trip over from Paris had been rough.

At the station that night Duke, as usual, was surrounded by his staff. Three footmen and two housemaids from his house in London were coming with us to reinforce the staff already at Affric Lodge.

I was no sooner settled in my compartment than Price, one of his valets, came and informed me, "with His Lordship's compliments," that dinner was ready whenever I was. Winking at Elise, I said, "My compliments to His Lordship. Please tell him I shall be along shortly."

"Well, Elise," I said, after the valet had left, "this is a far cry from our little house on Hawthorne Avenue in California."

"As it should be, Madame," Elise said approvingly.

The compartments on English trains are much smaller than ours in America, and I was surprised to see one of these turned into a dining room. The berth had been covered over with a white tablecloth and set as we should have expected it had we been dining at the Ritz in Paris. There was champagne in ice buckets. A picnic basket packed with delicacies had been ordered and brought aboard the train.

Duke and I solemnly sat down side by side on two suitcases and were served this "feast" by one of the footmen. Price did the honors with the champagne.

As I looked around, I said, "What, no plover eggs?"

"You wonderful darling," said Duke, taking me in his arms. "I love you so very much."

I don't remember that Duke ever asked me to marry him, but from that moment we both took it for granted that we would marry.

Davis, Duke's chauffeur, met us at Inverness in a gray open Rolls at the ungodly hour of 6 A.M. Inverness, the chief town of the Highlands, is at the mouth of the Ness on Beauly Firth. Rumor had it that the Loch-Ness monster had been sighted only recently. And as we drove past the Ness, I kept my eyes glued to it, but the monster did not pay His Lordship the compliment of a nod.

Duke's hunting lodge was some forty miles north of Inverness, and the road ran through some of the most beautiful country in Scotland. To me, at the time, it seemed the most beautiful country in the world. Craggy mountains climbed sharply from the clear blue water of the lochs to disappear into the gray-blue mists that banded the sky. Sitting next to Duke in the open car that early morning, I was completely happy. I wanted to tell him what I felt, but I was afraid of seeming sentimental; and I knew that Duke, like most Englishmen, had a horror of sentimentality.

Duke interrupted my thoughts. He apparently thought it wise to brief me on the household arrangements at Affric Lodge. "You know," he said, "though the place spreads over a few thousand acres, the house itself is small—and it's primitive. It has no electric lights and no telephone. So prepare yourself." The warning was unnecessary. Duke had already surrounded me with luxuries and with the service and attention that went with a feudal barony; who was I to carp now at a few discomforts? Besides, knowing Duke, I could well assume that he had substituted a thousand candles for each possible electric bulb and a private courier service for the absent telephone. "Besides you," he went on, "there will be only a handful of guests; there will be Lady Wodehouse, Dr. Gavin, Major Clark, Averill, a school friend of Averill's—and, of course, Dick."

The mention of the others suddenly brought me back to reality. In my excitement I had forgotten that there were other people; I was daydreaming in a fantasy world that had only us as inhabitants. Now I was reminded that Duke had a flesh-and-blood world of his own, and in this world were his children. "Darling," I said, now apprehensive, "what about Averill and Dick? Suppose they don't like me?"

Duke's reaction to my fears was typical. "Why the bloody hell shouldn't they like you?" he spluttered, then went on telling me about the fine points of stalking, about the number of stags that had been bagged last season, and something or other about the "far beat"—whatever that is. But I listened with only one ear; I had my worries. I could think of at least three reasons why the children might not like me. Suppose they didn't want their father to remarry? Suppose Averill didn't cotton to the idea of a stepmother only two or three years older than herself? Even worse, suppose they just didn't take to me?

I was thankful to see we were turning into the driveway. All these supposings were making me wretched. Duke noticed that I looked worried. Thinking it was because I was shy at meeting Margaret Wodehouse and Dr. Gavin, he said, "They're old friends of mine and I know you will like them. Anyway, they won't get here till the day after tomorrow. There's only Charlie Clark and the children here now."

Charlie Clark, Duke's controller, I had met in Paris, and I liked him. It was the children that worried me.

When we entered the drawing room, the only person there was a handsome young boy of fourteen, tall and slender, with the merriest, bluest eyes and the reddest red hair.

Duke introduced us. "Thelma," he said, "this is Dick. I want you two to be good friends."

Dick responded in choicest Etonese. "Dad has talked about you often," he said. "Topping you could come up." Then turning to his father, he added, "Averill is out stalking. The old girl said something about she'd try and be home early and was sorry not to be here to meet you, but one of the gillies had spotted a good ten pointer on the home beat and she and Olivia have gone out after it."

After freshening up, Duke, Dick, Charlie Clark, and I sat down to a most delicious breakfast of porridge, kippers, and hot scones. The long drive in the open car had made me ravenous, and I ate almost as much as Dick did. This, for some unknown reason, seemed to please him. As we finished, Dick asked me if I would like to walk over to the stables and see the new stag pony his father had just given him.

I noticed Duke smiled a little as he said, "Run along, I have some business to talk over with Charlie. We'll join you later."

As we walked toward the stables, Dick talked a mile a minute. How he loved being up here! How he hated Eton! How he wished he could hunt every winter! It was only during the Chrismas holidays, he told me, when he went to Burrough Court, their home near Melton Mowbray in Leicestershire, that he ever got a chance to hunt. Averill had all the luck. "Have you ever seen her out hunting? No, of course not. How silly of me. You've never been to Melton. She's top-ho! The very best."

Little did I know then, and how thankful I am I didn't, that this boy I was to get to know and love so much, walking and chatting so gaily about when he would be old enough to hunt all winter, would one day give up his life selflessly and heroically for his country.

Averill and Olivia (whose surname I can't remember) arrived while we were having tea. They were both in tweed suits, but it wasn't hard to tell which was Duke's daughter. Averill was tall and slender with a rather boyish figure; and she had the same pale blue eyes as her father. She wasn't what one would call a beautiful girl. Her features were sharp. Her walk gave the impression she would be happier in a riding habit than in a ball gown. Her beautiful long auburn curly hair reached halfway down her back.

As Duke introduced us, I was quite sure the two girls had discussed me and had made up their minds they weren't going to like me. I realized that Averill wasn't going to be won over easily.

Dinner that night was not as pleasant as breakfast had been. The atmosphere was a little strained. Averill and Olivia talked and giggled together and only included me in their conversation every now and then, when politeness demanded it. I was sorry that Averill seemed so distant, for I knew how important it was to Duke that she should like me. In his way he loved Averill and Dick very much; ever since their mother, whom he had married when only twenty, died, he had done all that he could to make them happy. I say "in his way," because he had a funny way of showing his affection. The way he would bully them and swear at them shocked me. But it didn't take me long to realize that his swearing and cursing were often terms of endearment. His hatred—or fear—of sentimentality caused him to express his deepest feelings in reverse English.

It had been planned that the following day Duke, Dick, and Charlie Clark were to go stalking. Averill and Olivia were to keep me company. I was quite sure that this was the last thing the girls wanted to do, but they were stuck with me. I remember they left me severely alone all that morning, and it was only during lunch that I decided something had to be done about the tension. I suggested that, after lunch, we might take a little walk. I could see this idea didn't please them at all; I was sure they had made other plans, in which I was not included.

I didn't blame Averill too much. Her only interests were riding, hunting, and the outdoor life; and here was a woman who talked about "taking a little walk," a woman who did not even know which side of a horse to get on. And this woman had come into her father's life.

The lodge was situated on the edge of Loch Affric, which was some fifteen miles long. A motorboat was used to take guests to the "Far Beat," which was where Duke was stalking that day. I suggested we walk up a bit along the loch. Averill and Olivia started off at a brisk pace; I kept right along with them. After a little while Averill said, with the solemnity of a Galileo announcing that the earth moves, "Funny, your stride is the same as ours." Then, the ice broken, she transformed her discovery into a philosophical observation. "It's so much more fun walking when one doesn't have to wait for those lagging behind, don't you think?"

I thought so, indeed, and from that moment on we were all friends. It seems strange, in retrospect, that an event as insignificant as this could demolish the psychological barrier that stood between us; but the emotional lines that pull people together or apart seem linked with the small, not the outstanding, incidents of life; and their workings often seem indifferent to logic or sense.

We chatted together like three schoolgirls on a picnic. I told them about the life Gloria and I had had at the Convent, and about Reverend Mother Dammen. (This seemed to have a special interest for Averill, who had never even been to a boarding school.) I told them about Hollywood, about Gloria's and my experience as "Northern Lights." I ended with the account of my fantastic experience with a horse in Central Park. "Thelma," Averill said, "tomorrow I'm going to teach you to ride." I was now plain "Thelma"—all the stiffness, all the formality, all hostility were gone.

"How much farther is it," I asked, "to the place where Duke is to meet the motorboat?"

"Some four or five miles from here, I think," said Averill.

"Let's go meet him and surprise him."

And so it was that when Duke came along he saw three tired, laughing friends. We may have surprised Duke, but I had surprised myself even more. I had walked fifteen miles—and every one to me was worth the walking.

Lady Wodehouse and Dr. Gavin arrived the next day. Margaret Wodehouse later became—at the death of her father-in-law—Lady Kimberley. She was tall, slender, and fair, a typical English beauty.

G. T. Bulkley Gavin, a Scotsman, was Duke's best friend and his confidant. I thought he looked at me appraisingly through his monocled eye. I was sure Duke had told him about us, and I was sure that he did not approve of Duke's marrying such a young woman and, what was worse, an American. Yet, as he stood there, I thought his courtly manners and old-world turn of phrase were charming; he was like a character in some Edwardian novel.

Averill, true to her promise, started giving me riding lessons. This time I wasn't nervous; Averill was an angel of patience with me, and anyway all I rode were ponies. After I was married, she tried very hard to teach me to hunt, but finally gave it up as a hopeless job. I certainly was never meant to go careering over five-foot fences across open country. As she tactfully put it, "You sit a fauteuil more gracefully than a hunter, darling." Nor did I enjoy stalking, but I often went with Duke; it pleased him and I loved being with him.

The Highlanders around Glen Affric are mostly all Catholics. And unlike other Catholic countries, where Sunday after church is a day of fun and play, Highland Scotland dedicates this day to prayer and solemnity. Duke, who had no fixed ideas about religion, and was accustomed to doing what he wanted, was frustrated on Sundays, when nothing would persuade the Highlanders even to saddle a pony.

Time hung heavily on these days—at least until Charlie Clark came up with the idea of throwing empty tin cans a little way up the loch. As they came drifting down past us, we'd take pot shots at them. It was great fun, and I discovered to my amazement that I was a very good shot. I was delighted when Duke and the children applauded my marksmanship.

In time Gav's reserve began to thaw. We would take long walks through the heather, and he would talk about Duke and their friendship through the years. He also told me all about the death of Daisy, Duke's first wife, on Duke's yacht, *The Sapphire*, on their way to Cannes—after Daisy's unsuccessful brain operation in London. They were forced to bury her at sea. There were no embalming facilities on the yacht, and they were too far out to turn back to England and not near enough to Cannes to make port. Gav told me the doctors who had attended Daisy in London realized she did not have long to live, but they had told her the operation was successful. Her one desire was to go to the South of France to recuperate. Duke had taken the Grand Duke Michael's Villa Kasbeck in Cannes, and *The Sapphire* was chosen as the best and most comfortable means of getting Daisy there. Dear Gav must have been very fond of her; there was a deep sadness in his eyes as he reminisced.

By the time we left Affric Lodge Gav and I were friends— a friendship I prize above all others. There has never been a time in the last thirty years that, when I needed him, Gav has not been there, ready to advise, sometimes to scold, but always to understand.

DUKE

Duke and I came back one beautiful September evening tired and happy. Duke had bagged a record "Royal" stag that we had been stalking for days. As I went up to change for tea, I noticed that Charlie Clark looked preoccupied, and I heard him ask Duke if he could talk to him. I didn't pay much attention; I thought this had something to do with business. When I came down, however, I found Duke sitting alone, head bent, a telegram in his hand.

"Thelma, darling, come sit here beside me," he said quietly, "I have bad news for you." As if reading my mind, he added, "No, dear, not Gloria."

CHAPTER X

"I'll See You Tomorrow"

Gloria

When Reggie and I arrived in New York, I telephoned his mother at once to tell her how successful the cure at Vichy had been, and how well Reggie looked. Mrs. Vanderbilt was overjoyed to hear the good news. I also told her we were motoring to Sandy Point the next day. She suggested that on the way we stop at The Breakers for dinner. "That would be wonderful," I said. "We're both longing to see you. Expect us around six-thirty."

Before we left, Reggie had made arrangements for Mamma, little Gloria, and the nurse to leave on the one-o'clock train for Providence, where a car was to meet them and take them on to the farm. It was all so simple, we thought; but nothing was simple with Mamma around. At the last moment she decided she had an errand to run. She sent the nurse on ahead with little Gloria, telling her she would meet them in the compartment.

Mamma boarded the train a few seconds before it pulled out. Reaching the drawing room, she found it empty. Pressing every bell she could find, she screamed that the baby had been kidnaped. The conductor and the porter both tried to tell her that no baby had gotten on at Grand Central.

It was at this point that Margaret Power, who by chance was also on the train, realized that it was Mamma who was causing all the trouble. Margaret was very funny when she

"I'LL SEE YOU TOMORROW"

told us about it later on. It seemed that Mamma kept on screaming that the baby had been kidnaped, demanded the train be stopped at once, yelled at everybody to "do something, not just stand there!" Conductors and porters scattered in every direction, only to come back and report—no baby! "Oh, my poor baby, what have they done to her?" Mamma wailed. "If I ever get hold of that fool of a nurse, I'll cut her throat. I'll kill her."

Margaret tried to calm her and sagely suggested they get off at One Hundred and Twenty-fifth Street and telephone the hotel. Something may have detained them. "Don't tell me that," Mamma protested, "I've always said you can't trust nurses, and this fool is always picking up and talking with strange people. Oh, why did I ever leave my baby alone?"

By this time they had reached One Hundred and Twenty-fifth Street, left the train, and gotten to a telephone. Mamma shouted half in Spanish, half in English to the poor telephone operator, who couldn't make head or tail of what she was saying. Margaret finally took the phone from her and got the Ritz Hotel. The manager informed her that Reggie and I had left by car, and that the nurse and the baby were on their way to meet Mrs. Morgan.

"I knew it! I told you so!" Mamma raved. "She's been kidnaped." Snatching the phone from Margaret, she ordered the startled operator to give her the nearest police station. "My baby, Gloria Morgan Vanderbilt," she announced to the police clerk, "is being kidnaped and nobody is doing anything about it."

The Daily News the following day reported: "Enough action was crowded in the next half-hour to cause the director of a motion-picture thriller to turn handsprings from sheer elation."

What had really happened was that Mamma's "fool of a nurse" had taken the wrong train, but she and the baby by then were safely on their way to Providence.

When we left the Ritz early that morning it was hot, humid, and gummy. The road from New York to Newport certainly cannot, even in the wildest stretch of the imagination, be called one of the scenic wonders of the world. It is flat, dull, uninteresting. But I did enjoy the breeze as the fast-moving car got into open country. Reggie, on the other hand, did not seem to enjoy anything. He groused all the way up. For hours he talked of nothing but the horse show—how he had let everybody down, all on account of that "damn cure" he had needed as much as he needed a hole in his head. After all, he should have been back three weeks ago. Now he would have to cram hours of work, naturally badly done, into a few days.

I listened to this tirade with a sympathetic ear, but remembering Dr. Binet's words, I was uneasy. The last thing I wanted was to have him throw himself headlong into the old routine. I had made up my mind to do very little entertaining and accept as few invitations as possible. I was determined Reggie should get all the rest he could.

As we were nearing Newport, Reggie, to my consternation, announced that he had to see the secretary of the horse show at the Reading Room. Would I mind dropping him and going on to The Breakers alone? He would join me there later.

"Reggie," I pleaded, "your mother will be so hurt! The drive has been so long, you must be tired. Can't it wait till the morning?" But nothing I said would make him change his mind.

It was not till long after eight that he finally arrived.

The next two weeks were easygoing, carefree. Reggie and I would watch the morning exercise of the horses at the Ring, have long conversations with Mr. Bone about the management of the farm, have informal buffet luncheons, then take a dip in the Seaconnet River from our private little beach that we all enjoyed so much more than stuffy Bailey's Beach. Even Reggie begrudged the time he had to spend on his beloved horse show during these lovely, lazy days.

Little Gloria and I had a wonderful time exploring the farm, followed by little Fortitude yapping at our heels. Little Fortitude was a tiny golden-brown Pomeranian that Reggie had brought up to my room one morning, the year before, in one of Fortitude's championship cups. It was very funny to see Fortitude being chased around the paddock by his diminutive namesake.

Little Gloria loved chasing the geese. I had a hard time keeping myself from laughing as I watched her waddling after them. She was so little and trying so hard to keep up with them.

The horse show over and a great success, Newport prepared to close its shutters for another year, another season. Reggie and I had planned to remain a few weeks longer so that he could tie up loose ends, and also get ready for the National Horse Show in New York. "After that," he said apologetically, "I promise you you won't even know there is such an animal as a horse."

Reggie and I were playing with little Gloria one afternoon in the garden when I saw Mamma coming toward us, sobbing. I was afraid that she might not be able to control herself and that she might scare little Gloria; I asked Reggie to take the baby indoors.

Between sobs she told me she had just received a cable from her Aunt Rosa in Santiago, Chile, telling her that her mother was dying and that if she ever wanted to see her alive again she had better come at once. I was surprised at the tone of the cable. Then I remembered that her twin aunts, Rosa Blanca and Blanca Rosa, had never forgiven her for not making the slightest effort to see their sister, her mother, for the past thirty years. Mamma's recent excuse, they wrote, was even more ludicrous than the ones in the past. "Ridiculous!" Aunt Rosa had written at the time Papa had gone to Buenos Aires. "Your place is with your husband. At least you would be on the South American continent and could come and see your ailing mother as a dutiful daughter should." Mamma had shown me this letter. But the only impression it had made on me at the time was that my Great-Aunt Rosa and Mamma were very much alike. They both had a genius for melodrama.

Mamma was crying hysterically when Reggie rejoined us. "Oh, my poor mother. What shall I do? I have sacrificed my whole life to my children. And now *she* is dying thousands of miles away, with nobody near to close those dear eyes. What am I going to do? How can I go so far away alone?"

Reggie looked at me inquiringly and whispered, "What is your mother raving about?"

"Mamma has just received a cable and it's bad news. Her mother is seriously ill and is not expected to live."

"Oh, I'm so sorry, Laura, to hear it." Reggie was genuinely affected. "Is there anything we can do?"

To my surprise, Mamma asked Reggie if he would let me go with her. I must say this request staggered Reggie, too, but seeing Mamma so distressed, he consented.

I was torn between my desire to be of help to Mamma and my unwillingness to leave Reggie, knowing that he also needed me.

Later in our room that night I told Reggie of my feelings. But he argued that Mamma had done so much for us when I was ill after the baby; now that she needed me, I ought to go. "She really should not be alone on the trip down there," he said.

I loved my mother very much and really wanted to be with her; I was also grateful to Reggie for his unselfishness.

In no time all arrangements were made. Two days before we were to sail Mamma and I left early in the morning for New York. Reggie had an important meeting that afternoon. It was decided that he would join us the following day, Wednesday, the fifth of September, to see us off for Valparaiso.

Mamma was already waiting impatiently in the car when Reggie and I came out of the house. I had at that moment a strange presentiment that if I should leave something dreadful might happen. But I put aside my feeling; what could happen?

"I'LL SEE YOU TOMORROW"

Besides, I knew Mamma would not go to Santiago without me, and I felt that she should go. After all, Grandmamma was in her nineties, and even if she were not actually dying now, this would probably be the last time Mamma would see her alive.

As Reggie and I were standing by the car waiting for my maid to come with the last-minute things one always seems to forget, Reggie told me that Forest March, a friend of ours, had just called, and learning that I would be in New York, had suggested taking me to the theater. Reggie had tentatively accepted for me. He also told me he had telephoned Colton, his secretary, to instruct him to meet us at the Marguery Hotel with our passports and to stand by in case I should need him for anything. Kissing me good-by, he said, "I'll see you tomorrow."

Mamma went straight to the hotel on our arrival in New York, and I went off to do some last-minute shopping. On my return to the apartment, I telephoned Forest to tell him I would be ready by seven. I also cabled Thelma, telling her that our grandmother was ill, and that Mamma and I were leaving for Chile. Then I telephoned Reggie to tell him we were all set and to kiss the baby good night for me. But when I asked to speak to him, Norton told me that Reggie was resting; he had not been feeling well all day, and had complained of a sore throat. Should he put the call through or could Mr. Vanderbilt call me later? I told him not to disturb him.

As I hung up, the same strange feeling I'd had earlier in the day came over me. Was Norton telling me the truth? Was it just a sore throat? Had Reggie told him to tell me this?

I knew that his mother would know and tell me. I telephoned her. "Hello, is that you, Gloria dear?" I heard my mother-in-law's calm, sweet voice. "I'm so sorry to hear about your grandmother's illness and hope it is not as serious as you think, dear."

Before she could go on, I interrupted, "Please, Mrs. Vanderbilt, I'm worried. I've just spoken to Norton and he tells me

Reggie is not well. I didn't want to disturb him, but I must know. Have you heard from him? Is he all right?"

"Yes, Gloria. There's nothing to worry about," Mrs. Vanderbilt said. "Reggie is perfectly all right. I talked with him just a little over an hour ago."

As I hung up, I said to myself I must really stop this nonsense, making mountains out of molehills.

Forest March picked me up at seven on the dot. We had a quick but excellent dinner at Jack and Charlie's, better known as "21."

Forest was one of the tallest men I have ever known; he must have been well over six foot four. We had been friends for ages. It was he who took me to my very first prize fight, the Dempsey-Firpo match. I had never seen such an enormous crowd. When Dempsey came into the ring, the crowd stood up en masse, and kept standing and screaming through the entire first round. I couldn't see a thing. "I wish I were as tall as you are," I told Forest, "I can't see anything." "We'll soon fix that," he said, as the bell sounded for the second round. Everybody stood cheering and yelling. Forest picked me up and stood me on my chair. Just at this moment a roar went up from the crowd. We turned to see what had happened, and saw Firpo flat on his face, the referee counting him out. Poor Forest, I had made him miss the most sensational fight of the century.

I don't know how it happened, but when we were in the theater, just before the end of the second act, I was gripped with such a premonition of disaster that I turned to Forest, and, clutching his arm, hardly being able to get my words out, I said, "Take me out of here. I want to go home at once." Before he could answer me I was halfway out of the theater. This time I knew I was right. This time I knew it wasn't my imagination. I just had to go to Reggie.

In the car on the way to the hotel Forest anxiously asked me if I were ill. "No, it's Reggie," I said. "I know something has happened to him."

"Don't be silly, Gloria! Reggie's fine. I talked to him only this morning."

"What's happened to you?" Mamma asked, as I rushed into our hotel suite. I rushed on to my bedroom without answering her. Slamming the door, I made straight for the telephone. I really must try to control myself, I thought, as I waited for the long-distance telephone operator to put me through. Would they never answer? After what seemed to be an eternity, I heard a strange, impersonal woman's voice.

"I'm Mrs. Vanderbilt," I said. "Who are you?"

"I'm Mr. Vanderbilt's nurse."

"Oh, my God!" I screamed. "What's happened?"

"Please, Mrs. Vanderbilt, don't get upset. Mr. Vanderbilt has had a slight hemorrhage. I would let you speak to him, but the doctor gave him a sedative and he is now sleeping."

I didn't care who told me not to get upset or worried, I was determined to go to Reggie at once. I asked the nurse to tell Norton to have the car meet the midnight train from New York at Providence, I would be on it.

"But, Mrs. Vanderbilt," she protested, "Mr. Vanderbilt told me that should you phone, I was to tell you not to worry, that he would meet you in New York as planned."

"Please, nurse, do as I ask," I said. Nothing, neither she, Reggie, nor anyone else could have prevented my going to Newport.

The first thing I saw as I pulled up to the house, at five the next morning, was my mother-in-law's car. My heart nearly stopped. Reggie was worse; otherwise why would Mrs. Vanderbilt be at the house at this hour?

I rang the bell and waited. Norton let me in. He stared at me, and there was a strange, bewildered look on his face, as if he didn't know me.

DOUBLE EXPOSURE

"What is it?" I asked. "What is the matter?"

Norton's lips trembled. "Mr. Vanderbilt died three minutes ago."

I was shivering; my head ached. I was vaguely aware that Mrs. Vanderbilt was gently stroking my hand. I felt myself floating through vast empty space. The only thing that seemed real was Norton's voice repeating over and over in an endless monotone, "Mr. Vanderbilt died three minutes ago, three minutes ago, three minutes ago."

I tried to force myself to think clearly. This was nonsense. It was only yesterday morning that Reggie had said so confidently, "I'll see you tomorrow, dearest." The word "tomorrow" brought me back with a start. This wasn't a dream; this was cold reality. Reggie was dead. I would never see him again.

I turned my face to the wall and sobbed wildly. Mrs. Vanderbilt turned me around. "Gloria, dear," she said, with what seemed to me unbelievable composure, "you must really try to pull yourself together."

I was shocked. Her words sounded so cold and harsh. How could this mother sit there so calmly and tell me to pull myself together? Had she no feelings at all?

I sat up and looked at her. It was only then that I realized the agony she, too, was going through. Yet her face looked as if it had been carved out of marble. Not a muscle moved. Only her tragic, tearless eyes reflected the anguish and despair she felt.

I was a little ashamed as she took me in her arms. I shouldn't have been so quick in my criticism of this mother, whose heart I knew must be breaking. She held me tight. And for the first and only time I saw great tears roll down her cheeks. She didn't sob. She didn't say a word. She didn't make a sound.

After Mrs. Vanderbilt left, I tried my best to control myself. I knew I should not go on like this but, try as I might, my mind kept racing back to the tragic events of the past few hours. I blamed Mamma, myself—everyone. "I should never have left him!" I cried.

I was still reproaching myself when I heard a knock on the door. "What is it?" I asked. "What's happened?"

It was Dr. George Bolling-Lee. "You really should be lying down and resting, Gloria. You have had a terrible shock," he said kindly, as he led me to the sofa.

I was surprised at the calmness of my own voice as I asked him please to tell me what had happened. He probably realized that any further words of sympathy would only make me break down again. He told me that Norton had telephoned him at about ten the night before, and said that Mr. Vanderbilt was ill. Would he please come at once? On his arrival he found Reggie had had a slight hemorrhage, no worse than any of the others he had treated him for. But he thought it advisable for Reggie to go to the hospital in the morning for a general checkup. Reggie, he told me, had refused point-blank. He had insisted there was nothing the matter with him and that Norton was nothing but a fuddy-duddy and a meddlesome old maid. He was going to New York in the morning as planned, and that was that!

It was not until Dr. Lee told him that he was going to get in touch with me that Reggie agreed at least to have a nurse that night.

At two in the morning the nurse had telephoned him that Reggie was hemorrhaging badly; she thought it advisable for him to come at once. After calling the hospital to have someone stand by to give a blood transfusion, should it prove necessary, Dr. Lee had tried to reach me in New York and was told I had already left for Newport.

I had been crying softly as the doctor spoke. All of a sudden I felt faint; my hands were cold and clammy; I was trembling, and I could hardly breathe.

"Come, Gloria," Dr. Lee said. "I'm going to get you a sedative. You really must rest or you'll crack up." As he rang for the nurse, he told me to please believe him that everything had been done that possibly could have been done.

Drowsily I said, "Doctor, I want to go and see Reggie."

Vaguely I heard him say, "A little later, Gloria."

The next thing I remember was sitting up in bed and hearing Dr. Bolling-Lee's voice saying, "Would you like me to take you to your husband now?"

When we reached Reggie's room, I told the doctor I would prefer to go in alone.

During the hours that followed, the house became a maelstrom. People kept arriving and leaving; wreaths and flowers were delivered every few minutes; the telephone was constantly ringing. Sooner or later, I realized, I must attend to all the obligations these attentions involved; and I would have to face the hundred responsibilities suddenly thrust upon me.

Mrs. Vanderbilt returned to The Breakers, taking little Gloria with her. I was thankful. As Gloria was only a year and a half old, she could not realize the loss of her father, but she might sense the oppressive sorrow in this house of mourning.

While I was having breakfast the following morning, the maid announced that Harry Payne Whitney was downstairs. I asked her to hand me a bed jacket and told her to bring fresh coffee and show Mr. Whitney up. I was relieved he had come. From our very first meeting I had liked Harry Whitney and sensed that this feeling was reciprocated. For all his impetuosity, his jocular ways, and his quick wit, Harry was one of the men most respected in Wall Street for business acumen and integrity. I was going to need all the help and advice he could give me.

Over our coffee he was telling me of the arrangements he had made for the funeral when Mamma unexpectedly entered the room and saw him sitting on the edge of the bed. I can no longer recall the precise words Mamma used at this terrible moment, but the gist of her outburst was this: I had lost all sense of decency. It was unbelievable that I, dressed only in my nightgown, should receive a man in my bedroom, and it was all the more unbelievable that such shameless behavior should occur at this of all times.

I have never in my life seen a man angrier than Harry was at that moment. His face turned white. He rose and faced her. "That's enough, Mrs. Morgan!" he said. "I will not stand for any more of your damned insinuations. You are a meddlesome old woman, and, what's more, you are a horrible one." Then he walked out of the room.

Naturally I was in tears. I had gone through too much. Mamma then suddenly reversed her stand; she became the obsessed sentimentalist, the maudlin mother doing only what was best for darling daughter. She tried to explain that I was very young, that I didn't understand the ways of the world, and that she was only looking after her baby. I interrupted this flow of pathos. I asked her to leave me alone; I could not take any more.

Later that morning Harry returned to my room to resume our conversation. He apologized to me for losing his temper. "But really, Gloria," he said, "what kind of a mind has your mother got?"

I explained lamely that Mamma was more foreign than American in her ways, and that her "dear grandmamma" would never have approved of such lack of formality.

"Well, you may be right, Gloria," Harry said dubiously, "but watch out. She'll cause you trouble yet. Women like her always do."

Then abruptly he changed the subject. "This I know will be trying, Gloria, but there are some details that I must talk to you about. I have ordered a bronze casket, silvered to Reggie's gray. Later this afternoon he will be laid in the large drawing room downstairs. I know it will be hard, but you must be down there, my dear. Neely and Grace are here. Gertrude went straight to her mother at The Breakers from the yacht, after we docked this morning. I've located Reggie's daughter, Cathleen, in Montana. She and her husband are on an extended trip with the Clarence Mackays in the Canadian Rockies, but Mackay is rushing them here by private trains for the funeral. The William H. Vanderbilts are now across the way at Oakland Farms. All of them will expect to see you this afternoon."

Reggie was now lying in the large drawing room downstairs. As I entered, I felt the contrast with the still gray room upstairs. Masses of American Beauties and lilies banked the walls, and the many floral tributes seemed to make death look less grim. Norton came quietly in and told me Gertrude and Harry Whitney were in the library. Gertrude embraced me warmly saying her mother and little Gloria sent their love and reassuring me that the baby was getting on famously in her new surroundings.

The next two days were among the most difficult I have ever spent, but I was grateful for the kindness of the many relatives and friends who came to offer their condolences. I was especially touched when a spokesman for the tradespeople phoned to ask if they might call to pay their last respects.

After a night of fitful sleeping I awoke early on the morning of September 7, 1925. The funeral service was to be at St. Mary's Episcopal Church in South Portsmouth at ten o'clock. Harry had promised to be at the house early to relieve me of any last-minute arrangements. The plans were that Gertrude would come with her mother before the others arrived.

It was comforting to see Harry waiting for me in the library and hear his matter-of-fact voice as he said, "Now, Gloria, everything has been attended to and will go off like clockwork. There is nothing for you to worry about except yourself." Patting me on the shoulder, he added, "Hang on, old girl."

I went into the hall to meet Mrs. Vanderbilt as I heard her car in the driveway. She looked so very little in her deep mourning as she lifted her veil from her face and kissed me. One could see the pain she had suffered the last two days; her eyes were sunken and red from many tears. No words passed between us as I took her to the drawing-room door, opened it, and left her. A short time after this Reggie's coffin, blanketed with orchids, was placed in the hearse and the funeral cortege left for St. Mary's some two miles away.

The small St. Mary's Church was filled with Reggie's many friends. I was impressed with the simplicity and dignity of the service conducted by the Reverend James Conover.

I have little recollection of boarding our private train, which was to take us to New York. I do remember removing my hat with its heavy crepe veil, and lying down. The train stopped at New Haven, where I received the condolences of members of the Yale faculty who placed on the coffin a beautiful Yale blue floral wreath, with white flowers forming the numerals 1902-1925.

(The Vanderbilt family has a close association with Yale. After the death in college of Reggie's brother, William H., the Vanderbilts erected a memorial hall there in his name.)

We journeyed on to New York. There was a short religious ceremony, attended only by members of the immediate family, at the Vanderbilt mausoleum in the Moravian Cemetery on Staten Island.

Few words passed between Mamma and me on our way back to the house on Seventy-seventh Street. In one of her rare moments of understanding, she left me alone with my thoughts. I suddenly remembered a touching thing that had occurred, and the tears that up to then I had been able to control poured forth. I saw before me old Norton, who, instead of riding with the rest of the staff, had insisted upon walking the whole distance from Sandy Point to Portsmouth beside the hearse of the master he had loved so well.

DOUBLE EXPOSURE

I still remember with gratitude the wonderful tribute paid Reggie by his many friends in Newport. As I write this, I have before me a clipping from the *Sun* of September 5, 1925:

NEWPORT SOCIETY CANCELS ALL ITS SOCIAL EVENTS

REGINALD C. VANDERBILT'S MEMORY HONORED BY COLONY

Special Dispatch to the *Sun*:

Newport, R.I., Sept. 5.—Because of the unexpected death of Reginald C. Vanderbilt at Sandy Point Farm yesterday morning, the various social events planned have been canceled. All luncheons and dinners yesterday were called off. The annual luncheon and shoot at the Clambake Club, of which he was president for a number of years, were canceled. The shoot this afternoon was to have been for the Cup offered by Walter S. Andrews, the treasurer, and was to have been preceded by luncheons there.

On arriving at the house, Mamma noticed I was near collapse. The long, sad day had overtaxed my strength. She immediately called the doctor. The diphtheria of two years ago had weakened my heart so that the doctor insisted I remain in bed for the next three weeks. Little Gloria stayed on at The Breakers with Grandmother Vanderbilt until I was well.

These weeks gave me a chance to straighten out my thoughts. I had a lot of decisions to make. The major one centered around my year-and-a-half-old baby. Until she legally came of age her education and her religious training were my responsibility. I was ignorant of the tenets of the Episcopal faith, and after much thought I decided I could give Gloria better religious guidance in my own faith. I discussed this step with my dear Mother Dammen; and on April 7, 1926, I took little Gloria to be baptized in the Roman Catholic Church, at Manhattanville, Convent of the Sacred Heart, in the same beautiful chapel that held so many fond childhood memories for me. Gloria behaved like a perfect little angel as Father Evan Duffy of Fordham University christened her. Throughout the ceremony, for no reason that I could see, Mamma was in tears.

During this period the only people I saw were James Deering, our friend and Reggie's lawyer, and "Uncle George" Wickersham, acting as my attorney at the reading of Reggie's will.

"Uncle George" was a small, thin, gray-haired man with a remarkable resemblance to Clemenceau. He had been one of the most eminent attorney generals of the United States and was now a member of the firm of Cadwalader, Wickersham & Taft. He brought with him Thomas B. Gilchrist, whom he had assigned to handle my affairs under his supervision.

Reggie left me five hundred thousand dollars. Several thousand dollars in bequests were left to friends and servants. The five-million-dollar trust fund was divided equally between his two daughters, Cathleen and Gloria.

Reggie named James Deering, W. K. Vanderbilt, and me as executors of the estate. Willie K., for business reasons, was unable to serve. Since I was not twenty-one, the Probate Court held I was ineligible.

"Uncle George" advised me not to accept the five hundred thousand dollars left me under the terms of the will; Reggie's debts were excessive—one item alone was a butcher's bill for $14,000. He suggested, instead, that I exercise my dower rights. This, as it was explained to me, meant that after the houses, stables, and other properties were sold, my rights as a widow would entitle me to a prior claim, no matter how deeply indebted the estate was.

After little Gloria returned from The Breakers, Harry Whitney came to see me several times. I told him how worried I was about the condition of the estate, and asked him what would happen to the creditors if I were to accept my dower rights. He told me not to give these obligations another thought; he had seen Mrs. Vanderbilt and her lawyers, and Mrs. Vanderbilt had arranged to pay any debts still owing after the sale of Reggie's properties.

Harry also very generously told me that I could count on him for all the money I needed, until my lawyers could make other arrangements. This was a great relief to me; I don't know how I would have managed financially without his help.

Many people, including my friends, have never understood why Reggie did not leave me amply provided for. I shall try to explain.

At his father's death, Reggie inherited a five-million-dollar irrevocable trust, the income of this trust to be enjoyed by him during his lifetime. At his death the capital or principal was to be divided, as he saw fit, among any legitimate children he might have. Therefore, following the terms of his father's will, he left his two daughters this trust, in equal shares of two and one-half million each.

Cathleen Cushing, being of age at the time of Reggie's death, inherited her share outright. Since Gloria was then still a minor, her share of the estate was placed in trust for her until her twenty-first birthday, at which time she was to receive the principal together with the accumulated interest. At no time could Reggie legally have left any of this money to me or anyone else.

Reggie's way with money had, to many, been a puzzle. Beside this five-million-dollar trust fund, he had also inherited from his father an outright five million. And this he had spent—some said "squandered"—before our marriage. It is not easy to understand how a man can actually spend five million dollars. But Reggie was a man who loved living well and saw no reason not to gratify his whims. After his first marriage, which was not a happy one, he did not intend to remarry. His daughter, Cathleen, was more than amply provided for. All that he might require to satisfy his own future needs was guaranteed by the trust fund. There was no reason not to indulge himself; he chose to live fully, on his own terms, believing that he could not possibly hurt anyone but himself. I was an unplanned addition to his otherwise well-ordered life, and I entered this marriage knowing what the financial situation was, and knowing that I loved Reggie as he was and for what he was. I am certain that Reggie had no regrets about his life except one—that of leaving me, as he put it, "a Mrs. Vanderbilt without money."

The following weeks were soul-trying. Because of the Vanderbilt name, I became front-page news. Reporters, unable to get any information out of me, sought it elsewhere. And what they came up with was not always accurate.

On September 24, when Reggie's will was probated, every paper carried the news that I had inherited seven million dollars.

In this instance there was some basis for their deductions: the inheritance could have been a fact. Mrs. Vanderbilt had a life interest in the house on Fifth Avenue between Fifty-seventh and Fifty-eighth Streets. This Reggie would have inherited had he outlived his mother. But since Reggie did not survive his mother, this property at Mrs. Vanderbilt's death reverted to Reggie's sister, Mrs. Whitney.

A few days after the probating of the will, "Uncle George" and I went to see Surrogate Foley in his chambers adjoining Surrogate Court. I was making application to have George Wickersham appointed guardian of the property of Gloria and myself, as we were both minors. I would not be of age until the following August. At "Uncle George's" suggestion I also applied for forty-eight thousand dollars a year from the trust for the support and maintenance of my daughter and myself. I did not realize it then, but future events were to prove that from this moment on I had the sword of Damocles hanging over my head.

I was exhausted. All these legal matters were foreign to me, and difficult to understand. How I wished Thelma were with me to help me face these problems, help me make the decisions that were required; but Thelma was in England with Duke. I naturally would have liked to have turned to Mamma; but I had learned, only too well, that Mamma's reactions were not to be relied upon. I had only recently had too vivid a demonstration of this when Mamma accused me of "shameless" behavior with Harry Whitney. I loved Mamma deeply, maybe too much, but I was now well alerted to her strange ways, her obsessions, her mad flashes of jealousy and suspicion; I knew she was the last person to whom I could turn.

I told "Uncle George" that I intended to make my home in France until Gloria was old enough to go to school. I would then enroll her in a school in America, where I wanted her to be brought up. Meanwhile, Mamma had received a letter from Papa, telling her that he would retire from the diplomatic service the following June, and that he wanted to make his future home in France. Consuelo was living in Paris, Benny had been transferred to the Embassy there. All my family, in short, were now to be on the other side of the Atlantic; and I, no longer having any ties to hold me in New York or Newport, wanted to be with them.

Still vivid in my mind is the tiny figure of Mrs. Vanderbilt, sitting by a window in her upstairs drawing room the day I went to tell her I was going to make my home in Paris. She came forward, kissed me on both cheeks, and motioned me to a chair beside her. I didn't know how she would take my news. Although she had always shown me affection and kindness, I still stood a little in awe of her. After all, I was only twenty; she was in her eighties.

I told her of my decision as simply and directly as I could. I need not have been afraid; she agreed with me that, for the time being, I would probably find more peace and contentment near my family. Mrs. Vanderbilt, I had suspected, never liked Mamma; I had noticed in times past that Mamma's name never came up in her conversation. I knew, too, that she did not believe that it was wise for the older and younger generations to live together. I carefully avoided this subject, and Mrs. Vanderbilt tactfully or considerately did the same.

Just before I sailed, Mamma announced to me, in the most matter-of-fact way, that she had received a cable from her Aunt Rosa telling her that her mother had died. There were no hysterics; there were no tears; there was not even a change in the tone of Mamma's voice. When I thought back to the scene Mamma had created not long before, this total absence of any sign of emotion was to me incomprehensible. But that was Mamma!

Eventually I arrived in Paris; and Thelma, as would be expected, was waiting for me at the Gare du Nord. On the way to our hotel she told me that Duke Furness was coming over from London that evening, and that we were dining with him. I was still in deep mourning, and Thelma suggested that, when Duke arrived, we go to Prunier, a quiet but famous restaurant specializing in sea food. She could not have made a more welcome suggestion: this was the last of the "R" months, and Thelma knew I was a glutton for oysters, especially the French marennes. Their coppery taste is not liked by most Americans, but I have a special affinity for them; I've been known to eat three dozen at a sitting.

An amusing thing happened that evening—almost a repetition of Thelma's experience with Junior Converse. Thelma and I had so much to say to each other that we kept talking long past the time to dress for dinner, and Thelma was not ready when Elise announced Duke. "You receive him," Thelma said. "Pour him a drink and tell him I'll be right out."

I entered the sitting room, said a quick hello to Duke, then started to explain; but before I got three words out I found myself in Duke's arms. "Why, Duke!" I said teasingly, "I didn't know you cared." Never have I seen a man suddenly so flustered. Then he joined in my quick laughter as we waited for Thelma.

Thelma and I spent the next few weeks house hunting. After seeing practically every available house and apartment in Paris, I decided on a charming triplex on the Avenue Charles Floquet, facing the Champs-de-Mars.

A few days later Thelma and I returned to the United States.

Little Gloria had grown by leaps and bounds since Thelma had last seen her, and she chattered away like a little magpie. I don't know how it happened, but Thelma became Aunt Toto to her. We spent many happy hours with her in the nursery, playing games, and though neither of us can sing, she loved to hear the old Spanish and French nursery songs of our youth.

I saw very few friends during this time. My days were filled with lawyers, arrangements regarding the sale of both the Newport and New York houses and all the furniture. Problems were piling up on me, one after the other.

Thelma rarely accepted invitations; she spent almost all her time with me. To Mamma's disapproval, claiming it would ruin our eyes, we did jigsaw puzzles far into the night. Maybe I found a therapy of my own, for, believe me, the fitting together of a thousand or more little curved, pointed, angled, odd-shaped pieces of wood to form a finished picture is soothing to a troubled mind.

We made a flying trip to Sandy Point Farm to sort out the things to be sold, and to pack and ship my personal effects to Paris.

CHAPTER XI

Stormy Weather

Thelma

Although Duke had seemed to be perfectly willing to let me go at the time, I had no sooner arrived in New York than he started cabling me, asking when I intended to return. The longer I was away from him, the more I realized how much he really meant to me.

Duke hated writing letters. I don't believe in all the years I knew him I received more than six from him. But he certainly made up in cables and telegrams for his letter-writing deficiencies; he bombarded me with cables, pleading, begging, then demanding my return. These and my many talks with myself decided me: Duke Furness was the man I loved.

I had said very little to Gloria about my feelings. I wanted to be terribly sure myself; besides, I hated to talk of my happiness when she herself was so unhappy.

A few days after I'd made up my mind, Gloria came to me and said, "Darling, why don't you go back? I know Duke loves you and you love him." Putting her arms about me, she whispered, "Life is so short, dear; go to him."

That afternoon I cabled Duke I was sailing on the *Leviathan* April 30, and would land at Southampton. Would he engage rooms at Claridge's for me and Elise? He wired back, "You have made me very happy Stop Rooms reserved for you and maid at

Claridge's Stop If not too much trouble bring record of 'Who' Stop Love to Gloria Stop Always Duke."

Elise and I sailed with the promise from Gloria that she would be in Paris late in May.

In my desire to get to Duke the trip seemed endless. I wished somebody would make an airplane that would fly me across this wretched Atlantic; little did I guess that a few months later Lindbergh was to make his historic flight nonstop to Paris. I deluded myself that the days were shorter when they put the clock ahead an hour at midnight. I tried to sleep late in the morning, hoping it would make them shorter still.

The night before we reached port, the passengers were told that England was in the throes of a general strike and that we would not be able to land as announced. We were to pull up beside the dock the following morning and, if arrangements could be made for transportation and unloading of passengers' luggage, we would be able to leave the ship. If not, we would be taken on to Cherbourg.

When we docked that morning, I was pacing my cabin like a caged animal. "This is too much!" I screamed at Elise.

"Calm yourself, Madame. Lord Furness will join you in Paris, I am sure, if we can't land here."

"What do you mean, Paris?" I said, looking out of the porthole at an empty quay. "Why, look, I could almost jump the distance."

Just then I saw a solitary figure and I nearly did jump. There was Duke calmly walking up the gangway. Before I knew it he was in my stateroom.

I should have known that nothing short of an act of God would have prevented Duke from doing what he wanted to do. A strike, even a general strike, was certainly not going to stand in his way. I suppose owning a ship line, as well as the largest shipyard in England, and a few steel works and collieries to boot, didn't hurt any.

Duke told me that when he had heard we might not be able to land, he had decided to come and get me. But how were we going to get all my luggage in the car, I wondered. Again I should have known better. Duke had come down to Southampton with what seemed to me a caravan of Rolls-Royces. To be exact, there were three. Davis, Duke's chauffeur, was to drive us. Killips, who later became my chauffeur and remained with me till I left England in 1940, was to drive Elise and transport some of the hand luggage. The bigger pieces were to follow in the station break.

As we started on our way up to London, Duke nearly scared me to death by pulling a revolver out of his pocket and placing it on his lap. "Now," he said, "I'd like to see any bastard try to stop this car."

What in the world did he mean, stop the car? Seeing my look of surprise, he told me how the strikers had been overturning cars—in some cases even burning them—in their efforts to keep food and other necessities from reaching London. He also told me what a magnificent job the young men at Oxford and Cambridge were doing, manning the trains, driving trucks; even the Eton and Harrow boys were doing their bit at strike-breaking. I thought of Dick and could almost hear him say, "Jolly good show."

Just then Davis pulled up short. A long line of cars and trucks in front of us had stopped. Duke, waving his revolver in the air, got out of the car. "I'll soon see what the bloody hell is holding us up."

"I wish His Lordship wouldn't do that," Davis said, turning around to me. "He's sure to get hurt. These blokes really mean business. Anyway, these Rolls don't help any."

Oh, for heaven's sake, Duke, I thought, stop playing hero and come back here to me.

When Duke returned, he looked a little sheepish. One of the large trucks had merely got a flat tire, and our brave amateurs were having trouble putting a new one on. I was thankful when we reached Claridge's without any further incidents.

Duke had arranged for Averill and Gav to pick me up at the hotel before taking me to lunch at 17 Arlington Street. I was anxious to see this house Duke had rented for one night from Lady Yarborough for a dance—and was still occupying six years later.

The door was opened for us by a liveried footman who ushered us down a long corridor lined with marble statues on marble pedestals. "Horrible, don't you think?" said Averill, and I must say I agreed with her. I felt as if I were walking through a graveyard and hoped the rest of the house was more inviting.

I found out later that Duke had taken the house furnished and, in the course of years, had added some of his own things. The result was a potpourri of every known period from William and Mary to good old Queen Victoria. Still the house had a certain grandeur about it. Its lovely high ceilings and beautifully paneled walls gave it an old-world grace. I had never lived in such a big house and wondered what it would be like. It didn't take me long to find out that a taste for luxury and prodigality is easily acquired—though not so readily forgotten.

Duke met us in the library, a charming room. Its walls were lined with beautifully bound books. It also had a superb Adam mantelpiece. At the far end two big French windows opened on the Green Park.

At lunch the conversation naturally turned to the strike. Dear Gav seemed to take it as a personal insult. He intensely disliked the inconvenience of it all. The government, as far as he was concerned, was allowing England, as well as the whole British Empire, to go to the dogs—and not doing a damned thing about it. Placing his monocle firmly on his glass eye, he glared at me out of his good one. "Queen Victoria," he shouted, "certainly would never have allowed any such nonsense!"

Duke suggested we dine at the Embassy Club that night. The

Embassy was the smartest and most popular restaurant in London. The incomparable Luigi ran it with the innate tact of a born restaurateur. English married people, I found out later, thought nothing of accepting dinner invitations separately, and it was Luigi's feat never to seat husband and wife at adjoining tables.

The room itself had not been decorated with imagination. The banquettes against the wall were upholstered in red velvet. Above them were walls entirely mirrored, reflecting the much-too-bright lights. The table on the right as one came in was reserved for the Prince of Wales or other visiting royalty. The table to the left Luigi usually kept for us.

We might as well have been alone in the restaurant that night for all the attention we paid to the others. But I didn't realize that I had caused quite a sensation as, beside Duke, I entered in a long evening gown.

An amusing article came out in one of the Paris newspapers just before I left for New York: "With Ganna Walska and Thelma Morgan Converse leading one side, and with Julia Thompson and Jean Nash leading the other, the long versus short skirt war goes on," and ended by saying, "Mrs. Converse's skirts actually touched the ground!"

We had finished dancing and were back at our table when Duke blurted out, "When is that bloody divorce of yours final, anyway?" It was so like Duke to pick the Embassy Club to inquire. I looked around to see if anybody had overheard him. The newspaper reporters had been hot on my trail before I left New York, and I, of course, had been denying all rumors of an engagement to Duke or to anybody else. I had only just made up my mind myself; I had not even told Duke of my decision. "The latter part of June," I whispered. "I'll tell you all about it at lunch tomorrow."

Averill's coming-out ball was to take place on June 24. Dear Averill hated the very idea of "coming out." She told me she had not said a word to her father because she knew how disappointed he would be at the way she felt about this ball—which she called "a waste of time and money." She loathed London and was only happy at Burrough Court with her hunters and dogs. I was glad she had not told him. He was so proud of her, and he had gone to such infinite trouble to make this ball *the* ball of the London season. Duke, as a widower, found it awkward to bring out a young girl in society, and was grateful when Lady Sarah Wilson, the aunt of the late Duke of Marlborough, a great friend of his, came to the rescue and offered to help chaperon Averill. Lady Sarah and I became great friends after my marriage, in spite of the difference in our ages. It was this wonderful, charming, worldly lady who took me under her wing and led me through the maze of London society and its bewildering names and titles.

Before I had a chance to say anything, when I arrived at No. 17 for lunch that day, Duke placed a beautiful diamond ring on my finger and said, "I think we had better be married in Paris, rather than in London. That way I believe we can avoid publicity."

I sat down hard on the nearest chair. I was flabbergasted. I looked at him in amazement. He hadn't even taken the time to kiss me, much less ask me what I thought of his plans. When I finally got my voice, I said, "You know, a girl likes to be proposed to. It gives her a chance to say no."

It was Duke who then stared at me in shock; this was a response he had not expected. Suddenly he leaned over and kissed me, and at that moment Averill walked in. "Well," she said, "at last you two are making sense. When is the happy day to be?"

Some newspapers in America at the time hinted that Averill opposed this marriage. Nothing could have been further from the truth. Ever since my visit to Scotland she and I had been close friends. We couldn't have been more unlike in looks and temperament. I suppose that is why we got on so well; we were not competitive.

I decided not to cable Gloria my news. She was arriving in Paris the end of May, and I wanted to tell her myself. Dick, Duke's son, was also to be kept in the dark; he might talk at Eton. The only ones who knew were Averill, Gav, Lady Sarah Wilson, and, of course, Elise, who I knew would keep our secret.

Elise and I went back to Paris within the next few days. There was so much to be done.

I had been told by my lawyer that if I were to be married in France I would have to get certain papers from the American Consul General in Paris. I didn't give this much thought; I knew that Mr. Skinner was a great friend of Papa's and would do all he could to expedite matters, and also to keep our secret. I remembered him well; he had been American Consul General in London during the war.

But first I wanted to order my gown for Averill's coming-out party, as well as my wedding gown. I knew I wouldn't have time to get much else.

I went to Patou for my wedding dress—a lovely bois-de-rose crepe de Chine with a matching long coat bordered at the sleeves and hem with soft, silky lynx. Reboux designed a very pretty turban of the same material. For Averill's party I chose at Lanvin a beautiful wide white slipper-satin robe-de-style, very tight at the waist and touching the ground. Halfway down the skirt on either side was a cluster of round black-velvet appliquéd circles the size of a small pancake. These were circled by little round mirrors which, when I danced, reflected the lights.

The lease was almost up on my apartment; I decided to move to the Hôtel du Rhin, on the Place Vendôme opposite the Ritz, hoping that the change of address might help me to avoid the press. Ever since my return from London reporters had been deluging me with calls and begging for interviews. I was at my wit's end, dodging questions.

Monday, June 7, the New York *American* came out with, "Reports reaching New York from Paris today tell of the secret marriage in London last week of Mrs. Thelma Morgan Converse and Lord Furness, multimillionaire steamship owner. While confirmation is lacking and Mrs. Converse has denied that the ceremony has taken place..."

I don't know whether it was the move or that the reporters had tired of hearing me say, "No comment." At any rate, they now gave me a breathing spell.

Before I left London, Duke and I had agreed that he was not to come to Paris until the day before we were to be married; and the marriage was scheduled to follow Averill's party. Our high romantic moment, in short, was precisely geared to the clockwork of social events. In the interim, we kept in touch by telephone.

One evening Duke called to say that he had just talked, long distance, to his lawyer in Paris. "When you go to see Mr. Skinner," he said, "I suggest you take him with you."

I didn't see any reason for this lawyer to go with me and told Duke so. "After all, darling, it isn't as if I did not know the Consul. He's an old friend." But Duke insisted.

The next morning I telephoned the Consulate and made an appointment for that afternoon. Duke's lawyer picked me up at the hotel and together we went to the Consulate. Mr. Skinner couldn't have been sweeter. He asked about Papa and Mamma. He reminisced a little about the war and then said, "Well, Thelma, what can I do for you?"

I told him all about my wedding plans, how wonderful Duke was, how happy I was, and that I understood I needed some papers from him before I could get married in France.

I looked over at Duke's lawyer and wondered why he didn't say anything. Surely, I thought, that was what he was here for—to talk about those papers I was to get.

"Of course, Thelma," Mr. Skinner said, "I'll see to it that

everything is in order for you." Then, turning to Duke's lawyer, he asked, "What is the marriage settlement to be?"

I looked at him in amazement. "I don't understand. What do you mean, marriage settlement?"

Finally Duke's lawyer spoke up. "Mrs. Converse, Lord Furness asked me to come here with you, knowing Mr. Skinner is a friend of your family; he thought perhaps Mr. Skinner would advise you on the marriage settlement."

I was getting furious. "I still don't understand."

Mr. Skinner tried to calm me. "Listen, Thelma, in England it is the custom for a woman to get a marriage settlement when she marries. It doesn't mean anything, really. It doesn't matter whether you're very rich or not, there is still a little marriage settlement. It can be a few hundred pounds a year or a few thousand pounds a year."

To me this was horrible. "So I'm being bought!" I cried. "I certainly won't take a marriage settlement. I'm not marrying Duke because of a settlement. This is absurd!"

Mr. Skinner tried to explain once more that this was the custom in England. "Nobody is buying you," he said. "Nobody is doing anything. This has been done since time immemorial."

"Just the same," I declared, "I'm not going to accept it."

This exasperated the lawyer. He called my stand ridiculous. I stood up. "It may be ridiculous to you, but in America things are not done that way, and I'm an American and that's that."

Again Mr. Skinner interrupted. "After all, Thelma, I'm your father's friend. He happens to be in South America. If he were here, he would advise you just the way I'm advising you."

"If God himself were to advise me, I wouldn't do it," I insisted. "I don't want a settlement."

Mr. Skinner looked at me as if I'd lost my mind. "In that case, I won't give you the papers you need."

"Very well, Mr. Skinner. Thank you just the same." I stalked out of the room with Duke's lawyer following behind me, not knowing what kind of lunatic his client was marrying.

As soon as I got back to the hotel, I telephoned Duke and told him he had better come over to Paris at once. I had something to say to him that could not be said on the phone.

"What's wrong, darling? You sound angry."

I surprised him by saying, "You're bloody well right I'm angry!"

"Darling, that doesn't sound like you. I'll be over on the first plane in the morning," Duke said. "Whatever has upset you I'm sure can be ironed out."

As I hung up, I was a little ashamed. Duke was right. This didn't sound like me.

The next day Duke stormed into my apartment and took me in his arms. "What's this nonsense about my buying you?" he asked, laughing. "My solicitor met me at the airport and told me all about your meeting with Mr. Skinner. Frankly, darling, he thinks you are a little bit off the beam."

I pulled away from him. "Look here, Duke," I said, "I don't want a settlement from you. I'm marrying you because I love you, and that's that!"

"Listen to me, darling. In England it's only a normal procedure—it's expected—that a man should settle a certain amount of money on the woman he marries. This isn't wife-buying; it's insurance."

I started to cry. "I know I'm being ridiculous," I said, "but I can't help it. It's all so businesslike."

At this point Duke was ready to do anything to calm me. "Don't worry, darling," he said soothingly. "Whatever you want, you can have. And if you want no settlement, that's the way it will be. I'll go to see Mr. Skinner and explain."

"No, you won't!" I shouted. "We're not going to be married in Paris. We're going to be married in London; I don't know the

American Consul there, but whoever he is, I'm sure he isn't interested in playing second father to me."

Gloria

I don't believe I ever felt more alone than I did, sitting in my deck chair, when the *Majestic* was three days out of New York. My thoughts were as troubled as the waves that beat frantically against the side of the ship. I missed Reggie so very, very much.

I had just come from Mamma's cabin—and one of Mamma's characteristic scenes. Mamma had turned on me suddenly, violently, vituperatively. The reason? I wanted to take Gloria on deck with me. The sea was too rough, Mamma said; the baby might get hurt. The way she described the state of the sea at this moment you would have thought that the next roll of the *Majestic* would be her last, and that we were all bobbing over Davy Jones's locker. But this was not all; Mamma, in a rage, accused me of deliberately trying to harm little Gloria. If I was totally lacking in concern for Gloria's safety, Mamma went on, she at least would see to it that "the little one" was protected. I had tried to explain to her that all the other children on board were playing on deck, and having a wonderful time. Mamma's voice then rose to a scream: "This might be so, but they are not Gloria Vanderbilt!"

I know now that this was a turning point in my life. By a strange twist in her disordered mind Mamma had come to assume that my child was hers, and that I, her actual child, had become a force of evil, threatening the safety of her fantasy child; I should have recognized this pathological trait for what it was, and asserted my authority. But I did not. It is not easy, at this writing, to account for my inaction. Perhaps the shock of Reggie's death had left me emotionally inert. Perhaps I was still under the spell of Mamma's authoritative personality. Perhaps, not yet aware of the tragic implications of Mamma's delusional flights, I still believed everything she did was based, at heart, on a deep although confused love—a love that I could trust. I prefer to think that the last is the most reasonable explanation. In spite of all that I have since experienced, I still believe that it is unnatural for a child to turn—without a devastating cause or fright—against her own mother. But whatever the reason, I left Gloria in Mamma's hands; she did not come on deck that day.

The nurse, Emma Keislich, was also giving me trouble. She had adopted toward little Gloria—and in some respects toward me—an attitude that seemed patterned on my mother's; to Keislich, Gloria was an especially delicate child whose fragile nature was not properly respected by me; she was, moreover, an heiress whose privileged status was not adequately acknowledged by those whose duty it was to serve her. Only the day before, the chief dining-room steward had come to me to say, with apologies, that no matter what the chef prepared, Keislich returned it to the kitchen: it was not right for Gloria. The baked potatoes were either too mealy or not mealy enough; the meat was invariably too rare or too well done; the fruit was too green or too ripe. This, too, was the beginning of a trend, a warning symbol of emotional disturbance which I should have dealt with at the outset.

There was a time, later, when we were at the Ritz, in London, that Keislich tangled with the chef there. When Dr. Gavin came to visit us, he found Keislich cooking a chicken for little Gloria—in a hot plate resting on the toilet seat. The nurse told Dr. Gavin, in all seriousness, that the Ritz food was not fit for anyone to eat—much less a sick child. "Of course," she added, "Mrs. Vanderbilt does not agree with me; but I for one am going to see that little Gloria Vanderbilt has the best." Gav suggested, sarcastically, that perhaps she, when younger, had the privilege of acquiring a culinary skill superior to that of the Ritz's Cordon Bleu chef, but he doubted it. Then, turning, he saw the washbasin heaped with carrot and onion parings. The sight spurred him to exercise his medical authority. "What the hell do you mean by using the washbasin as a kitchen sink?" he bellowed. "As a registered nurse, you should know that a bathroom is for other purposes."

Thelma

The night of Averill's ball, Lady Sarah Wilson gave a dinner in a private room at the Ritz and had graciously included me. I write "graciously" with purpose, for although Duke and I planned to be married within the next few days this fact was obviously not known to most of the others who would be present. To those who knew of me at all, I was merely Mrs. Morgan Converse, a young American divorcée whose name had been linked by gossip with Duke Furness. As a consequence I must say that, as I was dressing for dinner, I felt apprehensive. I had been told who some of the guests would be; some I already knew—among them Lady Emerald Cunard and Sir Thomas Beecham; the Brazilian Ambassador and Madame Regis de Oliveira, whom I had known in Paris; Sir Hugh Seely, now Lord Sherwood; and the late Viscount Tredegar, a very distant relative of ours through the Morgans. I hoped they would take pity on me and help me navigate these strange and treacherous channels.

I was a frightened young woman when I entered the drawing room and discovered that at least sixty others had been invited for dinner, some fifty of whom were strangers to me. Among others I recognized H. R. H. Prince Henry, now the Duke of Gloucester, and realized that this was to be my first encounter with British royalty. Averill, seeing me hesitate as I stood in the doorway, came up to me and led me to Duke and Lady Sarah. En route across the floor, I observed that I was the target for many inquiring glances.

After dinner we all went to 17 Arlington Street, where the

ball was to be held. The house was festive. Constance Spry, the famous London florist, had blanketed the rooms with flowers. There were two orchestras and two supper rooms. In all, Duke had invited some eight hundred guests; and taken as an ensemble, they provided a sight as impressive as it was exciting—the women in their gala gowns, the men, all handsome it seemed to me, with their many decorations. Among those who stand out in memory are the Duchess of Westminster, Sir John and Lady Milbanke, Lady Loughborough, Viscount and Lady Ednam (Lady Ednam was later killed in a plane crash on a flight to Le Touquet), and Mme. Martinez de Hoz, one of the most beautiful and best-dressed women in international society.

Viscountess Wimborne also gave a dinner before the ball. Among her guests were Prince and Princess Obolensky; the Earl and Countess of Brecknock; the beautiful Lady Dalkeith, now the Duchess of Buccleuch; and the equally beautiful Lady Diana Cooper. Sir John, the famous portrait painter and his wife, Lady Lavery—whose face can be seen on Irish stamps—also come to mind. I was to come to know most of them well in the next few years and many of them became my friends.

At lunch the following day Duke told me he had made arrangements to have the registrar's office at St. George, Hanover Square, which ordinarily is closed on Sundays, opened especially for our marriage. He hoped by this stratagem to avoid the press, and he succeeded. One of the New York papers came out the day following our wedding with, "A Triumph of Secrecy—the society gossips are still ignorant of many of the details—all reports of the affair thus far have been secondhand." Duke, as usual, had got his way.

Mamma and Gloria arrived from Paris the morning before the wedding and were staying at the Ritz with me. Duke had asked all those who were to be at the ceremony for cocktails that afternoon. Lady Sarah, Gav, Mamma, Gloria, Averill, Dick, and Bettine Abingdon.

We decided not to go to the registrar's in our cars, but to use taxis instead. A flock of private cars in front of the registrar's on a quiet Sunday morning might attract too much attention.

Gav, Duke's best man, was to go with Duke. Mamma and Lady Sarah were to go together. Bettine, Averill, and Dick were to share a taxi. Gloria was to come with me.

Averill looked disappointed. "Oh, Thelma dear," she said, "can't I be the one to go with you?"

I didn't have to look at Gloria, for I was sure she was as pleased as I was at the pretty compliment, and so it was decided that Gloria should go with Dick and Bettine.

That night Mamma, Gloria, and I dined quietly in my apartment. The next morning, the twenty-seventh of June, at nine-thirty sharp, Averill arrived, loking very pretty in an almond-green suit that set off her red hair. Elise was trying her best to keep me still long enough to fasten the line of little buttons down the back of my gown.

"Well, how does the bride feel on this bright sunny day?" Averill asked with matter-of-fact briskness.

"Oh, Averill, I'm so glad you're here. I'm so nervous I don't know what I'm doing."

Averill sat down on the bed. "*You're* nervous! You should see Dad. I've just poured half a tumbler of brandy down his throat and he was still shaking apart when I left."

I must say I don't think a registrar's office is the most romantic setting in the world for a wedding. It all seemed so cold and businesslike. But before I knew it I was signing the wedding certificate; and it was only then that everybody became natural. Duke kissed me. Dick said rather shyly, "You look simply topping." Averill whispered, "The brandy must have done the trick." They all flocked around us, congratulating Duke, wishing us both all sorts of luck and happiness. Mamma took me in her arms and, as usual when emotional, spoke Spanish. "*Mi deseo, querida, es de verte siempre felice como ahora*—my wish, darling, is to see you always as happy as you are now."

When we arrived at No. 17 I was touched to see all the servants in the hall, waiting to wish us happiness. Watson, the butler, made a charming little speech as he handed me a bouquet of flowers that he "respectfully hoped I would accept from the staff." I thought I was going to cry when I thanked them.

Mrs. Vanderbilt, Gloria's mother-in-law, was staying at Claridge's in London at the time and had asked Gloria, if it weren't a large reception, whether she could come and wish us luck; it would please her very much. Though I didn't know this charming old lady well, I was of course delighted. She was still in mourning for Reggie, and I'm sure it must have been an effort for her.

It all seemed like a dream as Duke and I drove off to Burrough Court, his place in Leicestershire, where we were to spend the night.

The next morning Elise woke me with my breakfast. "Good morning, Milady! It's a beautiful day."

"Oh, Elise, darling," I said, "it is indeed a beautiful day!"

With a little sly smile, Elise, as usual, went about her chores.

On our return to London I opened, with excitement, the first invitation addressed to me as a peeress. The card read: "The Marquess and Marchioness of Londonderry request the pleasure of Viscount and Viscountess Furness' presence...." At the bottom corner was the single word, "Decorations." By this time even I knew that this meant royalty would be present.

I was terribly nervous as I got ready for the dinner, and I tried to imagine who the royalty would be: Princess Mary? The Duke of York and his bride? Could it possibly be the Prince of Wales? Later, when Averill joined me, she announced, "I'm nervous as a cat." I smiled reassuringly and said, "You needn't be, dear; you look lovely." But little did she know how nervous I was.

Londonderry House was magnificent that night. Flowers were massed everywhere. There were footmen with powdered wigs, knee breeches, and long white stockings. What a tale this house could tell were it only able to speak, I thought. Kings and queens had strolled through its stately rooms; lords and statesmen had made history there over glasses of port.

Duke's friends all came up to meet me, and to congratulate Duke. Everybody was very kind and very flattering, and I soon got over my nervousness. Duke seemed pleased when his friends called him a "lucky dog."

I looked around for Averill. She, too, seemed to have gotten over her nervousness and was happily dancing with a handsome young guardsman.

"Come on, darling, let's dance, too," Duke said as he led me to the dance floor.

We hadn't been dancing long when all of a sudden there was a murmur and then a little hush. Lord and Lady Londonderry had entered the ballroom with the Prince of Wales at their side.

I whispered to Duke, "Look, darling, the Prince of Wales!"

As he stood in the doorway, the Prince seemed a little shy. His hand went often to his white tie. He held his head a little to one side when spoken to. He looked younger than I had pictured him and very handsome.

The music had stopped. Duke and I were moving toward the supper room when I heard my name called close behind me. "Lady Furness." I looked around and there was Lady Londonderry with the Prince of Wales beside her.

"Sir, may I present Lady Furness, Duke Furness's young American bride. Lady Furness, His Royal Highness, the Prince of Wales."

I was thankful for my long, full dress. My knees would not stop shaking. I knew the Prince could not see them; I only hoped he could not hear them. He put out his hand and I put my gloved one in his, made a deep curtsy, and said nothing. I couldn't.

"Welcome to England," he said cordially. "I hope you will be happy here. May I have the next dance? I believe it's a Viennese waltz. I do hope you like them."

Like them! The Viennese waltz had always been my favorite. Again I thanked my lucky stars for my long dress. Waltzes and knee-length dresses never did go together.

The music stopped. The Prince thanked me. I curtsied, and did not see him again—at least really to talk to—for nearly three years.

Looking out the window just before we reached Inverness, I noticed a heavy mist and hoped it would lift. I so wanted it to be a perfect day. As the train pulled into the station, the sun came out. Davis was waiting for us again with the old gray Rolls.

Scotland in June I thought even more beautiful than in autumn. Long-haired sheep grazed peacefully, tended by little boys and their dogs. Wild flowers were to be seen everywhere. North toward Beauly, which is in the midst of one of the wildest regions in the Highlands, where red deer are plentiful, the glens were a mass of color, pale pink lavender to deep purple heather.

Duke and I spent four heavenly weeks doing nothing very much but being divinely happy. The hunting and shooting season was not open; I had Duke all to myself. On fine days we would get on our ponies with lunch baskets and ride through the moors for hours until we found just the right spot to picnic—usually near a cool stream. After lunch Duke sometimes would take out his spyglass and watch the stags and hinds as they roamed the moors; I wandered, picking wild flowers. At other times we would just lie on the heather in each other's arms.

One day I found some white heather. I was delighted; it's supposed to bring good luck. I took it home with me, carefully pressed it, and put it in a book of Rabindranath Tagore's poems. It is no longer green and fresh, and only a few of the little white flowers remain, but it brings back many happy memories. Memory is very kind. More often than not it lets one remember only the pleasant things.

There were days when we would take the motorboat to the end of the loch, and I'd go swimming in the cold, clear water. Duke always worried on these occasions; he himself couldn't swim. He would have a gillie in a rowboat follow me around. It wasn't much fun being supervised this way; so I didn't swim often.

I received a long letter from Papa, telling me that at long last my letter to him announcing and asking his blessings on my forthcoming marriage to Duke had caught up with him in Paris. He also enclosed a newspaper clipping dated July 7, 1926. The heading read: "Marriage of Mrs. Morgan Converse to Lord Furness a Surprise to Bride's Father, H. H. Morgan." The item read, in part:

The first intimation received by Harry Hays Morgan, retiring American Consul General at Buenos Aires, that his daughter had married Lord Furness, the British shipping magnate, came this week, when reporters meeting the Munson liner, *Southern Cross*, on which he arrived from South America, asked him if he were on his way to visit his son-in-law. "What son-in-law?" he demanded. "Lord Furness," he was told. "Did Thelma marry Lord Furness?" he said. "That's the first I ever heard of it. Well, I'm sure he'll make an excellent husband for her and I'll gladly give my blessing to them both."

Then in the interview he explained his ignorance by saying that he had been on the sea for more than fifteen days. "I suppose Thelma's message never reached me or else that I will find it waiting for me when I land."

That was what had happened. In the bustle and excitement before my marriage I hadn't stopped to think how long it took a letter to reach Buenos Aires from Paris. Papa sent his somewhat belated blessings and said he hoped to see us both in the fall on his return to Paris from Biarritz, where he was to spend a few weeks with Gloria and Mamma.

I was overjoyed at the thought of being with Papa once again. It had been nearly three years since I had last seen him, and I missed him. I was also eager to have Duke meet him.

Meanwhile, Duke and I decided to spend three or four weeks at Duke's country place, Burrough Court, then meet Papa in Paris.

We arrived at Burrough early one morning and were met by Averill and Dick. I was looking forward to the prospect of sinking roots in this country house, which had come to mean so much in Duke's life. When Duke bought it, Burrough was a small, two-storied hunting lodge. Duke had since added wings on either side, giving the house the shape of a square U. The dining room, drawing rooms, and library were on the ground floor. Our bedrooms and the guest rooms were above. We could put up some fifteen people, which seemed quite a lot to me; but by English standards this was not considered a large house. Still, it was roomy, and it was comfortable; every bedroom had its own bath, and there was central heating—a blessing in the cold winter months.

I was glad that most of our neighbors had not yet arrived for the season. It gave me a little time to get used to my new surroundings.

Gloria

On my return to Paris from Thelma's wedding, my brother Harry and I went to Biarritz to see about a house for the summer. We arrived early in the morning and were lucky enough to find a charming house called the Villa Ourida, near the Chiberta golf course.

The Villa Ourida was all I hoped it would be. Little Gloria, as usual, loved the beach and our picnics in the pinewoods nearby.

Papa arrived from Buenos Aires. I was happy to see him after so long a time, and pleased that he was now going to make his home with me. He had, of course, never seen his first grandchild, and it was a delight to behold his joy in her.

The summer passed pleasantly but quietly.

I celebrated my twenty-first birthday with a small dinner party. Among my guests was Angustias, the Marquesa San Carlos, who has remained a close friend ever since. Angustias was the mother of two handsome boys. Tall, gray-eyed, she has all the beauty and charm of her native Granada. Extremely chic herself, she surprised no one at the tremendous success she had as "Marie Christine"; from her very first showing, she established herself as one of the foremost modistes in Paris.

It was during this season that I met the Prince of Wales. As we entered the Reserve de Ciboure, one of the charming places to dine that dot the Basque coast, the air was vibrating with excitement.

"His Royal Highness, the Prince of Wales is here!" the maître d'hôtel excitedly told me.

As I sat down I glanced across the room and saw a slender, handsome young man. I thought him far handsomer than in the many pictures I had seen.

Nothing could have surprised me more than when, as we were dining, his aide-de-camp, General Trotter, came to our table and said, "His Royal Highness would like to know if you are related to Mrs. Benjamin Thaw."

"Yes," I answered, "I'm her sister, Gloria Vanderbilt."

As soon as the aide-de-camp returned to his table, the Prince arose and came over to me, saying, "I met your sister Consuelo in Buenos Aires. May this serve as a present introduction?" He sat and joined us for a few moments. He told me that when he was in Buenos Aires, the American Ambassador was away. All the entertaining had fallen on the shoulders of Benny and Consuelo. He saw a great deal of them and they became great friends.

We did not meet again until some time later at Thelma's house in London.

The end of September found Mamma, little Gloria, and me installed at the Avenue Charles Floquet. The newly decorated apartment looked lovely. The furniture and curtains I had chosen on previous trips fitted in beautifully.

At Thelma's wedding Mrs. Vanderbilt had told me she had bought for me all the silver, linens, and trophies from Reggie's estate, and had shipped them to me in Paris.

When I tried to thank her, she said, "They belong to you, Gloria dear. I want you to have them."

And now these had arrived as well, so that everything was in order in a house I hoped would be a happy one. It wasn't!

In October, when Thelma was back in London, I received word from "Uncle George" that my presence would be necessary in America, now that I was twenty-one, to sign certain papers that would wind up the settlement of the estate.

Harry, Angustias, and I sailed in November on the *Leviathan*.

Two days out, Captain Hartley asked me to lunch. The luncheon was in honor of the Queen of Romania, who was aboard with her daughter, Princess Eleana, her son, and her nephew, H. S. H. Prince Hohenlohe. Those present were Mrs. Woodrow Wilson, Baron Thyssen, and some of the Queen's entourage. I was seated next to Friedel Hohenlohe. He was not a handsome man, but distinguished. He had the long upper lip of his great-grandmother, Queen Victoria, which most of that family have. I marveled at his English, which he spoke with a perfection one rarely hears in a Continental.

This was his first trip to America, and I liked his enthusiasm. He wanted to know about the Metropolitan Opera. Was it as wonderful as he'd heard? It seemed his two loves were music and horses. The National Horse Show was opening, and, as I had a box, I asked him to join my party.

CHAPTER XII

Honeymoon

Thelma

After Christmas at Burrough Court, a hard frost set in and all hunting stopped. Duke and I decided to go to Monte Carlo. I was delighted. We arrived in brilliant sunshine at the Hôtel de Paris. I couldn't wait for Elise to unpack my things, I was so anxious to go exploring. As I looked out of my window I saw the famous Casino; even at eleven in the morning people were going in to gamble.

After lunch Duke and I took a stroll around the town. I was fascinated with the gendarmes in their cock-feathered helmets directing traffic as seriously as if they were in the very heart of Piccadilly. Bejeweled old dowagers, sitting at sidewalk cafés, were sipping hot chocolate and eating mountainous heaps of French pastry. Their finery must have been the fashion in Edward VII's time. Duke told me many of them were widows who found the climate of Monte Carlo pleasanter than England's; and, what was more important, there were no taxes.

Later that afternoon I asked Duke if he would like to go to the Sporting Club for a while before dinner. He told me he was expecting some calls from London; I should go on ahead and he would join me later. I went up to my room to change, and, as I was leaving, I realized I had no French money. Elise proudly handed me 4,000 francs. I knew that would not take me very far in a casino. But I decided, if I lost this, as I was sure to do, I

HONEYMOON

could always cash a check. Tucking the 4,000 francs in my purse, I went to the Sporting Club. After I had paid and signed for my entrance card, I had a little more than 3,000 francs left.

At the first table they were playing roulette. I watched for a while. This was a new game to me; in Deauville, or any of the other French casinos for that matter, roulette, at that time, was not allowed. People here seemed to be taking it seriously. All had a system. To me it looked like sheer luck. I placed 1,000 francs on zero, 1,000 francs on 17, and 1,000 on 32. To my amazement 17 popped up; I had won 32,000 francs. I played one or two more turns of the wheel and lost, then wandered off to play chemin de fer, which I understood and liked better. I was lucky there, too. When Duke arrived, I was the proud possessor of some 80,000 francs.

Monte Carlo in 1926 was a winter resort only. It wasn't till a year or so later that Elsa Maxwell, after her tremendous success in attracting summer tourists to Venice, was asked to do the same for Monte Carlo, and I think it was mainly her ideas that made it the world's most fashionable summer playground.

Duke wanted to show me all the beauty spots he knew so well. We'd drive toward Nice on the Upper Corniche over paralyzing hairpen bends the like of which I have never found anywhere else—except along the Costa Brava in Spain. Gloria, once when we were motoring there, had said, "This coast was certainly well named. One has to be brave to take it."

One beautiful day Duke and I stopped for lunch at the lovely little village of St. Paul high above the Mediterranean. Sitting over our coffee, we could see for miles up and down the coast. Yachts on their way to Monte Carlo or Cannes dotted the translucent blue sea. Majestic sailboats cruised leisurely by. The pungent scent of mimosa, so much a part of the south of France, was all around.

On our way back we followed the coast on the Lower Corniche. I am not sure which are the more petrifying, the hairpin bends on the Upper Corniche, or the lunatics that drive at a hundred miles an hour, or so it seemed to me, on the Lower.

When we reached the hotel, I was surprised and delighted to find Hannibal de Mesa. I had not seen him in ages. As he threw his arms about me, I noticed Duke bristle. It wasn't until I had introduced them and explained that Hannibal had practically bounced me on his knee as a little girl that Duke unruffled. Over cocktails Duke asked him if he would care to join us for dinner. I was pleased; I liked him to like my friends. We had already asked Sarah Wilson and the Duke of Westminster; though Hannibal protested he would make an odd number, Duke insisted.

"Ben-Dor" Westminster was one of the most attractive men I had ever met. In many respects he was very un-English. He adapted himself to the continental ways much better than most Englishmen. He entertained lavishly on his yacht, the *Cutty Sark*. He was a keen gambler, a good loser as well as a gracious winner. He loved beauty of any kind, especially beautiful women.

After dinner we all went to the Sporting Club. Duke was never very good at cards, but he did enjoy strolling through the rooms, chatting with friends, and every now and then taking a hand at chemin de fer or baccarat.

One of the pleasantest memories I have of these days is of a lunch at Lou Sueil, Madame Jacques Balsan's house at Eze. Madam Balsan, née Consuelo Vanderbilt, a first cousin of Reggie's, was and is one of the most beautiful women I have ever known. Should anyone ask me whom of all beautiful women I would pick to look like, I would unhesitatingly say Consuelo Balsan. Before she married Jacques Balsan she was married to the Duke of Marlborough. I once saw a photograph of her as canopy bearer to Queen Alexandra at the coronation of King Edward VII and I don't think I have ever seen anything more lovely.

One could see at once, as one entered Lou Sueil, that it was a loved house. The paneled walls were magnificent, the Chinese

HONEYMOON

fret and fine carvings of rare Chippendale chairs and tables blended beautifully with the more romantic and delicate Louis XVI low and comfortable sofas. Madame Balsan had somehow managed to make into a home what might have been a museum.

When Duke decided to push on to Cannes, I hated to leave. I thought Monte Carlo was lucky to me. I had won more than 100,000 francs, some $4,000 at the then rate of exchange. But at the same time I was anxious to see the place where Napoleon landed after his imprisonment in Elba, also the Île Ste. Marguerite, where the man in the Iron Mask was consigned to oblivion by Louis XIV.

On the way we lunched at the Reserve de Beaulieu, the famous restaurant which is mentioned in every guidebook as a gastronomic must, and indeed it is. I have never tasted anything more delicious than their trout, which they catch in the streams in the Alps, bring down alive, and place in a large fountain in the middle of the courtyard, to be seen as one enters the restaurant. The guests who choose to have trout for lunch are given nets and catch their own. This is easier said than done. I had set my heart on a particular one, but he kept eluding me. When I finally got him, I was as proud as if I had harpooned a whale.

Duke's mother, to get away from the cold English winter, was spending a few weeks in Nice. We had promised to stop for tea on our way to Cannes. I wasn't looking forward to this visit. Lady Furness, though she tried hard not to show it, I am sure never quite got over her son's marrying again. Duke in his way was very fond of his mother, but I soon realized his visits to her were largely duty calls.

He must have taken after his father, for there were never two people more unlike in appearance and character. Lady Furness had been an invalid for years, but I always suspected this was partly put on to attract attention and sympathy. She was short and stout and always dressed in black or gray, relieved by a lace fichu held in place by a pearl dog collar. Although Yorkshire born, she spoke with a slight cockney accent; and she had an exaggerated sense of the family importance, I thought, considering the fact that the Furness fortune and title were so new. But in full plumage and reinforced by relatives, she could be formidable. The Furness aunts, uncles, cousins, and in-laws, however much they might hate, kowtow, or envy separately, presented en masse a solid wall of respectability.

As we entered the Hôtel des Anglais in Nice, I squared my shoulders and took a deep breath. Lady Furness was reclining on a sofa. I was relieved to see Annette Bryan and Connie Furness there. Of all Duke's cousins, I liked them best. Annette was a sweet, comfortable, homey sort of person, without a mean streak in her nature. Her life rotated around her husband, Claud, whom she worshiped, and her two young sons, whom she adored. Connie Furness was young and acted as a sort of *dame de compagnie* to her aunt. As a matter of fact, I never knew if she was a niece or a cousin. They all always called Lady Furness "Auntie"—and as there were so many of them, I never did get to know which was which.

Connie always seemed pleased to see us and the children. Her life at best must have been very dull. It also must have been very difficult for her to please an old lady who frowned on anything modern and who believed the strait-laced Victorian Era was the only one in which to live—and lived accordingly.

Many a Sunday when we stayed at Hamels Park, my mother-in-law's place in the country, Connie would smuggle a pack of cards up to our apartment to while away a dull, rainy afternoon. Sunday, as far as Lady Furness was concerned, was a day only for prayer.

Duke's pungent vocabulary, a combination of the stables where he bred his horses, the Yorkshire collieries that formed the basis of the family fortune, and the docks where the Furness ships tied up, shocked his mother, but even she could do nothing about it but wince. The miracle of it all was that I did not pick up the phrases. Somehow Duke's swearing never registered—at least not with me. Outside of "bloody" and "hell," I don't remember one single word of that startling, picturesque vocabulary.

We arrived at the Carlton Hotel in Cannes just in time to dress for dinner. We dined at the Café de Paris a short distance from the hotel. Duke had ordered something he said he was sure I had never had before. When the waiter brought this *spécialité de la maison*, I was mystified. I couldn't make out what they were. They looked like little dark brown apples steaming in a dish, but they turned out to be immense truffles cooked in champagne. They were delicious. For years after, whenever I was in Cannes, one of the very first things I'd do was go to the Café de Paris for their *spécialité*.

One morning I saw in one of the shopwindows an exquisite old rose-point lace shawl. I wasn't surprised, but I was a little disappointed when I asked the price and was told it was 45,000 francs. I wanted it, but thought it an unnecessary extravagance.

I had tucked my 100,000 francs in my purse just before leaving the hotel. We were dining at the Casino that second night in Cannes and were sure to go to the gambling rooms later.

The Casino at Cannes was much larger than the Sporting Club at Monte Carlo, much more impersonal. I supposed that it was like the Municipal Casino at Monte Carlo, which I hadn't had a chance to see when we were there. As I strolled through the rooms, I missed the friendly faces of the Sporting Club croupiers. I stopped for a while and watched the play at the big table, roped off to keep the spectators from crowding the players. What I saw scared me; if I had thought the betting high at Monte this was astronomical. I moved off to find a table where the play was lower, but I had no sooner sat down than the manager came up and said, "Lady Furness, there's a place at the big table now. Would you care to take it?"

I didn't, but I did not have the courage to say so. I was still young, inexperienced, and shy. I hesitated a second, then scooped up my 100,000 francs and with all the dignity I could muster followed him to the table as if it were the most natural thing in the world for me to play in hundreds of thousands.

As the flunkey held the chair for me to sit down, I looked at the card over the table to see what was the minimum wager. "Six thousand francs," it read. Well, that's not too bad, I thought to myself, but wished it had been my lucky 3,000.

As I settled down, I looked around the table to see whom I was to play against. The Aga Khan was the only one I had met. Some of the others I knew by sight: Jack Coats, sitting at the far end of the table from me, who I had been told was an English millionaire and an inveterate gambler; Gordon Selfridge, the American-born department-store tycoon of England; and Jenny Dolly. My eyes popped. I had never seen so many jewels on any one person in my life as on Jenny Dolly, and every one of them was an emerald. The magnificent necklace she wore around her neck must have cost a king's ransom. Her bracelets reached almost to her elbows. The solitary ring she wore on her right hand must have been the size of a small ice cube.

I turned and saw Duke standing behind me. The "sabot," or shoe, as the wooden box is called in chemin de fer, which holds the cards one is to deal from, was just coming around to me.

"Would you like to come in halves with me, darling?" I asked.

"No, thanks, I can lose quite enough on my own and have more fun doing it," Duke answered, I thought somewhat rudely.

As the croupier placed the sabot in front of me, I timidly put up 6,000 francs. The man on my right said, "Banco." I won. I now had 12,000 francs. At chemin de fer the bets are doubled every time one wins. At the time I am talking about, after the player had won 40,000 francs, he could ask the croupier to put 20,000 aside and play for the remaining 20,000. I was delighted when my luck held out and I had reached that point, as I was now playing on other people's money. I had the croupier say, "Twenty thousand in the Bank. Who makes this Banco?"

"Banco," someone said on my left. I turned and looked at the player. It was Gordon Selfridge. I dealt him his cards and waited.

"Card, please," I heard him say. I turned mine up. I had a nine, the highest you can have. I had won again.

"I will play again," he said, "if you leave the 40,000 in the bank."

I smiled sweetly. "Why, certainly, Mr. Selfridge," I said with forced nonchalance. My heart was pounding.

"Card," I heard him say. I slowly turned mine up. A little gasp went around the table. I had won again. It wasn't so much the amount, for much higher stakes had been won and lost that night. It was for the number of times I had won. Now I was playing for 80,000 francs.

Jack Coats was the next to Banco me. I won again! Jack, it seemed, had not learned a lesson from Mr. Selfridge. He also said he would Banco again if I left the 160,000 francs in the Bank. I won!

By this time my table was surrounded. The word had got around the Casino that there was a fantastic run at the big table. The players were beginning to think I was going on forever, and so did I. Again, again, and again I won!

The next hand was to be the seventeenth straight pass. How could I lose with my lucky 17? But by this time the players were frightened to play against me. Finally a few bets of some 10,000 francs were made up around the table. Confidently, I dealt the cards and to my surprise my opponent threw a nine on the table. I turned my cards over. Two Jacks stared me in the face. I had finally lost.

When the croupier handed me my winnings, I was amazed to find I had won a little under a million francs—about $250,000.

Duke had also heard of the run at the big table, but in the excitement I had not noticed him standing behind me. With a twinkle in his eye he said, "Did you say something about going halves?"

"Oh, go win your own money! It's more fun."

But when we went to the bar to celebrate I paid for the champagne.

The very first thing I did the following afternoon was go on a shopping spree. I bought the lovely rose-point lace shawl I had admired. Next, I went around to Révillon and chose a handsome ermine cape for Mamma. There's an amusing sequence to this gift. Four or five years before Mamma died she gave it back to me all wrapped up in its original blue linen bag, just as I had given it to her. "Darling," she said, "I think this beautiful ermine cape will look very nice on you. Would you like to have it?" She had forgotten completely that I had given it to her some twenty-three years before.

I next went around to Cartier and was lucky enough to find for Gloria an exceptionally lovely jeweled gold-and-enamel clock, the work of Faberge, the famous St. Petersburg jeweler. Also at Cartier I ordered a cigar case for Duke, specially made for the enormous cigars he always smoked.

Our stay at Cannes was coming to a close. A thaw had made hunting possible again at Melton and I knew Duke wanted to take advantage of the few remaining weeks. I hated to leave. We had had such a wonderful time. But I also realized how selfish it would be on my part to suggest that I should like to stay.

I had never been happier. Duke, I was convinced, was the ideal husband—intelligent, determined, worldly, and fun to be with. We were blissfully happy those first few months. I had never had so much attention showered on me. Duke's eyes rarely left me. He delighted in giving me gifts—large and small. Knowing my passion for flowers, hardly a day went by that he didn't send me some. I was utterly content in his love and firmly believed it would always be that way. People who didn't know Duke well may read this with some bewilderment. The impression he gave, I have been told, was that of a hardheaded businessman, finicky in his apparel, self-centered, arrogant, and quick-tempered. But to me who knew and loved him he was none of these things.

On our return to England, we settled down at Melton for the remaining weeks of hunting. As I did not hunt myself, time hung heavily on my hands. Following hounds in a pony cart or by car I found rather dull. What I needed was an interest of my own.

Walking down a lane one afternoon, I stopped to watch a mother hen and her chicks. They looked so fluffy, yellow, and sweet as they pecked at the ground. I decided then and there that that was what I was going to do—start a chicken farm!

Duke laughed when I told him about it, but agreed to let me have three acres of my own for my farm. I was terribly proud when at the end of the first year the books showed the magnificent net profit of sixpence—twenty-five American pennies.

Averill's interest, apart from hunting, was the management of the 400-acre estate that was Burrough Court. She bought and sold livestock, hired and fired farm hands, kept the books, and made the property pay, which I think quite wonderful for a girl of her age. She was also in many ways strong-headed and determined to have her own way. As devoted as Duke and Averill were to each other, there was bound to be a clash of wills. At times I inevitably found myself in the middle.

I remember as if it were today the terrible scene that took place when Averill asked permission of her father to cut her lovely red hair. "If you do," he stormed, "you'd better bloody well not come back here, and that's final."

But by the look in her eyes as she left the room, I knew she was not intimidated. I was right. She went straight to the beauty parlor and had her beautiful hair cut off. To make matters worse, she came back with an Eton bob. Poor Duke could do nothing about it.

A constant bone of contention between them was her insistence on riding astride and his determination she ride sidesaddle. I watched with some amusement, for I knew they were both stubborn and would not give in easily. I made little bets with myself as to who would be the victor. I should have known better, though. It took time and a good deal of maneuvering on her part, but Averill got her way in this, too.

Melton Mowbray is the focal point of three famous hunts: the Quorn, the Cottesmore, and the Belvoir. So it wasn't surprising that it attracted a good many American sportsmen. I was delighted to find among them some old friends. The Ambrose Clarks, Laddie Sanford, the Bostwick brothers, Freddie and Winston Guest, and the Phipps boys are some I remember. Particularly good friends were the Lawson-Johnstons. Although they didn't hunt, they stayed with us often and were very popular with the hunting set. I had met Betty through my sister, Consuelo, who had known her in Washington as the widow of Lyman Kendall.

London, that summer of 1927, was the gayest it had been in years, I was told. There was hardly a night without a ball or a dinner party. Hostesses had to pick their dates for these parties well in advance, lest they conflict with one another. Even then, more often than not, there were two or three balls on the same night.

I have never liked big parties, and rarely go to one if I can help it. The reason, I suppose, is that they frighten me. Though people, I am sure, will never believe me, both Gloria and I are shy. When I try to explain this to my friends, they only laugh and say, "You, *shy?* Don't be idiotic. I have never seen a woman enter a room with more poise and aplomb than you do." I may give that impression, but it's certainly not what I feel.

I had come up to London for my first season with some perturbation. I was aware that the English, unlike the Americans, are not apt to take strangers at face value only. They have to know you well before they give you their friendship; but once they have given it, I have found, they remain true and steadfast.

Another thing that disturbed me was their irritating custom of not introducing you. I suppose they take it for granted that everyone should know everyone else, but just the same the custom is nerve-racking to a stranger. Occasionally, however, you would encounter the reverse of this practice, the barbed introduction, which was even more disturbing. The arch devotee of this practice was Lady Cunard, one of whose aspirations was to maintain a salon on the style of Madame de Maintenon—and to a certain degree she succeeded. Her guests, never more than ten or twelve on any one occasion, were hand picked. The men were wits or lions; the women were chosen for their charm or beauty. Emerald herself was a witty conversationalist, although her *bons mots* were frequently at the expense of others.

As I got to know Emerald better, I realized that all her bravado and cutting remarks were merely a shield to hide a lack of assurance in herself.

Averill and I were shopping in Bond Street one day when I stopped to admire a lovely chiffon-and-lace nightgown.

"I don't understand how you can sleep in one of those things, Thelma."

"Why, what do you sleep in?" I turned around to her, surprised.

"Pajamas, of course."

All the way home we argued about nightgowns versus pajamas, with neither giving in an inch.

When Duke and I had married, I had insisted that Averill keep her mother's bedroom at Arlington Street, as well as the one at Burrough. I knew how much she had loved her mother and understood how she'd hate to have to give them up. I was glad I did. This little gesture made us come closer than anything else I could ever have done.

Coming home from a party that night, I started to get ready for bed. As I opened my door to go to the bathroom at the end of the hall, which Averill and I shared, I saw her come out and go to her bedroom. She had her back to me and I did not speak. As I said before, it was late and I didn't want to chat all night, which I was sure she'd want to do if she saw me. I chuckled to myself, for I noticed she was wearing a long, flowing white nightgown with a light blue sash around her waist. I could hardly wait for morning to tease her about it. At lunch the following day I said, "So you never wear nightgowns, do you?"

She looked up at me. "No, why?"

"Well, you certainly were wearing one last night when I saw you coming out of the bathroom."

"You must have been dreaming, darling," she said. "I never left my room at all last night."

I knew I hadn't been dreaming, but thought it best not to argue the point.

That afternoon Lady Furness phoned and asked me to tea. As I entered the house, in the hall I noticed a painting propped up against the wall. The portrait showed a young woman with red hair piled high on her head, dressed in a flowing white gown with a light blue sash around her waist. I was puzzled. I knew I had never seen it before, but the subject seemed very familiar to me. I vaguely wondered who she might be. A little later, as we were having tea, I asked Lady Furness who the lady was.

"I've just had it sent down from Hamels Park. I thought it would look rather nice hanging in the hall. It's my favorite portrait of Averill's mother."

I caught my breath. The cup in my hand crashed to the floor. I must have turned deathly pale, for Lady Furness anxiously said, "Why, dear, what's the matter with you? You look as if you'd seen a ghost."

With the greatest effort I regained my composure. I judged it wiser to say nothing about what I had seen.

To this day I wonder. Was it Averill—or the ghost of Averill's mother—that I saw in that hallway thirty years ago?

Toward the end of July London started to empty. The houses in Mayfair and Belgravia were beginning to close their shutters. The season was over. People were leaving for Deauville, Le Touquet, Biarritz, or Cannes—the newer vacation resort that was fast becoming popular.

Duke and I went over to Ireland for the Dublin Horse Show and the Phoenix Park races. He also wanted to show me Guildtown, a thoroughbred stud farm he owned near Dublin. Duke took a great deal of interest in the stud. It was his knowledge of breeding as well as that of George Smithwick, his able stud manager, that made Guildtown one of the best and more profitable studs of the day. For years it topped the sales at Doncaster in England. I believe it was in 1927 that Dorothy Paget bought one of Duke's yearlings for the staggering figure of 17,000 pounds, at that time the highest price ever paid for a yearling.

The late Aga Khan bought Guildtown from the estate shortly after Duke's death.

CHAPTER XIII

Friedel

Gloria

My return voyage, from New York to France, was to prove fateful. Harry, Angustias, and I sailed on the *Majestic* one cold December day. And entirely by coincidence Prince Hohenlohe was again on the same ship. He was on his way to Schloss Langenburg, to spend the Christmas holidays with his parents. Friedel had been my guest several times during his visit to America; we had been together at the horse show and at the opera—but always as part of a large party, and I had had no opportunity of knowing him well. On shipboard, however, we were together constantly; and by the time we approached Cherbourg, our casual friendship had developed into love.

We were together again in Paris; and before Friedel left for Langenburg he asked me to marry him. My impulse was at once to say that I would. But we were not the only ones to be considered. Facing me was my responsibility to little Gloria. And there was Mamma. To this day I have never fully understood Mamma's opposition to Friedel. I was still young; a new life was opening for me, full of promise for happiness and love with a man of character and integrity whose family name Mamma should have been proud to have me bear. But with Mamma, my happiness counted for nothing. I was not so much a daughter as an instrument for the manufacture of an heiress. And once that heiress had been given physical existence my former virtues became transformed into vices; for as a mother, with a mother's responsibilities, and a mother's love, I might—in Mamma's eyes—disturb the tender roots through which little Gloria was predestined to tap the subsoil of two-and-a-half million dollars.

It is not easy to account for the motivation of a woman who is mentally, or at least emotionally, disturbed. And although I do not know in what technical category my mother would fall, there is no question of the fact that she was disturbed. Although Mamma all her life was a miser, and made money—or the anticipated lack of it—the center of her concern, she came from one of the richest families in Chile. Never in her life had she lived in poverty; never had she wanted for anything. There may, however, be some subtle hereditary factor involved in this trait: my grandmother had also shown signs of miserliness, even, in her later years, hiding money under the mattress. In fairness, however, it should be pointed out that my grandmother's symptoms were not conspicuously evident until she was ninety, and at that age almost any oddity is excusable.

My father's behavior may have been a contributing factor. He was an extremely generous man. Money had no meaning for him other than the pleasantness it gave. Trips around the world, gigantic parties, entertainment of every sort—these were extravagances he delighted in, with no thought of the effect the costs might have on his financial reserve, or on his or the family's future. If Mamma had not restrained him, he would have spent everything he had; and this attitude may have had a bearing on her growing fears. She could never put out of her mind the fact that she had to take care of three daughters and a son—and later, of course, the one who replaced in her affections all of her own children, little Gloria.

After little Gloria was born I became to Mamma little more than a threat to Gloria's bank account. Perhaps this statement would be more apt if put in the negative: my chief function, as Mamma saw it, was not to interfere with the management, by others, of Gloria's inheritance. And this, at bottom, was her opposition to my marriage to Prince Hohenlohe.

Mamma's vision of an insidious "plot" had all the melodrama of an Alfred Hitchcock thriller—with a little of the atmosphere of *Richard III* thrown in for macabre effects. According to Mamma, Friedel would influence me to such an extent that I would so neglect the child as to bring about her the kind of natural death that would spare us both the threat of the electric chair.

My life at this time was a succession of hues and cries. Alarms were compounded with alarms. I could scarcely leave the house, even for a few days, without being bombarded with frightening telegrams from Mamma. I shall never forget one terrible trip I made to Biarritz. Angustias, Harry, Friedel, and I had motored from Paris, arriving at Biarritz in the late afternoon. A frantic message awaited me at the hotel: Gloria had developed tuberculosis. There was no train until late that night; so, over Harry's protest, I insisted on returning at once, by car.

We left for Paris, dashing through the night at racing speed. On reaching the apartment the next morning, I rushed into Gloria's room, only to find it empty. My heart sank. I was sure she had been taken to the hospital. Then I heard Mamma say, "Well, you're back."

I turned. "Where is Gloria, Mamma?"

The air became cold as ice.

"Why, in the park with her nurse. Where else would she be at this time of day?"

"But you told me she was dying."

"She is better," my mother replied, her mouth set tight.

Years later, when I saw the play *Gaslight*, I was reminded of this inhuman moment.

FRIEDEL

I received a charming letter from Princess Hohenlohe, Friedel's mother, inviting me to visit her at Langenburg and saying they would meet me in Munich.

Two lovely baskets of flowers greeted me when I entered my rooms in the Vier Jahreszeiten Hotel. The red and white roses I knew were from Friedel, the others must be from his family. Picking up the card, I read, "Welcome, Gloria."

Though Friedel and I were unofficially engaged, I had never met his father and mother. Knowing they must be aware of Mamma's attitude, I was touched by this greeting.

It had been arranged that we would spend a few days in Munich and then motor to Langenburg, about five hours distant. Friedel's sisters, Dolly and Baby, took me on long sight-seeing tours of this lovely town, to museums, shops, and historical monuments. At night we would all dine at the famous Wirtshäuser and beer gardens. Princess Hohenlohe, *grande dame* that she was, was one of the simplest women I have ever known, interested in everything that went on about her. She would chat gaily to total strangers sitting next to her, then laughingly turn to me and say, "Dear, you really must learn German. One misses so much fun in not understanding."

Prince Ernst Hohenlohe-Langenburg was a slight man with a long, thin face and aquiline nose. His manner was extremely quiet. His was the type of aristocracy, derived from centuries of authority and gentle breeding, that maintains a stoic serenity and detachment from the pettiness of worldly affairs. Princess Hohenlohe was the daughter of the Duke of Edinburgh, Queen Victoria's second son, who was later to become Duke of Saxe-Coburg-Gotha. Her sisters were Queen Marie of Romania, Grand Duchess Cyril, and the Infanta Beatrice of Spain.

Like all the hereditary princes of Germany, the Hohenlohes were great feudal landowners. Their estates included two castles, or *Schlösser*, in Bavaria, one at Weikersheim, the other at Langenburg. Between the castles is a stretch of thirty miles, dotted with small villages; all of this—farm lands, forests, houses, villages—comprises the Hohenlohe holdings.

The town of Langenburg is situated in a green valley between two mountains; it consists of a single street of little houses clustered together like the medieval houses in the engravings of Albrecht Dürer. Each building, if in miniature, might well be a museum piece. Although Langenburg does not have a population of more than four or five hundred, the Langenburg families have occupied these houses for generations. Everything in Langenburg appears to symbolize serenity, permanence, tradition—a weather-worn aesthetic completeness.

To approach the *Schloss*, you drive over a moat. About a hundred yards beyond, you come to an enormous stone archway on which the Hohenlohe arms are carved; on either side are entrances with carved escutcheons. As a gesture to me, the day I first visited Langenburg an American flag was flying alongside the flag of the German Republic.

The sheer weight of antiquity overwhelmed me when Friedel escorted me to the vast main hall, along whose walls were rows of antlers and stags' heads and collections of ancient arms and armor, and from whose hewn oaken beams were suspended huge iron candelabra. The thick, solid gray stones of the walls spoke of times when the *Schloss* was a bastion, and when remote Hohenlohe ancestors defended the castle with arbalests and halberds. In the corners of the large rooms were enormous stoves of colored tiles, some of which, brought from China in centuries past, are priceless. Early each morning, on cold days, the fires in the stoves were fed through openings from the outside hall.

During the time when I was first at Langenburg, Princess Hohenlohe had a birthday, and the ceremony which marked it was charming in its grace and courtesy. Tenant farmers assembled in the great hall, presenting as gifts their finest fruits and preserves. Gardeners came in carrying baskets piled high with bright flowers. All were dressed in the picturesque Bavarian costumes made from fabrics in brilliant hues of red and green and dyed, I later learned, by their own hands with pigments compounded according to formulas traditional to the village.

A formal dinner followed, attended by the Grand Duke and Grand Duchess Cyril and many friends from the surrounding countryside. A unique old custom is observed at these dinners. Behind the chair of each guest stand a man and a woman servitor. It is to them the butler or footman hands the food; they in turn serve the guests. This is a relic of the ancient service demanded by feudal chiefs, in which the underlings tasted the food first, to insure against poison.

Many things are famous about Langenburg, among them, in one of the turrets, an extraordinary library that contains a Gutenberg Bible and a collection of rare editions whose counterpart can be found nowhere else. The tapestry room has rare Gobelins and a fabulous collection of jade, a gift from an emperor of China.

Those few days spent at Schloss Langenburg were a harvest of peace and contentment. Bolts of emotional lightning and strong physical attraction, as we know, have marked most of the history-making and world-shaking romances. But Friedel and I were not writing history or trying to shake the universe. We were two people in love who wanted desperately to gain happiness. It was as simple as that.

As simple as that? There were a dozen different complexities attendant upon it, both on Friedel's side and on mine. Could I, in all fairness to Gloria, bring her up entirely in a foreign country? What would the Surrogate's point of view be? Friedel, on the other hand, was the son of a semi-royal house whose income was derived from vast forest lands which one day he would inherit and manage. And last but not least, there was Mamma's idiotic, unaccountable attitude.

If life was secure and placid at Langenburg, in contrast it simmered with an undercurrent of bitterness and venom in my own home.

My trip to Langenburg had given me much room for thought. I knew I was deeply in love with Friedel and hoped to marry him soon.

On my return to Paris, Mamma met me at the station. Her face was set in a calm, cold mask. I was surprised and worried. "Come, Mamma," I said, "it's not as tragic as all that. After all, Friedel is half English." I took her hand in mind, hoping to avert the scene I was sure was coming.

Mamma pulled her hand away. "Gloria," she said, "I have come to meet you because several serious things have happened since you went away which you must know at once." Here it comes, I thought. Back from the peaceful life at Langenburg, the perfect understanding of a family pulling together, each thinking of the others' happiness. It was so very unlike my own, where every move, every action was looked on with suspicion.

I heard Mamma say, "Are you listening to me? The nurse's mother is dying and she wants to return to New York immediately. This I want you to prevent at once. That poor unfortunate child could not stand the shock of a strange nurse."

Turning down the glass partition in the car, she ordered George to drive around the Bois until she told him to go home.

I don't get mad easily, but the combination of my mother's ridiculous notion of the harm which could come to Gloria from a new nurse and her highhanded manner of ordering George made me see red. Countermanding her order and closing the partition, I turned to her and said, "You forget you are a guest in my house."

Not another word was spoken until we reached the apartment. Entering the drawing room, Mamma took off her gloves and said, smiling, "You're right, Gloria, this is better. Now, we can talk."

"There is nothing to say. I'm going up to see the nurse."

I found Keislich in tears over a letter she had received from a friend of her mother's telling her that her old mother was dying and that there was no one to care for her. I told her not to worry. I would make arrangements for her to sail at once. Meanwhile, I would cable Forest March, whom she knew well and liked, and ask him to do everything possible for her mother.

"Oh, but Mrs. Vanderbilt," Keislich said, "I can't leave the baby. What will happen to her? I can't, I must not."

At this moment a thought glimmered in the back of my mind that it was not so much her love for Gloria as the realization that this might mean the end of her service.

Before Keislich could sail, however, I received a cable from Forest saying that her mother had died and that he would attend to all funeral arrangements.

Several days later Keislich received a sweet and kind letter from Forest March with details of her mother's last hours and stating that the funeral had been everything she could have wished. Unfortunately, her mother's friend was ill, but he, Forest, personally had gone to the burial and had been the only one present. Keislich wrote him a long letter full of undying gratitude for everything he had done for her "poor mother" and wept copiously as she read it to me.

(Her "undying gratitude" was not long-lived, for on the witness stand six years later she kept repeating that no decent person ever crossed my threshold. On being asked whether Forest March had visited Mrs. Vanderbilt, she sneered, "Forest March? Oh, you mean that big butter-and-egg man from the West? Yes, he came.")

Life after this became almost unbearable. I couldn't even talk to Papa about Mamma's irrational behavior. Peace-loving Papa, not being able to stand her tirades, had long since left for quieter surroundings.

That summer of 1928 I rented the Villa Aice Colpea in Biarritz. This was the last summer Mamma was to spend with me.

CHAPTER XIV

Wings of Love

Thelma

Duke seldom raced any of the horses he had bred. All yearlings were sent to the Doncaster Sales and offered to prospective buyers. Duke argued that if he made a practice of racing his own horses, the buyers would suppose, with good reason, that he had kept his best horses as his own entries. The only time he raced his own colors was when he bought a mare or two in the hope that they could win a good race before being sent out to stud.

We were all quite excited on Derby Day in 1928 when Orwell —a beautiful horse by Gainsborough out of Golden Hair—which had been bred and sold by Duke, was an odds-on favorite. Orwell, until then, had won nearly every race in which he had been entered; we were certain that he was going to win the Derby as well.

Papa had come over to London from Paris to visit us for the summer. For the first time I was getting to know my own father for what he really was—a kind, understanding, sensitive, gentle man. I began to realize more and more that Mamma's subtle insinuations about his not wanting us with him were pure fabrications. It was a joy to me to see Papa and Duke together; and Averill and Dick adored him. I had at last found a friend in my father.

Lady Kimberly and her husband, Jack, Papa, Gav, Hugh Seeley, Lady Sarah Wilson and her son Randolph, Averill, Duke, and I set off in high spirits for the Derby in brilliant sunshine. Epsom Downs was gay and colorful. The costermongers were out in full force; their traditional red, yellow, purple, and green ostrich-feathered hats and their pearly coats seemed to dance in the sun. There were bright red busses filled with merry people who had come out to enjoy themselves and see one of the greatest races in the world. The bookmakers, yelling their odds on the horses, the immense crowds, made everything very exciting.

But nobody was more excited than I. It is the dream of every thoroughbred breeder to have bred a Derby winner, and I was hoping and praying for Duke's sake that Orwell would win for him that day.

Friends came in and out of our box, wishing us luck. Everybody was sure Orwell was a dead certainty. I felt a little sorry for Lady Cunliffe-Owen in the adjacent box. She was obviously very nervous. Her husband, Sir Hugo, president of British American Tobacco, was running a rank outsider named Felstead. To make matters worse, her baby was just about due.

As the horses came out on the course, she leaned over and said, "Orwell looks magnificent. There doesn't seem to be anything to touch him. Good luck."

I was embarrassed. I didn't know just what to answer. With a forced smile I said, "Thank you, Lady Cunliffe-Owen, but you know one never can tell till they're past the finishing post, can one?"

As I said it, I knew it sounded insincere and rather smug, but I didn't have time to say anything else. The roar of "They're off!" got me to my feet.

Orwell got off to a good start. Through my field glasses I could see his jockey confidently holding him back, but as they came to Taterham Corner he gave him his head and Orwell jumped into the lead. Coming around the bend, he looked as though he were flying. The crowd was shouting itself hoarse. The favorite was bound to win.

Then all of a sudden there was a deathly silence. Orwell seemed to have stopped dead. For a second everything stood still. It was just as when a moving-picture projector stops suddenly, leaving the players caught in half-finished movements. Then the voices of thousands rose like a thunderclap. "Come on, Orwell!" "Come on, Orwell!" I couldn't believe my eyes. What had happened to Orwell? The crowd kept on shouting for the favorite to come on, but as I followed him through my glasses, I realized he was finished.

As the horses were coming up to the finishing post, I forced myself to look. To my amazement, as well as that of others, I saw Felstead win.

Pandemonium broke loose in the Cunliffe-Owen box. Friends rushed in to congratulate them. Lady Cunliffe-Owen was very near hysterics. Somebody gave her smelling salts. Her husband was anxiously hovering over her.

As they got up to go to the winner's enclosure, I said with a smile I'm sure must have looked as if it had been painted on, it was so artificial, "Congratulations. I told you one could never tell."

Going home that evening our little party was very subdued. The talk was all about Orwell and what could have happened to him. As a rule I'm a good loser, but this time I couldn't resist saying sarcastically, "Well, it must be very gratifying to win the Derby, but I don't see why one has to have hysterics about it."

"Oh, come, Thelma," Averill said, laughing. "In the excitement she might have had the baby then and there."

"Quite so," I snapped back. "And I suppose they would have cracked a bottle of champagne over its head and christened it Felstead for good measure."

Not long after I believe poor Orwell was found dead in his stall of a heart attack.

A few weeks later we went to Ascot to watch a little filly owned by Duke, called Wings of Love. The race she was entering in wasn't especially important, but it was the first time I'd seen one of Duke's horses run under our colors, and I was very excited.

Royal Ascot with all its traditional glory is really a most impressive sight. This opening day was perfect; the sun had come out after days of rain. The flowers banked against the royal box looked as if the dew were still on them. The course was as green as an emerald as the King and Queen drove along it in an open landau drawn by the famous Windsor Greys. Following were members of the royal family; and, behind them, the royal house party.

Just before Wings of Love's race, Averill and I went to the paddock to give her a little pat of encouragement and wish her luck. As we got back to the royal enclosure I tried to look cool and collected, but my heart was beyond my control.

The horses were at the post when Averill turned to me and said, "What's the matter, dear, aren't you feeling well? You look so pale."

I was quite all right, I assured her—just a little nervous. "Anyway, with a name like that, she should fly, shouldn't she?" I said and hoped I was right.

I don't remember any part of that race except that when the horses were coming up to the winning post, Wings of Love was neck and neck with another horse. It looked as though it would be a dead heat. I stood frozen, trembling, waiting for the winner's number to go up. Wings of Love had won by a nose. I grabbed Averill, who was jumping up and down with joy. "Darling, I think I'm going to faint."

"Don't you dare!" she said. "Now you know how Lady Cunliffe-Owen felt when she won the Derby."

Duke and I went up to Scotland early in August 1928. Not long after, I thought a miracle had taken place. I was convinced I was going to have a baby. I couldn't believe it. The doctors in

New York had told me when I lost Junior's baby that it would be very unlikely for me ever to bear children. Now I wanted to run and tell Duke. I wanted to shout the news across the moors. But I didn't do any of those things. I decided first to be certain.

I told Duke that night that I was going to London for a few days. I explained I'd been feeling rather tired and run down the last week or so and thought it advisable to get a checkup. Duke looked worried. He at once suggested coming with me. He didn't want me traveling alone when I wasn't well. "Nonsense," I said. "The doctor will probably give me a tonic and tell me to get on with it. Anyway, I won't be alone. Elise will be with me."

As I left my doctor, Sir Charles Stevens' office, my feet hardly touched the ground. I had just been told, "Your baby will be born early in May."

As I got on the train to go back to Scotland, I thought to myself, this is every woman's *raison d'être*. I now had everything in the world I had ever hoped for. This time I felt secure; my husband wanted the baby as much as I.

Christmas and New Year's we spent quietly at Burrough. Averill and Dick, as well as Duke, were out hunting most days. Time hung heavily on my hands, and though I did not expect my baby until May, I tired easily. I was both happy and grateful to have Papa and Gav to keep me company. Our leisurely walks around the garden or down to the chicken farm were pleasant ones. Puff, a little papillon dog Gloria had given me on my birthday that year, danced like a ballerina at my feet.

The holidays were over. Duke, Dick, and I went up to London, Dick to go back to Eton and I to get the nursery ready at 17 Arlington Street, where I planned to have my baby.

What a joy it was to see the nursery take shape! The crib, all pink and white, the bassinet—everything that could be dreamed up for a baby—were waiting for me when we arrived.

The Grande Maison de Blanc on Bond Street was filled with

all sorts of enchanting baby clothes to choose from. I picked out the most beautiful layette and an exquisite christening robe, which they promised faithfully to deliver the second week in April.

We returned to Burrough Court, intending to stay there through Easter, which was very early that year, and then go back to London to await the baby.

Toward the end of March Dick arrived for the holidays. Although the weather was still chilly, the hawthorne hedges were budding. Tiny green spikes of hyacinth and daffodil bulbs pierced the black earth. As I walked through the garden with Puff, I noticed Averill painting some garden furniture. It looked like fun, and I decided to help her.

"Don't be ridiculous," she said. "This is no work for a woman in your condition."

"Oh, stop fussing! I feel wonderful," I answered. I took a brush and went to work.

An hour or so later I suddenly felt very tired. "I think I'll go and freshen up for tea," I said, looking at my watch thankfully.

When I got to my room, I felt very ill indeed. I lay down on my bed, hoping the uneasiness would pass, but it didn't. I put a call through to Gav in London and was told he was out. I asked them to have him call as soon as he came in. I then called Sir Charles Stevens, my own gynecologist, and was told he was out of town. I asked them to please try to reach him and have him call me.

For the first and only time Elise lost her aplomb. Before I could stop her she dashed out to find Duke, though I had forbidden her to leave me. I knew just how he would react. Cars and servants would be sent in every direction. When he dashed into my room, I tried to reassure him but nothing I said made any difference.

"Why aren't those bloody doctors where they're supposed to be?" he stormed.

He telephoned Dr. Mould at Melton, who said he'd be right over. Duke had no sooner hung up than Gav came through and told him to tell me to stay in bed, that he was on his way.

When Dr. Mould arrived and examined me, he told me the baby would be born within twenty-four hours.

Gav arrived late that night and Dr. Stevens early the following morning. The nurses who had been engaged for the month of May were, of course, not available. In the excitement all the doctors had engaged their own nurses. In consequence, I had four of them—and three doctors—hovering over me that morning.

Dr. Stevens gave me an injection. I heard Gav say, "It will be some hours yet." The next thing I was aware of was a little whimper which seemed to come from a clothes basket next to me. "Yes, Lady Furness," said a faraway voice, "a beautiful little baby boy."

CHAPTER XV

Renunciation

Gloria

It was early in October of 1928 that one day, as little Gloria was going out to play in the Bois, I noticed she was wearing white kid gloves. I told the nurse to change them. Gloria burst out crying, insisting she wanted to wear her new gloves. This in itself was quite normal. What child does not want to put on the newest thing, no matter how inappropriate? What *was* abnormal was that at just that moment Mamma rushed into the room, picked up the child, and sat her on her lap. There and then took place one of the most disgraceful scenes one could imagine.

Holding Gloria so close to her I thought she would stop breathing, Mamma faced me hurling a barrage of bitter charges.

In my astonishment and horror I heard her tell little Gloria she could wear whatever she wanted at any time. Wasn't it the Vanderbilt money—*her money*—that paid for everything? "Your mother would be in the streets were it not for you, my darling, my poor little orphan," she said. "But I will protect you. As long as I live no one will take a penny of yours." Turning to me, white with rage, she yelled, "I know what you and that Boche are trying to do. You are trying to kill this poor, unfortunate child."

Seeing my look of stunned incredulity, she shouted, "Oh, yes! I know! It will be an accident. A little push down the stairs—seeing that she is left in a draft—a million ways! And you,

Gloria, will weep like a Magdalen, but just the same, the Vanderbilt millions will be yours!"

(Five years later, in a bedroom in Gertrude Whitney's Fifth Avenue house, practically verbatim, the same scene was repeated, but this time the words came from my own child.)

The nurse stood quietly by, smug, placid, saying nothing. I took Gloria from Mamma and said, "Nanny is only play-acting, darling! It's time for you to go to the Bois and play now."

After they left, I followed Mamma to her room where she threw herself on the bed and sobbed. "It's only because I love that poor, unfortunate orphan so much. Don't you understand that, Gloria?"

Suddenly changing her tactics she sat up, her sobs now a thing of the past. Trying to put her arms around me, she said, "Gloria, my darling, don't you know how much I love that poor, unfortunate little orphan...."

I cut her short. "Mamma, once and for all, I want you to understand that my daughter is *not* an orphan. I don't know what you are trying to do. You are doing everything you can to alienate my daughter from me. Your insane idea that I am deliberately planning to murder my child is bad enough. But the inhuman, horrible thing is that you dare to frighten little Gloria with your evil mind." She tried to take my hand. "I see you now for the first time," I added. "And I realize *now* that it is not love for what you term 'that poor, unfortunate orphan,' but the Vanderbilt money which goes with her that is behind all this. You must be sick in your mind!"

The next day I rented a small house at 14 Rue Alfred Roll, with room only for Gloria and myself. I at once advised Mamma of my decision to move. Her reaction was ominous. "I understand, Gloria; but mark my words, I will see to it that you regret this for the rest of your life." A few weeks later little Gloria and I sailed for New York.

Mrs. Vanderbilt asked me to lunch and a matinee. I was surprised at her choice, for the subject of the play was hardly one I should think this rather strait-laced, Victorian lady would have chosen. It dealt with a *mariage de convenance*, and, I had been told, was a bit risqué. But I was delighted, as it was the big hit of the season and tickets were at a premium.

On my way to Mrs. Vanderbilt's, my thoughts were on Mrs. George Gould, for 845 Fifth Avenue, where I was going, had also once been her home. Gloria Gould, Mrs. Gould's youngest daughter, and we had been great friends and Thelma and I had often been in this house as children. This was to be my first visit to it with its new chatelaine. I wondered if I would find it much changed. It was an interesting question, for here were two women as different as day and night—Edith Gould, sophisticated, worldly-wise, and a great beauty; the other quiet, reserved, upholding all the attributes of a society that was fast disappearing. Mrs. Vanderbilt was not beautiful, unless you count the beauty that comes from character.

Mrs. Vanderbilt came toward me as I entered the drawing room. It was a never-ending source of wonderment to me that so small and frail a woman could always dominate a room—no matter how large. Objects seemed to dwarf themselves, recede into the shadows, but she always seemed to emerge clearly into focus, and there she was. I felt that she knew she had this gift and took advantage of it, for there is a little ham in all of us, no matter how exalted.

Mrs. Reginald De Koven, the widow of the well-known composer, was the other guest. Mrs. De Koven and my mother-in-law were old friends. Halfway through lunch the conversation, as conversations with older people often do, reverted to the past. They were remembering an era I had not known. My thoughts were elsewhere; I heard only snatches of their gossip, as if from far away. I heard Mrs. De Koven say, "Alice, do you

RENUNCIATION

remember the famous feud between Mrs. Stuyvesant Fish and Mrs. Goelet?" And later, "Newport certainly has changed."

The butler was standing beside me. As I helped myself to dessert, I heard Mrs. Vanderbilt say, "No, I do not approve of these marriages of convenience." She must have been referring to the play we were going to see. "And what's more, they lead to a great deal of unhappiness. Take poor Consuelo Vanderbilt. She was made miserable for years because of it."

Like a whip snapping, my mind went back to another scene. The room was the same, but like a fade-out and fade-in, as in a motion picture, the well-remembered dining room of old slowly came into view. The faces, the furniture, the time were different, the room lighter in *décor,* the people younger. As I looked around the table, I saw beautiful Edith Gould, gay, talkative, chic; on her right Mamma, effervescent, obviously enjoying herself. Mrs. Gould and Mamma had been friends for years. Mrs. Gould's clear voice came back to me. "I do agree with you, Laura. Love in a rose-covered cottage is very well, but such feelings as the undying passion of a Paul and Virginia should remain in books."

Mamma interrupted. "Not only that, Edith, but I firmly believe that arranged marriages tend to maintain a pure line of ancestry, and besides, they are the only way to control fortunes and keep them in the hands of the aristocrats where they belong."

This was the first time we had heard anybody else express Mamma's often-repeated ideas, and we wondered if Mrs. Gould's next remark would be, "It's just as easy to marry a rich man as a poor one."

I had been fascinated by this adult conversation, and waited breathlessly for further pearls of wisdom. They came:

"I wonder, Laura, if we don't put too much stress on breeding," Mrs. Gould went on. "I had a provocative thought the other day. George and I were dining at Sherry's when one of his odd acquaintances came over to our table and without a by-your-leave sat down. His voice was loud, his tuxedo badly tailored, his manners crude. A good-looking devil, really, but a diamond in the rough. While he was talking to George, I studied him and wondered: suppose this man were to be dressed by Savile Row, given a title, plenty of money, and polished manners—well, I might even picture myself in his arms."

"Oh, Edith, you couldn't!" I heard Mamma say.

The butler's voice announcing, "Mrs. Vanderbilt, the car is at the door," brought me back to the present.

As we rose from the table, sneaking a glance at Mrs. Vanderbilt, I wondered, Oh, dear, what would she say if she could have read my thoughts?

I returned to the Sherry-Netherland Hotel one day to find little Gloria just back from the park. She looked so cute and innocent in her little white fur coat. And she bubbled with chatter about the exciting things she had seen at the zoo.

Only that morning I had received a letter from Friedel begging me to set a date for our marriage—a marriage I now knew could never take place. The many talks I had had with the Surrogate and Mr. Wickersham made me realize that this alliance would eventually mean a separation from my child.

The next few months were sad ones. I could not bear the thought of writing Friedel the letter I knew I must write. It was not until the first of December that I finally got the courage to act.

Strange indeed are the things one remembers. I can still hear the little thump my letter made as I dropped it in the letter box.

Friedel's answer came in a twenty-page letter which said, in part:

Your lines have just arrived and you must understand that I cannot possibly comply with your wish to leave it unanswered. There you are asking too much of me and my love for you.

RENUNCIATION

Above all I must insist upon your telling Mrs. Vanderbilt the exact details. I want her to know and to see no blame has fallen on the name she bears so proudly—through the fact of its being mentioned frequently with mine; and that it was not the glamor of a fortune that surrounded it that drew me toward you, nor will its absence make me drop its neighborhood.

Both my father and my mother, who have informed you of this, are willing to do anything in their power for us. It would be of vital importance to know that that indomitable old lady sees you and her granddaughter taking up relations with our house *de bonne grace et de bonne foi*. I insist you tell Mrs. Vanderbilt our whole story, with all its details, and acquaint her with what we intend doing in the future.

As I read and reread his words, my heart and mind were at odds. I could not understand my own motives. Was I being strong in giving up a deep and sincere love for the sake of my child? Or was I weak in that I was giving in to the emotional pressure of Mamma and the prejudiced views of Mr. Wickersham and the Surrogate? Was I being a fool to turn aside a love which would have given me what, after the welfare of Gloria, I wanted and needed most in this world? Perhaps I did not think long enough or hard enough. Perhaps I did not delve deeply enough into the legal tangle in which I was involved. I cabled Friedel that my decision, terrible as it was for me to make, must stand: there could be no marriage.

Shortly after this we sailed back to Paris. A long letter awaited me from Princess Hohenlohe saying she would be in Paris the following week and that she had to see me.

I waited in the high-ceilinged drawing room with foreboding and sorrow. Her letter had been so tender, so full of understanding, yet I knew why she had wanted to see me, and my answer would still have to be the same.

Fernand, the butler who had been with me for several years, interrupted my mood by announcing that Her Royal Highness

Princess Hohenlohe's car had just driven up. I got up and met her at the door.

Her face, framed by the long, black crepe mourning veil she wore for her brother-in-law, King Ferdinand of Romania, looked troubled as she put her arms about me.

"Gloria, my dear," she said, "do you realize you are breaking Friedel's heart? I'm his mother and I can't bear to see him so unhappy. Both my husband and I, you know full well, would receive and love little Gloria." Then with a little smile she added, "After all, Schloss Langenburg is not such a terrible place to bring up a child. I'm sure," and her voice gave evidence for the first and only time of how hurt she was, "not even the Vanderbilts with their wealth could deny that."

Putting my hand on Princess Hohenlohe's, I said, "Please, ma'am, it is not that, but as I told Friedel it just would not be fair to you, to him, or to Gloria. Please, ma'am, I love Friedel with all my heart. I'm only doing what I think is right." And I buried my face in my hands.

"Gloria, my dear," she said softly, "I don't agree with you. I am sure Friedel could have made you and your little daughter very happy. But I admire you." Getting up, she added, "It would please Friedel and myself if you would lunch with us tomorrow."

Returning to the drawing room after seeing her out, I sat numbly in front of the fireplace, watching the flames leap up, hearing the sharp crack, crack of the long silver-birch logs. Then wearily I went upstairs. Her words came back to me—"But I admire you." Admire? What empty solace the word implied!

CHAPTER XVI

Enter the Prince

Thelma

My premature delivery had been more difficult than I realized. It was more than a month before I was allowed to get up, and then for only a few hours at a time.

Duke was away a good deal that early spring, coming to Burrough only for weekends, and sometimes not even then.

Although I had lived in England nearly three years, I had never got quite used to the idea of husbands and wives accepting invitations separately. I remember shortly after I married having lunch with Lady Carisbrook at Claridge's one day and asking her about it. In New York, I told her, it was rare to see one's married friends having lunch or dinner tête à tête with a man other than their husband. In London it seemed quite the natural thing to do. She laughed and said that many of her American friends had asked her the same question. She explained that in England divorces were a much more serious matter than in the United States. A man, if divorced, would have to resign from his regiment, and, of course, was not allowed at Court; hence married couples stayed married.

A few months after my son Tony's birth Duke, Gav, and I were dining at the Embassy Club when Peggy Hopkins Joyce walked in. I turned to Duke and said, "Oh, there's Peggy Hopkins." Duke looked at her appraisingly, then asked, "Who the bloody hell is Peggy Hopkins?" I laughed and told him that she was supposed to be one of the most glamorous women in America, and that she had had three or four husbands and many admirers—including my first husband. I also told him that I had gone to California for my divorce because of her. (She was the unnamed woman in whose apartment, so the detectives informed me, Junior had whiled away so many nights.) Duke did not seem particularly impressed with her beauty, and took pains to make this point clear. I don't know what insane impulse took possession of me at that moment, but I turned to him and said, "I'll bet you ten pounds you can't get her to dance with you."

"Don't be silly," Duke said. "Why should I want to dance with her?"

"Oh, come on, old boy," Gav put in, "are you afraid she'll turn you down?"

That did it. "All right," Duke said to me, "you've got yourself a bet."

Duke caught her eye and smiled. Peggy Hopkins looked surprised and a little uneasy. She, of course, knew who I was, but was not sure of Duke. I noticed her beckon to the headwaiter and obviously ask who Duke was. I turned to Gav and said, "Now that she knows who he is, watch me lose my bet." And sure enough, the next time Duke smiled at her, she smiled right back. Duke got up and walked over to her table; in a few minutes they were together on the dance floor.

Duke began to be away more and more. Rumors started to get about that all was not well in the Furness household. I, of course, was the last to hear the gossip, and even if I had heard it, I would not have believed it.

A month or so after this dinner Duke came to me and said he was going to Monte Carlo. He had been working very hard and needed a rest. I, of course, thought he meant me to go as well, but then he informed me that he had planned to go on his own. I was surprised, but did not think too much about it.

ENTER THE PRINCE

A few days later, as I was walking down Bond Street, an acquaintance of mine stopped me and said, "I'm so sorry to hear about you and Duke." It seemed that everyone but me knew Duke was staying at Peggy Hopkins' villa in Monte Carlo, and not at the Hôtel de Paris, as he had given me to understand. I was stunned as I walked back home. It couldn't be! It was just malicious gossip, I thought. His daily telephone calls, I was sure, were from the hotel. But were they? I had blissfully believed him when he told me that business had kept him away from England so much. But was it business? I asked myself now. I had to find out. I placed a personal call to the Hôtel de Paris. My heart sank as I heard the operator say, "Viscount Furness is not registered here."

I lay back on my bed and tried to think. The telephone brought me back with a start. "Lord Furness calling Lady Furness," I heard from far away, and Duke was on the telephone. His voice sounded gay and happy, but mine must have been listless, for he said, "What's the matter, darling, aren't you well?"

I don't know what took possession of me, but I answered as cheerfully as I could. "Oh, I feel wonderful, just a little tired. I have been very gay since you've been away—parties night after night. Have you been having a nice rest?"

The phone seemed to go dead.

"Are you still there? Oh, I thought we had been cut off. I asked if you'd been having a nice rest."

"Yes, dear; and the weather's been lovely."

"That's nice for you. It's been terrible here. I must dash! Call me tomorrow." I placed the receiver back on its cradle and cried.

Parties night after night, indeed! An occasional dinner with Gav or Papa in London, weekends at Burrough with Tony and Averill, a theater party or two with Lady Sarah—this had been the extent of my gaiety.

Duke returned a few days after this telephone conversation.

I had had time to think, and had decided to say nothing about his affair, but at the same time I wanted him somehow to know that I knew.

The day after his arrival Gav, Papa, Duke, and I were having a glass of sherry before lunch when I nonchalantly opened my purse and took out a check made out to Duke for the sum of ten pounds.

"What's this for?"

"Have you forgotten, dear? At the Embassy Club some weeks ago I bet you ten pounds you would not get Peggy Hopkins Joyce to dance with you. Well, you won."

He looked puzzled as I smiled at him sweetly, adding, "You know, dear, it was only last week that I remembered the bet."

"This is ridiculous," he said as he tore the check up and threw it into the fireplace. "It was a silly bet anyway, just a joke."

"Yes, I know, dear," I said, still smiling, "but the joke is on me. I lost the bet."

Turning to Gav, I said, "What a pity. I can't ever make a bet with Duke again, if he's going to tear my checks up. It only means I will have to do the same with his should I win, and I had hoped to win this one back soon."

My attitude was not as flippant as it may seem. I was trying desperately to grow up, to conform to my new milieu. The remark: "We don't take things like this as seriously as you do in your country," had fixed itself in my mind.

But soon there was more gossip. This time it was more difficult for me to close my eyes. The lady in question, now happily married, I will call Mrs. X. She was a pretty young widow we had met at parties in London. I was heartsick when word got back to me that Duke was being seen with her. What had happened to us? Where had I failed? I wanted to ask Duke, but obviously this was impossible.

Our lives went on outwardly more or less the same; but Duke

made several trips that season—and not always alone. I was now deeply hurt. I had been so content. Now I found myself terribly alone and lost. I did not know what to do, or where to turn. .

One day, as I was making up a guest list for a dinner party I was planning, Duke asked me to include Mrs. X. I was stunned. I looked at him in amazement. "Are you seriously asking me to invite that woman to our house, Duke?"

He looked surprised. "Why, yes. Why not?"

Why not! Didn't he realize that I knew of those numerous trips abroad with Mrs. X? Didn't he realize how miserable he had made me the past few months? And now he wanted me to receive her. "You can make a fool of yourself if you want," I said, "but you're not going to make one of me."

I had to talk to somebody—somebody who understood Duke; somebody who could advise me. I called Lady Sarah and asked if I could come around and see her.

"Oh, Sarah darling, Duke has asked me to invite that woman to dinner," I said to her. "I won't do it! I won't have her in the house. And don't tell me anything about America. Hearts are broken there as well as everywhere else, but at least in America husbands don't bring their mistresses to pick up the pieces."

"Do sit down, darling. You're upset. Let me order you a cocktail."

When the butler left, Sarah sat next to me, taking my hands in hers. "Listen, Thelma dear," she said, "you know Duke well enough by this time. You know he really loves you. You mustn't take his little peccadillos so seriously. Many a time Daisy has cried on my shoulder as you are doing now, and I am going to advise you just as I did her. Duke has always been terribly spoiled. He's always had his own way. Neither she, nor you, nor anyone else could ever change him. You love him. Think of Tony; think of yourself. What good would a separation or a divorce do? He, I am sure, doesn't want one. Give him enough rope, dear, he'll come to his senses. Wait and see." I knew she was right, but it was difficult to wait, difficult to reorganize my life.

I spent most of that early summer of 1929 at Burrough with the children. Time hung heavily on my hands. Duke was away most of the time, and when he was there he was cool or distant and still persisted in going his own way. There were continuous arguments. My emotions ran the gamut from anger to self-pity and wounded pride. I found it more and more difficult to play second fiddle.

Averill knew that all was not well with her father and me. Her sympathy and understanding were a great help to me at that time although, of course, I never discussed my problem with her. One morning she came into my bedroom and asked me if I would like to go with her to the Leicester Fair where she was showing her favorite hunter. It was a thoughtful and kind gesture, for I was sure she must have sensed my unhappiness and loneliness and thought perhaps that the change would do me good. More to please her than anything else, I went.

The Leicester Fair is one of the big occasions in the Midlands. Breeders from all over the country bring their horses, hunters, cattle, poultry. There is also a flower show. When we arrived, it looked as though all rural England were on a holiday in Leicester. Yet with all the men, women, and children milling around me I felt more lonely than ever.

Averill had gone off to see about her hunter. I had walked through the flower show, when I saw a big crowd around one of the rings. I was curious to see what had attracted such a gathering. I put my arms on the railing of the ring and beheld nothing but five or six prize cows looking very soulful and bored. I sympathized with them; I, too, was soulful and bored. A young man was pinning a blue ribbon on one of the cows. My mind darted back to Londonderry House, to a Viennese waltz. I smiled to myself. Here was the Prince of Wales pinning rosettes on cows. He saw me and came over.

"This is the first opportunity I've had to congratulate you on the birth of your son, Lady Furness," he said graciously.

"Thank you, sir," I answered.

"Are you at Burrough for the summer, or do you plan to come up to London at all?"

"Oh, no, sir, I go to London often. As a matter of fact, I plan to be there next week."

I don't know what made me say it, for up to that moment I had had no intention of doing any such thing.

"How nice. Will you dine with me?"

"Why, thank you, sir," I said; "I should love to."

"Will Wednesday night be all right? Fine! St. James's Palace, eight o'clock. We'll have cocktails and then go out for dinner and a dance." There was not a word about Duke's joining us. Perhaps Duke was right, I concluded: English people thought nothing of inviting married people separately.

I never learned whether or not Averill won a ribbon that day. My mind was on other things. Had I been right in accepting the Prince's invitation? Was my pride or my heart hurt when Duke said he wanted to live his own life? Was I trying to get even? Or was I merely flattered, as I'm sure most women would have been, to be asked to dine with the Prince of Wales?

That weekend it rained almost continuously. I spent as much time with Tony as Nanny would let me. English nannies are a law unto themselves. From the moment you put your baby in their arms they nobly allow you to adore him, but nothing more; all other privileges are theirs.

I had said nothing to anyone about my dinner engagement with the Prince. The night before I was to go up to London, Duke, Averill, Dick, and I were dining alone. Halfway through dinner I turned to the butler and said, "Please tell Elise to pack a few things. I am going up to London for a few days."

Duke looked up. "You are going up to London?"

"Yes," I said coldly. "I have a dinner engagement tomorrow night."

Duke smiled. "May I ask with whom?"

I wanted to say, "I thought married people did not ask such silly questions." I wanted to say, "Yes, I, too, can lead my own life." There were so many things I wanted to say, but I said only, "Why, yes. If you really want to know, I am dining with the Prince of Wales."

Dick laughed. Averill looked up and winked. Duke repeated, "With whom?"

"The Prince of Wales, dear." I smiled as I took a sip of my champagne. I didn't know whether they believed me or not and I didn't care.

I arrived at York House, St. James's Palace, at eight o'clock sharp. To my surprise, there were no other guests. I looked around me. The room I found myself in was big; an enormous map of the world covered the entire far wall. A large and beautiful Empire desk dominated the corner of the room by the window. Comfortable quilted chintz sofas had been placed on each side of the fireplace, over which hung a portrait of Queen Mary in a white evening gown wearing the Order of the Garter, a magnificent diamond tiara on her head, and a fabulous diamond necklace around her neck. I found out later that this room was the Prince's private sitting room. The state rooms were on the ground floor.

It is exceedingly difficult, at this time, to recall the exact emotions I had as I entered the room. The moment is important; this was a turning point in my life, even if I was not fully aware of it at the time. It marked officially the beginning of the breakup of my marriage to Duke, although it was not until many months later, when I was sitting with the Prince beside a

ENTER THE PRINCE

campfire deep in the African veldt, that this fact became clear to me.

Naturally I was excited. I was conscious of the fluttering of my pulse, of a vague sense of expectancy. At such times we have a heightened excitement, a premonition of a significant change in our lives, even though the actual image of this change is not clear. The excitement was derived more from the situation than the man.

I had been terribly hurt when Duke told me that I was too American in my ideas about married life, that in England husbands and wives went on their own. This was something I simply didn't understand. If I had been wiser in those days, I would have understood, and taken Duke's words and actions for what they were worth. But as it was, I was simply hurt. And even though the Peggy Hopkins episode was no more than what I could call "a bit of fluff," and could ignore, there was the other woman who came in, a woman I could very well receive in my house, and Duke had asked me to receive her. It was then that I was really hurt. And all of this had occurred so soon after Tony's birth. And this is why, when I went to the Leicester Fair, and the Prince of Wales asked me to dine with him, my first reaction was: "Well, all right, if Duke wants me to lead my own life, I will."

When the Prince asked me, I had been flattered, of course. And my openness to the invitation was largely a matter of pique. I never dreamed, then, for a moment, that anything serious would come of it. A year earlier I would never have accepted; but, by the same token, I don't think that a year earlier the Prince would have asked me. But at this time he knew that Duke was running around; he must have—everybody knew it. And I am sure he would not have asked me for dinner without asking Duke, too, if things had been as before. At least I don't think he would have asked me.

The Prince seemed to me to be winsomely handsome. He was

the quintessence of charm. And after the swaggering earthiness of Duke, the Prince's natural shyness and reserve had a distinct appeal.

We sat by the fireplace and had cocktails, while the Prince chatted pleasantly about the small things one can discuss without strain or effort. In time he asked me where I would like to go for dinner. We decided on the Hotel Splendide, which was famous for its cuisine and its Viennese orchestra. It was a happy choice; we both loved to waltz, and it was significant to me that our first evening together should be in three-quarter time.

Aside from a little stir among waiters and guests as we entered, no one paid the slightest attention to us. We might have been any two young people out for an evening of pleasure. We talked of many things; of my sister, Consuelo, whom he had met in South America some years back. What fun he had had at her house; just little things like that. The admiration in his eyes as we danced, the frank, disarming way in which he spoke, as if there had never been a time when we did not know one another, quickened my heart. It all seemed so natural, so right.

As he drove me home that night, he said, "Thank you, Thelma, for a wonderful evening. Please let me call you soon again."

"Of course, sir." My reply was obvious.

CHAPTER XVII

The Trap

Gloria

I was in London, visiting Consuelo and her husband, Benny Thaw, when I received a letter from "Uncle George" Wickersham, announcing, in positive terms, that it was the wish of the Surrogate that, "in Gloria's best interest," I make my home in America. I returned at once, taking little Gloria with me, and talked with Mr. Wickersham. "Uncle George" was zealously paternal. And in the unctuous tones of a man giving fatherly advice to a rebellious daughter, he said, "I think you will have to comply with the Surrogate's wishes."

"I'm perfectly willing to live in America," I answered, "but I have a lease on the Paris house, and it still has three years to run."

"I'm sorry, but I can do nothing about it," Mr. Wickersham said. Nevertheless, after more discussion it appeared that he could do something about it. We reached a compromise: I would have one more year in which to wind up my affairs in Paris. Meanwhile, I made application to enter Gloria at Miss Chapin's school, for which there was a long waiting list.

When I got back to Paris I had a call from Consuelo in London. She and Benny were celebrating their wedding anniversary with a large dinner dance, and she wanted me to cross to London and be with them. Once again I packed.

A few days after the celebration, Consuelo called me, about five one afternoon, to ask if I would like to be presented at court the following day. She explained that one of the American girls who had a place on the presentation schedule of the American Embassy had come down with the mumps or measles, and I could take her place.

I was much too curious not to take advantage of the situation. But as soon as I hung up I suddenly said to myself, "Good heavens, what am I going to wear?" I immediately called Thelma, and Thelma offered me her train, the required three feathers, and a veil. Fortunately I had with me a gown which was elaborate enough for the occasion. But what of jewelry? I was only visiting in England; I had not brought any of my own jewels. I needed a tiara, and all the other things that make a lady look regally resplendent. I called up Nada Milford-Haven. "I shall look naked," I said.

"You're in the best of luck," Nada said. "I have just taken from the bank two tiaras, a pearl necklace, and a brooch to be cleaned, and appraised for re-evaluation by the insurance people. Come over and see me."

I went at once to her house. And there, sitting on a table, were two tiaras. One was a most beautiful tiara, with sapphires as big as plover eggs. The other was a combination of pearls and diamonds. There were also a sautoir and a brooch of pearls.

"May I borrow the diamond-and-pearl tiara?" I asked, "because I have my own pearls. And with the sautoir and the brooch, I'll be set."

"Certainly," said Nada; "take what you want."

These jewels came from her father, the Grand Duke Michael of Russia. What I was being loaned, consequently, if not Crown jewels, were at least "grand duke's" jewels; they were sensational.

As my car inched its way up the Mall toward Buckingham Palace the next day, I was fascinated with the crowds that had come out to see the ladies in their finery who were about to be presented. Some of the comments were very colorful and highly amusing. One little cockney woman poked her head into the car, took a quick look at my sparkling array, and announced: "Lord love a duck—it's the Queen of Sheba!"

I finally got to the palace and was presented. I curtsied to the King and Queen. And as I rose, I almost died. There, sitting to the left, among the members of the royal family, was Nada Milford-Haven, wearing the other tiara. She winked.

Mamma by this time had settled in New York. It later appeared that she had done much more than "settle"; she was in constant communication with Mr. Wickersham; and she informed Mr. Wickersham of every move I made.

I came back to America, in accordance with my agreement, and found a house I liked at 49 East Seventy-second Street—a house belonging to Schuyler Parsons. Before renting this, however, I called Mr. Wickersham. "I've found a house which I think will be rather nice," I said, "but under the circumstances—since you are the guardian of Gloria's property—I should like your approval."

Mr. Wickersham looked at the house with me. "Yes," he agreed, "this is a beautiful house; I think it will be perfect for you and Gloria." The following day I signed the lease. At that point, Mr. Gilchrist turned to me and said, "By the way, Mrs. Vanderbilt, you probably will be needing a butler. I have just the man for you. He wrote to me, recently, looking for a place. He was the butler of a client of mine, Mr. Shattuck, the owner of the Schrafft restaurants. He has been with the Shattucks for years; he is an excellent man."

"Certainly," I said, "I shall talk with him." The man came to see me. His name was Charles Zanck; he was very presentable, obviously a trained butler, and I engaged him. It was not until the trial that I learned that although Zanck had been the Shattucks' butler, he had also been put in their employ by Mr. Gilchrist.

I was also without a chauffeur at that time. Again Mr. Gilchrist was ready with a recommendation. "I have somebody whom I can recommend highly, a man called Theodore Beasley."

Sometime later, at a dinner party, my sister Consuelo found herself seated next to Mr. Taft of Cadwalader, Wickersham and Taft. Turning to him, she said sweetly, "By the way, Mr. Taft, how's the employment agency going?" Mr. Taft appeared to be quite bewildered. "Your Mr. Gilchrist," Consuelo said, "seems to be in charge of that department as far as my sister goes."

Nor were Mr. Gilchrist's extralegal activities confined to the hiring of household help. My mother once gave him for safekeeping my grandfather's West Point commission, drafted at West Point and signed by Abraham Lincoln, with a letter attached, written by Lincoln, complimenting my grandfather on his achievements. These papers, framed, hung on the wall of Mr. Gilchrist's home. None of us could get these family mementoes back because Mr. Gilchrist claimed my mother handed them to him not for safekeeping, but as a gift. I often wondered how Mr. Gilchrist could discover a way in which their presence on his wall did him honor.

It was necessary now for me to go to Paris to close the house there and ship the furniture to New York; I left little Gloria with Mrs. Whitney on Long Island. What followed was a barrage of alarms. On the ship to France I received a radiogram from Keislich saying that Gloria must be operated on at once—for infected tonsils. I immediately took the next ship back. As usual—another false alarm. Gertrude suggested that Gloria stay with her on Long Island, then join her cousins, the William H. Vanderbilts, at Newport. Again I sailed for France. No sooner had I arrived in Paris than a cable from Gertrude announced that Gloria had a severe pain on the right side, the doctor had diagnosed this as appendicitis, and was preparing to operate. Again I got ready to return. Before my ship sailed, however, a second cable from her explained that the doctor—by this time *doctors*—had discovered that Gloria did not have appendicitis, and there was no danger. And thus the cables volleyed back and forth across the Atlantic—all fulfilling a single purpose: to stir my fears, and to establish as fact that Gloria was a sickly child the extent of whose infirmities was not adequately appreciated by her mother.

By the end of August I had closed the Paris house and returned to New York. Immediately, on arriving here, I took a train to Newport, where little Gloria finally had been sent. I found her in radiant health. She was enjoying her summer, and she seemed to be delighted with the idea of moving into our new home in September and going to Miss Chapin's school. Only Keislich did not seem happy about these arrangements; but I attributed her disapproval to the fact that my household did not have the grandeur of Mrs. Whitney's.

I met Gloria at the station on her return from Newport. When I arrived, I saw Gertrude's car and chauffeur. I was not surprised at this as I did not as yet have a car of my own. I thought it a nice gesture on Gertrude's part. Nothing warned me or gave me the slightest hint that this was a prearranged move, not even when I told the chauffeur to go to Seventy-second Street and Keislich spoke up and said, "Mrs. Vanderbilt, the plans are to go to Mrs. Whitney's."

"Certainly not," I said. "We are going home."

We had not been in the house for long when Gertrude telephoned and asked if I had heard from Dr. St. Lawrence. (Dr. St. Lawrence, who had been highly recommended to me by Gertrude, was the doctor who also attended her grandchildren.)

I was surprised and asked, "Why?"

She then suggested I see him as soon as possible, as she was concerned about Gloria's health. I was surprised, for Gloria looked very well; but Gertrude's tone of voice worried me.

The following day I went to see Dr. St. Lawrence. This tall, distinguished, gray-haired man was in the category of doctors who address you as "little mother."

His first words to me were that Gloria was not a well child, the climate of New York City was bad for her, and she should return immediately to Westbury. When I protested that Gloria seemed the picture of health, he sighed and said, "Little mother, naturally it's up to you, but I strongly advise you that a winter in New York will be most detrimental to her health."

I should have had more sense and called for another opinion, but my trust in Mrs. Whitney led my steps straight to her house. Her attitude was sympathetic. "Now don't worry, Gloria," she said. "I'm sure the little one will be all right in time, and she'll surely be well enough to come to you in the spring. She can attend Greenvale School with my grandchildren and you can visit her. I know it's hard to have to be parted from your little girl, but this is the right thing and you *must* follow Dr. St. Lawrence's advice, dear."

There was no indication in her manner that she knew exactly what Dr. St. Lawrence had said to me, knew exactly what my reactions would be. Gloria went to Westbury that day. And in the months that followed I saw her only at the Whitney estate. Each time she was to return to me, Dr. St. Lawrence discovered some new symptom of frailty.

Meanwhile, a strange net began to close in around me. I was in constant anxiety about Gloria's health. The anxiety was accentuated by her absence, and the sequence of oddly accidental or coincidental conditions that seemingly made this prolonged absence necessary. Then one day "Uncle George" launched an attack from another quarter. He informed me that the Surrogate had objected to the fact that I was keeping up a house—with Gloria not in it!

I was livid. "Obviously," I said, "the Surrogate is not aware of the true situation. I have an appointment with Dr. St. Lawrence tomorrow and I insist that you or Mr. Gilchrist come with me and learn exactly what's what."

When we arrived at Dr. St. Lawrence's office, he was the same soothingly suave diplomat I had found him to be. He told Mr. Gilchrist that he admired me tremendously for sacrificing myself for Gloria's good, and that it was entirely on his advice that I had left the child all these months with Mrs. Whitney.

Suddenly his even, smooth voice changed. He looked at Mr. Gilchrist steadily, and emphatically said, "I will wash my hands of the whole case if my advice is disregarded and the child removed from the country. She must be left for the present where the climate agrees with her."

Mr. Gilchrist listened with attention as though weighing the evidence of the doctor's ultimatum.

"It is best to leave the child in Westbury," he said.

Returning in the car I said to Mr. Gilchrist, "Now that you see the situation, will you please make application to the Surrogate for sufficient funds for me to rent a house on Long Island, if that is where Gloria should live, so that I can finally have her with me? Perhaps I could rent the New York house."

(This application was denied on the ground that, since Mrs. Whitney was willing to have the child at no cost, it was unnecessary to incur added expense.)

On our return to the house, Mamma was waiting in the drawing room.

"Gloria," she said, "I want to talk to you and I want you to listen carefully to what I have to say. While you have been kind to me, no one knows how bitter it is to live on the charity of others. When your daughter is twenty-one you will have to live on hers, and I am telling you, you won't like it! If you will permit her to live with Mrs. Whitney, I am informed"—she shifted her words hurriedly—"I mean I feel sure Mrs. Whitney will support you for life if you will consent to this."

Many things of an impossible nature had been said by my mother in the past, but nothing to equal this.

"You must be mad to say such a thing to me. I am not selling my child."

"You use such big words," she replied, clamping her lips together.

She started toward the door. Then, turning to me, she said with a settled calm I found disquieting, "You had better reconsider, or you will be sorry."

With that she left.

The next day I sent the following letter to "Uncle George":

Sept. 20

Dear Mr. Wickersham:

I appreciate your expression of justification in sending Gloria to Long Island, and that I will be relieved of any criticism in accordance with the very generous offer of Mrs. Whitney of having Gloria with one added exception. My position in regard to the court as to the upkeep we have incurred in this house. I should like to know definitely how we are going to deal with this question.

Will I be subject to criticism, keeping up this house, since Gloria is not here? It is very essential for my peace of mind that you should clear up this situation so that I may know how I should act. I again stress the point, with her enforced absence both financial and moral not fall as a criticism from the court on me?

Hoping to hear from you at once on this subject, I am, as ever,

GLORIA.

To this came "Uncle George's" reply, dated the same day:

Sept. 20

My dear Gloria:

Mr. Gilchrist has told me of the interview which you and he had yesterday with Dr. St. Lawrence, at which the doctor expressed the opinion that little Gloria should not live in New York this coming winter but ought to be sent to Long Island as she was last year.

This being the advice of a competent physician I think you are

thoroughly justified accordingly, and that the interest of the child very properly leaves you to decide to send her to Long Island for the coming season. I understand there is an excellent school there to which she can be sent and thus her education will not suffer. I understand that Mrs. Whitney has offered to take the child for the winter without adding to her living expenses. This will, of course, relieve you of any criticism in that regard.
       Faithfully yours,
        GEORGE W. WICKERSHAM

The attitude of the guardians of the property in this circumstance could not be plainer than this letter of "Uncle George's" acquiescence.

The early winter of 1933 found me ill in bed. The removal of two wisdom teeth had resulted in an infection. The last person I wanted to see was Mr. Gilchrist, but "Uncle George" had phoned me to say that the yearly application to the Surrogate's Court for the guardianship of the property would have to be made in a few days, and as he had been ill for some time would I approve of Mr. Gilchrist acting in this capacity for the coming year?

I told him I would, and he said, "That's fine then. Mr. Gilchrist will call on you this afternoon for your signature."

Suave, businesslike, his brief case in hand, Mr. Gilchrist sat down beside my bed and presented a formidable array of legal documents. Seeing my startled terror, he smiled and said, "Oh, this won't take long, Mrs. Vanderbilt. Just sign here."

I don't know why, but I had a premonition, a strong feeling of mistrust. Why was he rushing me so? Looking sweetly at him, I answered through my locked teeth, "Why, Mr. Gilchrist, you surprise me. Papa always told me never to sign anything without reading it first."

"Yes, of course. I just didn't want to tire you needlessly," he said, handing me the papers.

I read carefully every legalistic word in the first half of a long sheet of foolscap. Then suddenly one word leaped from the page: the word "person." The passage read: "I, Gloria Morgan Vanderbilt, respectfully petition the Court to appoint Thomas B. Gilchrist as guardian of the *person* and property of my daughter, Gloria Laura Morgan Vanderbilt."

I put the paper down. "Mr. Gilchrist," I said, "Mr. Wickersham has, at my request, acted as guardian of the property of Gloria since Reggie's death, but never of the person of my child. That I am, naturally, myself!"

"Oh, Mrs. Vanderbilt, that never was intended," Mr. Gilchrist hastened to say. "That's just a slight error on the part of the secretary. I will cross it out."

I was now more than cautious. When Mr. Gilchrist had stricken out the offending word, I said sweetly, "Now please initial the change—on the margin." Meekly Mr. Gilchrist complied.

As the nurse showed him to the door, a frightening thought came to me: law offices do not often make mistakes of this kind.

I had met Nathan Burkan, the famous lawyer, at a large party given by A. C. Blumenthal, whom I had met with Will Stewart. Now, as soon as I was well enough, I went to see him. I told him of the incident with Mr. Gilchrist.

Mr. Burkan's face grew serious. "When," he asked, "were you appointed guardian of the child?"

"Never," I replied. I told him of my talks with "Uncle George" Wickersham, when I had returned from Europe, at his suggestion, to make my home in America. Mr. Wickersham, I explained, did not inform me that on becoming of age I was in a legal position to apply formally to the courts for the proper guardianship papers. If he had once said to me, "Gloria, you are of age now. You are the mother of the child, and now have the right to apply for the guardianship of her person," I certainly would have made the application. No word had ever been breathed to me then, or in the subsequent years, that this was my right.

"Well," said Mr. Burkan, "it is high time that you established your legal rights. You should apply to the court to be made sole guardian of the person of your child, and joint guardian of her property."

"Will you act for me?" I asked Mr. Burkan.

Mr. Burkan then took the necessary steps to establish as a legal fact the right every other mother assumes as a matter of course: the right of guardianship over her own child.

The petition filed by Mr. Burkan was to be heard on July 3, in the court of Surrogate Foley. I told Mr. Burkan I would like to go with him to the hearing; I had never been inside a court, and I was interested in seeing the procedure. Mr. Burkan smiled grimly. "The less you see of courts," he said prophetically, "the better." He also pointed out that it was in no way necessary for me to be present, the procedure was only a formality, but I insisted on attending.

There were three or four hundred spectators at the Surrogate's hearing. Mr. Burkan rose and addressed the bench. When he had finished speaking, a strange, small, impeccably dressed man who had been sitting in the back of the room jumped to his feet and said, "I object to the petition."

"On what grounds?" Mr. Burkan asked.

The man's answer was barked across the room. "On the grounds that Mrs. Vanderbilt is unfit."

All I remember of the moment that followed is the expression on the face of Surrogate Foley, who knew me well; his features were frozen, as if caught in a flash photograph. The Surrogate immediately banged the gavel. "Court adjourned," he said. Then, turning to Mr. Burkan, he added, "I will hear this case in my chambers after lunch."

Obviously, I was stunned. None of the events leading to this moment had made sense to me; there seemed to be no logic, no reason, no consistency or purpose in what I had seen happen; and now even the hearing made no sense.

I went to lunch with Mr. Burkan in a small restaurant a few blocks from the court. "Translate this to me," I said to Mr. Burkan. "In plain words, what does this accusation mean?"

Mr. Burkan was too direct a man to confuse the issue and too great a lawyer to jeopardize my interests at the expense of my feelings. "In plain words," he said, "the word 'unfit' in this connection alleges that the woman to whom it is applied is unmoral and immoral."

Before the hearing was resumed my accuser was identified. He was Walter Dunnington, of the Wall Street law firm, Dunnington and Gregg. Mr. Burkan challenged him as soon as we had assembled in Judge Foley's chambers. Addressing the Court, Mr. Burkan said, "I must refuse, Your Honor, to proceed in this case unless I am informed who is bringing the complaint objecting to the guardianship."

Surrogate Foley put the question to Mr. Dunnington. Mr. Dunnington flushed. "Does Mrs. Vanderbilt insist on knowing?" he asked, obviously embarrassed.

Mr. Burkan was adamant. "Mrs. Vanderbilt," he said, speaking for me, "insists on knowing."

Speechless, I nodded my head.

Mr. Dunnington lowered his voice, as if to conceal some unspeakable shame. "The complainant is Mrs. Vanderbilt's own mother, Mrs. Morgan."

I could not believe what I heard. "The complainant is Mrs. Vanderbilt's own mother...." I was stupefied. Such things do not happen. Here was Mamma—the mother I loved—now trying to destroy me. My own mother was calling me "unfit," immoral. The blow was too heavy to bear.

I drove directly from the courthouse to my mother's apartment hotel on East Sixtieth Street. The desk clerk informed me that Mamma was "not in." I insisted on being shown to her apartment. The clerk became flustered. "Just a minute, Mrs. Vanderbilt," he said, "I will have to call the manager."

The manager was extremely apologetic, but he apparently had orders and intended to act on them. "I'm terribly sorry, Mrs. Vanderbilt, but Mrs. Morgan's instructions are that if you even make an attempt to get into the elevator, I am to send for the police and have you ejected."

I wrote a note to Mamma saying that it was of great importance that I see her at once. I handed this to the manager and left.

I went back to my house. A short while later Mamma arrived. She was gay, genial, exuberant; and as soon as she caught sight of me she came up to me, as if nothing had happened at all, and tried to kiss me.

"Don't, Mamma," I said, cringing. "I can't bear that now."

Mamma looked at me in surprise.

"Why, why, Mamma? Why have you done this to me?"

Mamma's answer can be condensed into its standard form, her old, banal catch phrase: "What I have done, I have done only for the good of the child."

I looked at her and found myself almost speechless. There is a type of amazement that paralyzes the nerves of reaction—an amazement that comes from a sudden realization of the futility of an attempt to make sense. All I could do was to murmur vaguely, almost as if I were talking to myself, "For the child's good, Mamma? How can it be for the child's good if you destroy her mother?"

Finally I pulled my wits together, and as I did, I was seized with a blind rage. "Leave me, Mamma!" I shouted. "You must be mad; you don't know what you're doing!"

Mamma walked slowly to the door. Then pausing, with one hand on the doorknob, she said menacingly, "Gloria, I am advising you not to fight this. I have behind me money, political influence, and the Vanderbilt family. I am telling you this for your own good. If you try to fight it, you'll regret it."

When Mamma left, I scarcely knew what to do. In my confusion and panic I decided to talk face to face with Gertrude Whitney. I called on her at once.

The butler opened the front door of the Whitney house. I stumbled down the few steps in the front vestibule, passed the bronze doors in the lower hall, and ran up the marble stairs to her drawing room. I was too agitated to think strategically. I plunged immediately into my subject. "Gertrude," I said, "do you know what happened today in Judge Foley's court?"

"No," she said innocently. "What happened? Sit down and tell me."

I told her—in detail. Then I said, "I'm going to ask you something that may sound to you impertinent. I have just left my mother. She told me that she will oppose my guardianship of Gloria; and she said that behind her were money, political influence, and the Vanderbilt family. You know my mother says she has no money except what Thelma and I allow her, so someone is behind this case. Is it you?"

Gertrude's voice acquired the steel precision of a saw blade, controlled and cutting. "Gloria," she said, "if you were not so upset I would ask you to leave this house."

My breath left me; it was impossible for me to speak. Something about this reaction seemed to touch her. Her voice immediately softened. "I'm going to answer that directly," she said. "And the answer is emphatically no. I have always loved you. My mother loved you. I am horrified. Why, why should your mother want to do this to you?"

At this moment the butler came into the room. "Mrs. Morgan," he said, "is downstairs."

Gertrude put her hand on my arm. "That dreadful woman! I can't see her now. Go down, Gloria. Tell her you have been waiting for me, and that I'm not here. I'll get in touch with you later."

I met Mamma downstairs. She followed me to my car. In

silence I dropped her at her hotel. Gertrude called me later that evening and said, "Don't worry, dear, everything is all right."

Eventually there was a meeting in Surrogate Foley's chambers. At this meeting were Gertrude Whitney and her lawyers, John Godfrey Saxe and Walter Dunnington, and my lawyer, Nathan Burkan, and myself. Surrogate Foley suggested a custody agreement, and this suggestion was accepted verbally by Mrs. Whitney and myself, and the witnesses to this were our lawyers. This was the substance of the agreement: that I was to be made sole guardian of Gloria's person and joint guardian of her property—to be effective immediately. But because of the doctor's advice, Gloria was to remain at the Whitney estate for one more year. In September she would stay with me for a month. At the end of the year I would have little Gloria with me for good.

This, it is to be emphasized, was a verbal agreement.

CHAPTER XVIII

Quick Sand

Gloria

After the conclusion of this agreement, I sailed with Consuelo for Europe. Consuelo left the ship at Le Havre, to join Benny Thaw who was then stationed in Oslo. I went on to London to be with Thelma.

Friedel Hohenlohe, who recently had married Princess Margarita of Greece, wrote that it would give him and Margarita much pleasure if Thelma and I would visit them in Langenburg. I had previously met Margarita when she was staying at Kensington Palace with her grandmother, the dowager Marchioness of Milford-Haven. Her mother was George Milford-Haven's sister; her father, Prince Andrew of Greece, was first cousin to the late King George of England. Margarita is the sister of the Duke of Edinburgh. The last time I had seen her was in Paris, at a large dinner Papa had given at the Russian Eagle.

Thelma and I accepted the invitation. We spent many delightful days at the *Schloss*. We walked happily through the formal gardens planted in the old moat, sometimes alone, sometimes with Friedel and Margarita; and in this medieval setting we felt that we had been transported back to another century. Meanwhile, I came to know what a lovely human being Margarita is; I appreciated her beauty, which seems to come from an inner radiance; I felt the purity of character and the loyalty and devotion which are such signal parts of her nature. We became firm friends.

Thelma and I later went to Paris, where we were the guests of Aly Khan and his father, the late Aga Khan; and, together with Daisy Fellowes and Lady Granard, attended one of the most important sporting events of the Paris season—a night race at Longchamp. This occasion was unusually festive. In front of our box in the grandstand was a platform, and on this were staged dance performances by the Corps de Ballet of the Paris Opera and of the Imperial Russian Ballet. At other points around the racecourse nine different orchestras were playing. In the last race Aly himself rode, although, to the disappointment of our party, he did not win.

We then went back to London.

Papa at this time was staying with Thelma. One morning, when Thelma and I were sitting in her dressing room, Papa entered. He sat down, looking very tired and worn. For the first time I was aware of the fact that he had aged.

"Here you are sitting together," Papa said sadly, "and yet there is not a word about it from either of you."

We had no idea what he was referring to.

"What are you talking about, Papa?" I asked.

"Don't you know?" he said. "Your mother has divorced me."

The statement did not make sense to us. "How could Mamma have divorced? What are you talking about?" Thelma asked. "First, she would have had to serve you with papers."

"She has served me by publication, which she could do under Maryland law," Papa announced. It seems that she had divorced him on the grounds of desertion, and she had served notice of it by publishing an item in the Baltimore papers, which, of course, none of us saw. The unforgivable part of this action was not the divorce itself but the unnecessarily underhanded methods Mamma had used to obtain it. There was then no open breach between Mamma and my father, or between Mamma and her children. She was writing constantly to Thelma; she knew Papa was living with her. She knew exactly where to find him. And while Mamma and my father had not lived together since Papa was stationed at Brussels, there never had been an actual separation between them. They had been married thirty-three years.

My father never recovered from this blow.

I returned to New York. Eventually, when I judged the moment proper, I asked Mamma how she could have brought herself to do such a thing. Her answer was unpredictable, as usual—to her the divorce was just a "joke." "You know your father," she said. "He's always gallivanting about, and I wouldn't want to stand in his way should he want to marry someone else."

A few months later our father died. Consuelo arrived in London too late to see Papa alive. After the funeral, I went with her to Oslo and stayed two weeks with her and Benny Thaw. When the time came for me to return to New York, she refused to let me go alone. She made the trip with me, and we both settled down in the Seventy-second Street house. Meanwhile, Mrs. Vanderbilt had died, leaving me $100,000.

In September, at long last Gloria was to move in with me. She had spent the summer in the Adirondacks with Mrs. Whitney, and now that she was to come to a home of her own, I had done everything I could to fix her room the way I thought she would like it. I had gotten her a Louis XVI bed—much like mine, which in Paris she had loved. I had it upholstered in flowered chintz, to make it seem cheerful and inviting. And when Gloria saw the room, she put her arms around me and said, "Oh, Mummy, how grand. I feel like a grown-up lady in this room."

I was overjoyed that Gloria was at last with me; and I was so happy that she was pleased. Now there would be no more separation, no more worries for either of us.

We had lunch together. Then Gloria went out in Central

Park with her nurse, Keislich, and the chauffeur, Beasley, who had been hired through Mr. Gilchrist.

Consuelo was with me that afternoon. We played bezique. We were deep in our game when suddenly I realized that the afternoon had grown late—it was five thirty—and there was as yet no sign of Gloria. I assumed that she must have slipped into the house without announcing herself, and that at this moment she was in her room. I ran upstairs to Gloria's room; however, I found not Gloria—but Charles Zanck, the butler, opening Gloria's top bureau drawer. "What are you doing here?" I asked.

"The chauffeur is downstairs, Madam," Zanck replied. "They have sent for Miss Gloria's clock."

When I returned downstairs, I found Beasley standing in the hallway. "What have you done with Miss Gloria?" I demanded.

Beasley shifted his eyes uneasily. "She is at Mrs. Whitney's," he said. "She's very sick."

"What do you mean by taking her to Mrs. Whitney's?" I shouted at him. "Why didn't you bring her to her own home?"

Beasley muttered something. I did not stop to listen to him. I rushed in to Consuelo. "Put on your hat and coat quickly," I said. "We are going to Gertrude Whitney's."

Mrs. Whitney received us in the library. Her face seemed worried. "This is horrible, Gloria," she said to me. "I can't understand the child, but she is in hysterics. Dr. Craig is here looking after her now."

"Why Dr. Craig?" I asked. Dr. Stuart Craig was an ear, nose, and throat specialist. Moreover, he was not Gloria's regular doctor; Gloria was always treated by Dr. St. Lawrence. Mrs. Whitney explained that she had not been able to get hold of Dr. St. Lawrence, that Gloria knew Dr. Craig, and that, anyway, he was a doctor, which for the moment was all that mattered.

Mrs. Whitney took us to Gloria's bedroom. And as we entered, and Gloria caught sight of me, there was a spectacle so unexpected, so shocking to me—and at that time so inexplicable—that

I could do nothing but shrink back in horror. "For God's sake, don't let that woman come near me!" Gloria screamed, using the phrasing of a mature woman. "Don't let her come near, she wants to kill me!"

The doctor as well as the nurse tried to quiet her. But Gloria was beyond simple quieting. She threw herself on the floor, kicking and shrieking. Then, as if seized by a sudden inspiration, she got up, ran to the window, pointed toward me, and screamed, "If she comes near me, I'll jump."

Suddenly, in the midst of my shock, a great sense of calm came over me. I saw with startling clarity that little Gloria's emotions had been worked on until they had surged beyond her control; I understood how Keislich and others had played on the child's fears until in Gloria's eyes I—her own mother—appeared as a monster.

We returned to the library—Mrs. Whitney, Consuelo, and I. "I can't understand this," Mrs. Whitney said to me. "Gloria seemed anxious to be with you, and so pleased about going to the Chapin School—some of her friends from the Greenville School were going to be with her there. She's been looking forward to all this. I can't understand it."

Dr. Craig then joined us. He explained that this was just the child's reaction to sudden change, and that she would soon be over it. "However," he added, "I think it would be a good idea if you let her stay here tonight, and came back for her tomorrow."

"Is that all right with you, Gloria?" Mrs. Whitney asked.

The question was rhetorical. What could I do? I couldn't very well take away a child screaming and yelling and threatening to throw herself out the window. I agreed to come back the following morning.

The next day, at twelve, Consuelo and I went back to Mrs. Whitney's to get Gloria. Mrs. Whitney received us cordially. We sat down in the library, and the three of us had sherry. Then

Gloria came in, holding a cute little puppy her aunt had given her. She put the puppy on the floor and threw her arms around me. "Oh, Mummy, darling," she said, "isn't the puppy beautiful?" I held her tight. Last night must have been a bad dream. Gloria then sat on the floor and played with the puppy while Mrs. Whitney, Consuelo, and I chatted. Just in time, I looked at my watch; it was almost one o'clock—lunch, at home, had been ordered for quarter past one. I said to Mrs. Whitney, "Gertrude, don't you think Gloria had better go and get her coat on?"

"Oh, yes, Mummy," Gloria said, picking herself up from the floor. "I won't be long."

"Be sure and wrap yourself up well, dear," Mrs. Whitney said.

Gloria took the puppy with her and went out of the room. Meanwhile, Mrs. Whitney served us another glass of sherry. Then we waited for what seemed to be a very long time. Finally I turned to Mrs. Whitney and said, "Gertrude, dear, don't you think it would be better if you sent for Gloria? She's probably dawdling, and, really, lunch will be ruined."

At this Mrs. Whitney stood up in all her grandeur. All her affability vanished; her features froze. "I'm very sorry, Gloria," she said, "but little Gloria is halfway to Westbury by now. I'm not going to let you have her."

In retrospect, it seems to me that little Gloria's fear of me and the outbursts at this time were a cumulative effect of Mamma's anxieties and phobias and deliberate plotting. From the time the child was old enough to understand any of the realities of life, it was drilled into her that "This is your money, Gloria, not hers. Don't ever let her do this... or do that. If she says 'no' to what you want, don't listen to her—because she has to listen to you." Fears were drilled into her. Gloria was made to believe that sooner or later I was going to marry Prince Hohenlohe and, I am sure, that I would put her in a convent; she was terrified by the thought of being put in a convent, and Mamma played on this idea, suggesting that I wanted her out of the way. Every terror of the old fairy tales was dredged up by Mamma to frighten Gloria: I was going to marry Prince Hohenlohe, the cruel stepfather, and even if she escaped imprisonment in a nunnery, she would find herself locked behind the cold, thick stone walls of a medieval castle, catacombed with eerie vaults and dungeons. I am certain that the child actually had a deadly fear of me at that time.

From what I gathered later, this was the sequence of events which occurred: when Gloria left my house after lunch, the day she was to come and live with me, the chauffeur and nurse drove her around Central Park. When Gloria was finally taken to Mrs. Whitney's she was actually in a state of hysteria. She had not been the least frightened at lunch. Something must have happened, something so dreadful, so upsetting, that she was thrown into a state of shock. No matter how good an actress she might have been, that night there was no doubt of one fact: Gloria was thoroughly scared!

I began to realize then that all this had been an act for my benefit—a cold, sadistic act. Every detail had been planned cleverly, deviously, cruelly. And what was the purpose? To separate me from my child. It is my guess that it was the hope of many close to the picture that this maneuver would unfold smoothly, and that sooner or later events would force me to yield without protest to the ever mounting pressure, that I would eventually say to Gertrude Whitney, "You are right, Gertrude—Gloria is a sick, hysterical, unhappy child, and for her own good I want her to stay with you always." But what neither Mrs. Whitney nor my mother understood was how deeply I loved Gloria, and how convinced I was that it was they who were undermining her health emotionally. A neurosis can be induced; and it can be so carefully cultivated that it produces a permanent state of fear and hysteria.

When Consuelo and I got back to my house, I called Mr. Burkan. He was amazed by what had happened. He immediately prepared to serve Mrs. Whitney with a writ of habeas corpus.

A day later he reported to me that Mrs. Whitney had refused service of the writ, and that he had called Mrs. Whitney's lawyer, Frank L. Crocker, and announced that if Mrs. Whitney would not accept the papers in person he would have the summons plastered all over her front door. Mr. Crocker, foreseeing the newspaper headlines that would follow such a frontal attack, agreed to accept the papers for Mrs. Whitney. The papers were duly served.

I had three telephones in my house; and that night each was kept going. I was at war, and I needed support. I called Thelma in London, Harry in Paris, and Prince Hohenlohe in Langenburg. I can never forget those dramatic moments, and the feeling of comfort I had when those closest to me announced without hesitation that they were rushing to my side. There was, for example, Friedel's voice:

"Yes, Prince Hohenlohe speaking."

"Friedel," I said, "they have taken Gloria. I feel they will not give her back to me. We will need you. Will you ask Margarita if she will consent to your coming to me?"

There was not an instant of pause. "We will both be on the next boat," Friedel said. And they were.

The maid at Thelma's house told me that Thelma was not at home. Where was she? She was at a ball being given at the Hotel Claridge by Aly Khan for his father, the Aga Khan and the new Begum. I called Claridge's. When my twin came to the phone, I told her what had happened, and I asked her if she could come over at once—the *Empress of Britain* was sailing the next morning.

"Don't you realize," she said, "that it is already three o'clock in the morning here? If the boat sails tomorrow from Southampton, it will leave at about eight in the morning. That will give me only a few hours."

"Yes, darling, I realize it," I said, knowing well that I could count on Thelma for anything. "Catch that ship."

Thelma arrived in Southampton still in her silver lamé evening dress, but in time for the *Empress*. Thus, Thelma, Harry and his wife, Edith, Friedel and Margarita, were at my side during the grueling weeks that were to follow.

A few days after this the hearings began before Judge Carew of the New York Supreme Court—the hearings which the newspapers and the witnesses together turned into a *cause célèbre*. I have no desire at this late date to describe again the painful and ludicrous scenes, nor to relive the moments whose outcome had for me such tragic consequences. Time does not necessarily ease hurt; sometimes, however, it places persons and events in proper perspective. It also discloses subtleties which elude you when you are on stage, like one of Pirandello's *Six Characters*—playing a role in your own tragedy.

What now stands out in my memory is the scene of that dingy courtroom with its unwashed windows and its crowd of morbid spectators the morning Consuelo and I walked in. This was to be a sensational case; the public was hungry for details, the press was on hand ready to turn every crumb of innuendo into a tidbit of scandal. We had scarcely arrived when the room was engulfed in a wave of excitement. I turned. There was Mrs. Whitney entering with her daughter, Mrs. G. Macculoch Miller, and with her battery of lawyers, including Mr. Dunnington, Mr. Crocker, and Mr. Smythe. Mrs. Whitney and her daughter, however, did not sit with the Whitney lawyers; the counsel sat as an independent body, like a citizens' committee dedicated to the promotion of civic virtue. Then my mother entered, flanked by Keislich, the nurse, and Maria Caillot, the maid. Maria was a special surprise; when last I saw her, she was in Europe, where I had left her when her employment with me terminated. The three sat together, but at a distance from Mrs. Whitney and her daughter.

The hearing began.

First to take the stand was the nurse. She cried, explained to the Court how much she loved this child, and detailed the dozens of ways she claimed I had neglected Gloria. The substance of her testimony that morning was that the houses I had lived in—all of them—were unfit for Gloria. Some, she implied, were hovels. The house I had rented in the Rue Alfred Roll, in Paris, was "infested with rats." As her charges became more and more venomous, she moved to what she presented as an ultimate attack: the assertion that no decent person ever crossed my threshold.

To an objective observer little that Keislich said would have had any claim to significance. When Mr. Burkan cross-examined her on the "decent person" charge, for example, there was this exchange—quoted here from the Court record: Mr. Burkan reminded Keislich of a time I had a house in Biarritz, and of the period Consuelo was with me.

MR. BURKAN: Mrs. Thaw was there, was she not?

ANSWER: She calls herself Mrs. Thaw.

MR. BURKAN: What do you mean—'she calls herself Mrs. Thaw'? Do you not know this lady is married to Benjamin Thaw, then Secretary to the American Embassy in London?

ANSWER: She says she is.

She claimed she and my mother had peeked through the door to my room in the Biarritz house and had seen Prince Hohenlohe in deshabille early in the morning. When the facts were disproved by Mr. Burkan, her answer was, "We are not all liars—we are not of your sort." As the proceeding continued, her words grew in virulence. Finally Judge Carew himself interrupted the testimony to say, "Woman—woman, don't you know that God put teeth in your mouth to keep your tongue in?"

Eventually, even Herbert Smythe, attorney for Mrs. Whitney, was compelled to concede that Keislich was an unhealthy influence. Mr. Burkan, addressing the Court, said, "I wish to establish, Your Honor, that from this evidence alone this nurse is a dangerous woman to be around the appellant's child. Her influence for ten years accounts in a great measure for the child's attitude toward her mother."

Mr. Smythe immediately agreed. "We will let the nurse go," he said. "She will be of no help to the child."

Judge Carew at once concurred. "Then that is settled," he said. "The nurse goes."

The second witness against me was Beasley, the chauffeur. The substance of his early testimony was that I was presumably the mistress of Lawrence Copley Thaw. His contention was that he knew I was Larry Thaw's mistress because one night I went to the Thaw house, saying that I would be there only a short time, but actually stayed until three o'clock in the morning. Subsequent questioning disclosed that the occasion was a ball given by Larry Thaw and his wife. Beasley then tried to show that I was also the mistress of A. C. Blumenthal, and that he had once driven me to Blumie's place in Larchmont. Cross-examination developed the fact that this "rendezvous" was a party at which there was a showing of a motion picture in Blumie's projection room, and that Blumie, at my urging, had asked Beasley to come inside and see the picture, along with the rest of us.

A. C. Blumenthal was a fascinating little man—he stood about five feet one; he was charming, shockingly charming. I always found him great fun to be with.

The next witness was the maid, Maria Caillot. For a long while she disappointed the spectators who, after the earlier tidbits, were thirsting for blood. Maria accused me of a variety of trifling indiscretions, such as "drinking champagne." She supplemented this statement by saying that she had often seen me under the influence of alcohol ("*très gaie*" was the way she put it), and that this was evident because I always smiled when drinking excessively.

"Are you trying to imply," Mr. Burkan said, "that Mrs. Vanderbilt never smiles unless she is drunk?"

"When she is drinking," Maria said blandly, "she always smiles."

At this I could not keep a straight face. And Mr. Burkan, watching my expression, began an attack which was intended to show the absurdity of Maria's testimony. "You see Mrs. Vanderbilt smiling at you now," he said. "Would you call her intoxicated?"

There was a general titter in the courtroom. Mr. Burkan's sarcasm was an acid that clearly etched the quality if not the motives of the witness. He then turned to the motives. He made Maria admit that she had been brought from Paris as a witness by Frank L. Crocker, and that she had been coached in his office. "How much money did you ask, to give this evidence?" he asked.

Maria stiffened. "I did not ask for money."

"But you were promised it," Mr. Burkan suggested.

For a moment Maria hesitated. Then her answer, half-whispered but definite, was given for the record. "Yes."

By this time it seemed to most of us that Mr. Burkan had brought out, beyond question, the ludicrous nature of the issues that had been raised to keep me from having custody of my child, and had obtained from Maria a clear admission of bribery. The hearing had become a farce. Mr. Burkan moved to bring quickly into sharp focus the vague, wavering lines of innuendo. "And so all these months," he said, looking hard at Maria, "you saw nothing improper in her household?"

"No," said Maria, "I saw nothing."

Perhaps Mr. Burkan pressed his point too far; he was so certain of his position—our position—that he unconsciously sought emphasis in repetition. "Mrs. Vanderbilt always conducted herself in a perfectly respectacle and decent manner?"

"Always," Maria affirmed.

"So then," Mr. Burkan continued, probing for the repetition to confirm a repetition, "you never once saw evidence of improper conduct?"

Suddenly clapping her hand to her forehead as if straining to recover the details of some episode obscured in the fringe of the deep past, Maria said, "Oh, yes, I remember now something that once happened that was very *amusant*." Her word *amusant* was then translated, for the benefit of the Court, to "amusing."

Mr. Burkan was already putting away his papers, "Oh, yes?" he said, looking up, "and what was that?"

"Yes," Maria went on (and I quote from the record), "there was something struck me as very funny when we were at the Hotel Miramar in Cannes in 1929. Mrs. Vanderbilt called me one day and asked me to get breakfast. When I came back with breakfast, I saw Lady Milford-Haven and Mrs. Vanderbilt, and Lady Milford-Haven was kissing Mrs. Vanderbilt."

The silence that followed this statement was like the awesome quiet that separates a stroke of lightning from the thunder crash that is to follow. Not a cough, not a murmur was to be heard in the entire courtroom. Then Judge Carew banged his gavel like a sledge hammer. "In the interest of public decency," he said, "the press and the public will be barred from this courtroom."

At this point bedlam broke loose. It seemed to me that everyone in the courtroom was shouting. And the reporters, almost in a body, scurried to the telephones—all set on announcing to the world a succulent banner headline, big-name scandal. And simultaneously another world—my world—had without warning begun to crumble around me. And all of this, it seemed to me, without reason—except for the fact that a farce had been accepted as an authentic tragedy by those in authority, and this acceptance had automatically cast me in a role that combined the most lurid characters of Lucrezia Borgia and Lady Macbeth.

In moments of intense emotion one tends to remember, by some strange irony, not so much significant issues as the trivia—those little details of experience which become symbols for the experience itself. At lunch that day the only food I could bring myself to eat was sardines. Why this preference for sardines

I don't know; but I recall that I ate ravenously. To this day, because of the painful association, I can't bear the sight of a sardine.

"Mrs. Vanderbilt," Mr. Burkan finally said to me, "is there any truth at all to this accusation?"

I answered: "None whatever."

"Very well," Mr. Burkan said grimly, "we will go back into that courtroom and prove that what Maria Caillot said is false. I simply have to cross-examine her until the facts are brought out."

That afternoon Mr. Burkan fought to keep the hearings open. The press and the public had heard the damaging innuendos which had been made about me; it was now necessary that the press and the public hear them disproved. It was necessary that the world should know how false were the accusations made against me. But Judge Carew was adamant. He overruled all of Mr. Burkan's objections. The answers to these terrible and unfounded charges could not be made public.

That afternoon, in a courtroom containing only the judge, the lawyers, and the principals in the case, the hearings were resumed. Maria Caillot took the stand, and Judge Carew himself undertook the cross-examination of the witness. Unfortunately for me, the outcome of this testimony, which was shown to be unfounded, never appeared in the press; the press had already labeled me sensationally, and the labels were left in the mind of the public.

Here is that afternoon's testimony, quoted verbatim from the record:

HIS HONOR (to the witness): I want you now to tell me this whole account. I do not want to have to ask you about it. Tell me what you saw.

WITNESS: I saw Lady Milford-Haven kissing Mrs. Vanderbilt.

HIS HONOR: Where was Mrs. Vanderbilt?

WITNESS: In bed.

His Honor: Where was the other woman?

Witness: Standing next to the bed.

His Honor: Where were Mrs. Vanderbilt's hands?

Witness: They were holding a newspaper. She was sitting on a bed reading a newspaper, Mrs. Vanderbilt was.

His Honor: What is that you say—she had a newspaper in her hands?

Witness: Yes.

His Honor: So we have one woman sitting on a bed reading a newspaper and the other woman standing beside her giving her a kiss. They both had on nightgowns. Is that what you said?

Witness: Yes.

His Honor: And that is all there is to this incident?

Witness: Yes.

His Honor: What? Speak up.

Witness: That is all I saw.

I had Mr. Burkan point out to the judge that Maria had testified earlier that Lady Milford-Haven was wearing pajamas, not a nightgown. I then succeeded in having the question asked: "What kind of pajamas?" And the answer elicited was "beach pajamas"—an outfit which at that time was almost standard street apparel for most of the women in Cannes. And that was the story, told in secret, which branded me as a "Lesbian." (Or, as cautiously reported in the New York *Daily Mirror*, "Having alleged erotic interest in women.")

It is not to the point at this time to recount or analyze all the tedious and painful incidents of the hearing, which stretched out over seven weeks. The testimony varied in details of time and place. Most of the facts were not true, and those that were, were given meanings totally unrelated to the events. But all were coordinated to one end: to show me to the Court—and the world—as a scheming, immoral woman. I wish to say only that the charges brought against me at this hearing were altogether false and malicious, and that their purpose, as engineered by my mother with the support and collaboration of Mrs. Whitney, was to keep me away from Gloria.

Most vivid in my recollection of those long, trying weeks is the testimony of my mother. Although Mamma's face was generally heavy with make-up, she sat in court with cheeks as pale as white bread. Throughout the hearings she held her crucifix conspicuously in her hand. Her charges centered around Friedel Hohenlohe. "I hated him," she screamed when she was questioned; "he was trying to get my granddaughter's money. All that stood between her money and them was me."

Mrs. Whitney's lawyer, Mr. Smythe, then questioned her softly. "Is it not so, Mrs. Morgan," he said, "that you have asked me to refrain from questioning you about your daughter's morals?"

Mamma pressed the crucifix dramatically against her breast. "Yes, I did," she said hysterically. "I cannot speak of my daughter's shame. It was a Calvary on earth."

Pressed, however, Mamma spoke of her daughter's "shame" with much enthusiasm, detailing the bedroom farce she claimed to have witnessed between Friedel and me in the villa on the Côte Basque—a spectacle seen through a half-opened door and one apparently so entertaining that she, in her excitement, invited Keislich to leave her own bedroom and to share it.

Eventually even Mr. Smythe attempted to stifle her recital. Mamma had no desire to give up her Boccaccio role. Clutching her crucifix in one hand, she pulled Judge Carew's arm with the other. "They won't let me talk, you see," she shouted. "I have so much to tell—so much! I can never face my Maker if I don't do this. And they won't let me talk."

Nothing is to be gained, after all the years that have passed, to abstract the seven volumes of testimony that detailed this hearing. It is enough to say that the long weeks of ordeal—my ordeal—in which distortions, exaggerations, and bald lies had to be contested, phrase by phrase, were climaxed by the pontifical decision of Judge Carew. I was to be given the custody of Gloria every weekend, and for the entire month of July; the remaining days and months of the year, Gloria was to be with Mrs. Whitney. The opinion of the Court, in short, was that I was an unfit mother most weeks between Monday and Friday; but every weekend my shortcomings vanished—and in July I was practically perfect. We were forced to take this unreasonable decision to the Appellate Division of the New York Supreme Court. Five justices heard the appeal: Francis Martin, Edgar S. K. Merrell, Irwin Untermeyer, John W. McAvoy, and James O'Malley. The unanimous decision, written by Justice Untermeyer, read in part as follows: "We think that the charge which rests upon the testimony of the maid Caillot, elicited on cross-examination, is so detrimental to the relator and the evidence to support it so unsubstantial that she was entitled to unqualified and complete exoneration..."

The Appellate Court, however, did not change the lower court's order, which required my life—and Gloria's—to be transformed into an every-weekend game of battledore and shuttlecock. And the justification for this stand was again that ironic and by now almost meaningless phrase, "For the good and welfare of the child." The farcical aspect of the decision at that time was aptly expressed in a jingle written by the lawyer, Melville Cane, and published in the New York *Journal American:*

> Rockabye baby
> Up on a writ,
> Monday to Friday Mother's unfit.
> As the week ends she rises in virtue;
> Saturdays, Sundays,
> Mother won't hurt you.

It is not easy, at this late date, to account for Mrs. Whitney's attitude toward me. Some people have maintained that she was jealous of me. It was said that Mrs. Whitney believed that her husband had been in love with me. But whether or not this was an assumption on Mrs. Whitney's part, it had no basis whatever in fact. I did not see Harry Whitney more than twenty or thirty times in my entire life. He was charming; he was kind and helpful to me, especially in the months following Reggie's death. I was very fond of him; he was very fond of me—but so was Gertrude, at least so I thought. Personally, however, I believe that her attack on me was grounded simply on the fact that she accepted as truth the things said about me by my mother and the nurse. She believed, I suppose, that I was selfish and immoral and that I was planning to injure or neglect my child according to the tradition of melodrama, and hoping to take over the child's inheritance. Her turnabout was a stunning blow to me, because, up to the day she literally kidnaped Gloria and announced that she could never let me have her back, Mrs. Whitney had been my favorite sister-in-law, a woman I considered warm, worldly, charming, and understanding—an artist and a great friend, as well as my sister-in-law.

Mrs. Whitney was actually a very broad-minded woman, and even this is an understatement. She could not have been the sculptress that she was, nor moved among the people who composed the art and theater world, unless she were—not that I mean to imply that all artists are Bohemian or erotic. But there was nothing squeamish about Mrs. Whitney. The ordinary social taboos simply didn't exist in her life. Why, at the trial, she suddenly became "holier than thou" is an interesting psychological question—at least if you can approach it objectively.

Whatever patterns she chose had their own justifications; her life, however, was not exactly of the kind that put her in a position to call the kettle black. It is an understatement to say that Mrs. Whitney was at times quite unconventional.

How, then, can we account for Mrs. Whitney's behavior at the trial? I return to my first theory: I really believe that my mother, prompted by her strange compulsions and pathological fears, with the collaboration of the nurse, had actually convinced her that the acts I was accused of did occur, and that Gloria was made to suffer because of them. Even if my supposed "immorality" had been a matter of fact, she would not have raised an eyebrow at the events themselves. I am sure it was her credence of Mamma's insinuations that I intended to harm Gloria that moved her to act.

But once Mrs. Whitney found herself in court, other factors entered the case. She found herself riding on a tiger's back; and as a stubborn, strong egotist, she determined to ride the tiger, whatever the cost. After the third day of the trial—and this I learned from Frank Crocker who, years later, became my friend —Mrs. Whitney wanted to stop the trial; things were not going as smoothly as she had planned. But Gilchrist, Dunnington, my mother, and the nurse convinced her that she was already too deep in the case to back out. No matter how the witnesses fluttered, no matter how unreliable they proved to be, it was necessary for the sake of face to continue with the trial. And how trustworthy could these witnesses be? Who and what were they?—the nurse, the maid, my mother; the butler, and the chauffeur, both engaged through Mr. Gilchrist. Their word had to stand against the testimony of Thelma, of Consuelo, of Harry, of Larry Thaw, and of Prince and Princess Hohenlohe, who had crossed the Atlantic just to help me. These were obviously sane, responsible people; and Mrs. Whitney knew it. She realized what she had let herself in for, and that the testimony of prejudiced or bought servants had to be matched against that of people who moved in her own world and had no ax to grind.

I believe that this is why Mrs. Whitney, when she took the stand, said nothing whatever against me. On the contrary, she declared that I was a "charming" woman, that she had never known me, in speech or action, to do anything which was not the soul of propriety—I was just the paragon of American womanhood. Her mother "adored" me. This court action was not directed against me; it was taken merely "for the good and interests of the child." That phrase, I am sure, will be spelled out in neon lights on my grave.

I definitely claim that the nurse, the maid, and my mother were paid. Proof, naturally, I have not got. The only thing I do know beyond question is that until the day she died Mrs. Whitney supported the nurse. She also supported my mother. Oddly enough, all the money Mrs. Whitney and Gloria together gave my mother Mamma put away, and this was the $100,000 she left Gloria in her will. One of the many odd things about my mother I can never understand is why she took this money at all. She didn't need it; it was only put away in order to be returned.

CHAPTER XIX

Royal Romance

Thelma

Gloria's ordeal was the last thing I could have imagined as even remotely possible in those exciting days after my memorable first evening with the Prince of Wales. I dined and danced with him several times. And I found in him what at that time I most wanted and needed. Not only was he fascinating to me in terms of his own personality, but he was the perfect compensation for my emotional hurt. He was the antithesis to Duke; he was an antidote for Duke. Duke was rugged, blustering, carelessly self-indulgent; the Prince was shy, gracious, meticulously considerate.

I was still at this time living as Duke's wife in our town house, but I considered my life my own. I was living according to Duke's code—the single standard that I had, as a bride, found so difficult to understand.

The Prince and I spent a number of evenings dining and dancing in the fashionable London night clubs. Naturally, when we were seen together, eyebrows were raised and tongues began to wag.

We talked a great deal, but mostly about trivialities. The Prince was not a man for abstract ideas or ponderous thought; nor was he interested to any extent in the theater, books, or art. Our talk was mostly about people we knew or had known, and about places we knew and liked. And this was enough. There was a special rapport that seemed to exist between us, and this rapport was intuitive; we did not have to build it slowly through a discovery together of complex issues. This is not to say that the Prince is not complex; he is an extraordinarily complicated personality, but it is to say that his outward manner is simple and direct, and that it is easy to be with him and have an immediate liking for him, without going beyond the surface.

Long before my first dinner with the Prince, Duke and I had planned a safari in Africa. And by a coincidence, the Prince was to be in Nairobi, not far from us, at the time our safari was scheduled. I was not happy at the prospect of the protracted trip with Duke, or being separated a long time from the Prince; but Duke and I were still keeping up the appearances that society required and I consoled myself with the thought that the Prince would be there, too.

During this period, moreover, I was not always alone with the Prince. Duke took our friendship in stride—in the sophisticated Englishman's stride. My going out with the Prince was in no way extraordinary, and often Duke would join us—we would be seen together as a party of six or eight at the Embassy, the Kit Kat, or whatever other night spot we chose. At other times Duke and I would give parties at our house, and the Prince would be one of the guests.

Just before I left for Africa on my first safari, the Prince gave me a little St. Christopher's medal that he had always worn around his neck on a gold chain. His mother had given him the medal, and the Prince said it would protect me on my trip. I was deeply touched by this simple gift. I had it attached to a little diamond pin, and I carry it always with me.

Our East African port of call was damp, enervating, steaming Mombasa. A dispatch bag full of mail was handed Duke. He went through it casually. "Here are some letters for you, Thelma." I recognized the Prince's handwriting. I'm sure Duke did, too, but he made no comment. I was delighted to learn, from one of the Prince's letters, that we would have a chance to see each other in Nairobi.

As we left Mombasa for Nairobi, hot though it was, I was in high spirits; and I was fascinated by all that I saw. From the train window I had my first glimpse of big game—at least the first outside a zoo. Herds of giraffes galloped across the open ground. I saw zebras, kongonis, and other animals whose names I did not as yet know.

Nairobi, unlike Mombasa, was cool and dry, a divine oasis after the long, hot, trying trip. Duke had seen to it that our safari was the last word in comfort and luxury. When we were settled in our first camp, I must say that the setup was very impressive. Our tents, and those of the white hunters, Von Blixer, and Dickenson, were of green canvas and about the size of a small cabin on a ship. Behind these was a smaller tent that was used as a bathroom; the tubs were of canvas and, when not in use, were rolled up. The dining tent was made of netting; it was large enough to hold fourteen of us at a time. I was amazed at the quality of the meals served us in such a primitive setting.

The first night I slept in camp I was scared to death. Under my mosquito net, in the pitch darkness, I heard the growling of lions in the distance; to me the roars seemed to come from a place just outside my tent and at any moment, I believed, the lions would pounce on me. Why, I asked myself, did I have to be the big white hunter? Why couldn't I have stayed where I belonged—safe and sound in London? Once a wild animal actually did find his way into my tent. I woke with a start to see two shining eyes fixed on me. Was it a lion or a leopard? I didn't dare turn on my flashlight to find out. Finally, when I could stand the suspense no longer, I put on my light and fixed the beam on the creature, ready to scream my head off. There was a hyena, one of my shoes in its mouth, glaring back at me. By that time I was too petrified even to scream. Fortunately, the hyena bolted. It was only later that I learned that hyenas do not attack people—live people, anyway. Hyenas, I was told, are scavengers.

We plunged deep into the jungle. I shot an elephant, a lion, a rhino, and a water buffalo. I was surprised, not excited, when I shot the elephant. We were pushing through very tall grass. I walked ahead. All of a sudden a big bull stampeded in front of me, less than fifty yards away. When an elephant stampedes, ears out, trunk up, you think a house is falling on you. I raised my gun and fired; it kicked. I sat down, kerplunk, like a little child landing on its bottom. But I got the elephant.

On our way back to Nairobi a courier brought an invitation from the Governor, to be his guests at a special event. The Prince had arrived. I guessed that Duke must have surmised it, too, for he turned down the invitation, giving as an excuse that he had to stay in Nairobi for the disbanding of our safari, and I, in my excitement at the thought of seeing the Prince again, did not question his decision.

Natives were not allowed to spear lions unless given special permission by the government. But now, in honor of the Prince, two tribes were to compete with each other in a special lion hunt. The starting point of this safari was Government House in Nairobi, where the Prince had been staying. On the second day out a runner rushed into camp and said that he had sighted a lion.

The Governor and his guests perched themselves on a hilltop to watch the kill. But the Prince was not so passive. Camera in hand, he rushed out into the fray. Excitedly I took moving pictures of the Prince running all over the place, taking his own moving pictures. When the tribes closed in on the lion I got a wonderful, though rather harrowing, shot of a native boy being clawed by one of the lions. It was at that moment that another native boy raced up to the victim, spear poised, and destroyed the lion. In spite of my horror at the accident and the shaking of my hands, I kept my Bell & Howell trained on the scene—and ended the day with a remarkably good sequence. I am sorry that I lost these films in one of the blitz raids on London.

The Prince's safari was large; there were about forty of us, including the Governor and his wife, and the native guides and servants. No convenience for our comfort that could be transported and fitted into our nomadic life was overlooked: portable bath tubs, dining tables, wine coolers, and the finest mosquito-proofed tents. We even had a little Puss Moth Airplane to scout for lions, and each day began with the Prince buzzing my tent to wake me up before soaring off over the bush in search of game.

But fascinating as were the hunting, the natives, and the country, I was always glad when the Governor gave the signal to make camp, and the Prince returned from the hunt. The tents were always pitched at intervals of ten or twelve yards in a rough semicircle around a great central fire that was kept burning all night. In addition, there were smaller fires in front of every two or three tents to discourage animals that might have sneaked through the native camp in the rear of our line of tents or skirted the main blaze. The Prince's tent was always on one end of the line and mine next to his, and we shared a fire. After dinner was over our party soon broke up, each going to his own tent or gathering in small groups for a final pipe or nightcap. Early retiring and rising are the custom on safari.

But not for the Prince and me. This was our enchanted time to be together. As we sat by our own fire, now little more than glowing embers, the tropic African night would come closer and closer. It is hard to convey the quality of those nights. The stars seemed close enough to touch; the murmurous background sounds of innumerable insects were punctuated with the sudden hideous laughter of the hyena or the stealthy footfalls of larger animals moving through the underbrush. From time to time the eyes of "bushbabies,"—tiny furry animals—gleamed from the edge of the bush like little headlights. And the air was like a caress, silken soft. No one could remain insensitive to the vastness of the starry sky, the teeming, fecund sense of nature at its most prodigal. As the Prince and I would feel enveloped in all this, we would instinctively draw closer as if we were the only two people on Earth; our companions became as unreal, as remote from us, as the insubstantial shadows along the jungle's edge. This was our Eden, and we were alone in it. His arms about me were the only reality; his words of love my only bridge to life. Borne along on the mounting tide of his ardor, I felt myself being inexorably swept from the accustomed moorings of caution. Each night I felt more completely possessed by our love, carried ever more swiftly into uncharted seas of feeling, content to let the Prince chart the course, heedless of where the voyage would end.

But this enchanted time could not last. The Prince's itinerary was rigid, so many days for this, so many days for that. And Duke had arranged to retrieve me at the appointed time, and he was not less a slave to plans and timetables than the Prince. So it was that on the seventh day the Governor's safari came to an end. We were to proceed to the nearest town on the railroad, a tiny hamlet called Voi. There the Prince's private train would be waiting to carry him to the Belgian Congo and Duke to take me to Mombasa on the first leg of our journey back to England.

On the last day I was prepared for the briefest of farewells, assuming the Prince would proceed ahead to Voi while I followed with the others. Knowing that he detested scenes and sentimentality, I was determined that I would be gay and casual even if it killed me. Feeling much as Eve did on being faced with leaving her garden, I steeled myself to put on a good show as I saw him approaching, but I must confess I was hurt when I saw him coming toward me with even more bounce to his stride than usual, an even broader smile on his face. He didn't have to look that happy at leaving me, did he? But how wrong I was. He had arranged a delightful surprise. Brushing aside the alarmed protest of the Governor and the remonstrances of his equerry, he had arranged to drive me in an open car all by himself the forty or so miles across the trackless country between our camp and the railroad. Thus he had given us one more day to be together, one more day to be alone.

We started off in high spirits, looking on our expedition as quite a lark. And so it was for the first several hours. We met a rhinoceros with her "toto," as the cubs are called in Africa. We obtained some good movies, and after resting a while and having lunch we resumed the journey. I noticed that the Prince seemed very flushed, but I attributed that to the excitement over the rhinoceros and to the heat. But there was also something different in his manner. Gone were the gay badinage, the loving glances. He drove in silence, staring fixedly ahead. Finally he said: "Darling, I've got to stop for a bit; I feel frightfully seedy." When we stopped he slumped over the wheel, his eyes closed, his breath coming in short shallow gasps. My concern rapidly turned into near panic. What was I to do if he fainted? Nothing in my life had prepared me for such a crisis. I had no idea of what was wrong with him or what to do for him. I had learned to drive, haltingly, an old Marmon I had briefly possessed in California. But at best I could only manage the briefest of excursions along the then uncrowded boulevards of Beverly Hills—and that was a long time ago. Here I was in an utterly unfamiliar vehicle about whose workings I knew nothing—except that they seemed quite different from those of an American car. And I had only the vaguest idea in which direction the railroad lay. While the country was fairly open, one had continually to steer around clumps of bushes and tremendous ant hills. Could I maintain a sense of direction under these conditions? Worst of all was the ever-present danger of not spotting the frequent hyena burrows that disclosed their presence only by a slight lift of the ground forming their thin roofs. A wheel in one of these would be the end of the trip. I could never get the car out by myself. Above all I wanted to save the man I loved. I knew our failure to turn up at Voi would touch off a gigantic search operation and that we should eventually be found—but would it be in time? Then there was my responsibility to the Empire—here was my future king, the heir to the throne. If anything should happen to him through my stupidity in handling the car how could I ever forgive myself?

I finally decided that thinking about all that could happen was only making things worse. I had no choice but to put my shoulder, or rather my hands, to the wheel and take my chances. As I started to move the Prince away from the driver's seat, he rallied; his eyes came open, he shook his head and it seemed to clear. "Please don't look so upset, darling—it's just the heat; I feel fine now. We'll go on now, shall we?" he said and started the motor. Somehow he managed to keep the car going and to dodge the burrows. Finally I saw a faint smudge of white on the horizon and then a black dot at the end of it. The white railroad cars of the Prince's train and the black engine were at the siding. He increased the speed and in fifteen minutes we pulled up alongside the first car. To my relief I saw Dr. Breckenridge, the Prince's physician, standing on the platform; I beckoned to him and in a moment he was with us. "I feel terribly ill, Doctor," the Prince said quietly. But even then he was unwilling to give up; he led us through the first car, past bedroom and dining room, to the lounge. He refused to let the doctor take his temperature. That could be done after I left. But I insisted Dr. Breckenridge take it. I was horrified—it was 105°.

Then came a frightening ordeal: waiting for my train to come, knowing that I was on my way back to England, knowing that the Prince was ill—terribly ill—and that I was leaving him in the middle of Africa. Duke and I were not getting along, and there would be the voyage home together in emotional fog, while all that mattered to me was lying here in a strange place, at the edge of the bush. Yet civilized behavior requires sometimes that we hide our deepest feelings and pretend that life is a ballet danced by puppets whose gestures are made by strings, and whose words, projected from distant places, are always the proper words, although voiced by others.

Duke's train finally arrived and stopped on the siding. Duke joined us and had a drink with the Prince. Duke and I then got on the train and went down to Mombasa.

On the ship, a few days later, I had a cable from the Prince saying that his illness had been diagnosed—it was malaria—and that he had been taken back to Government House, at Nairobi, and that as soon as he was well enough he was going off on an elephant safari. When I reached London I received a letter filling me in on the details and saying all those things a woman in love wants to hear. He hadn't forgotten our time in Eden.

In time, the Prince and I began to spend long weekends at Fort Belvedere, the one place the Prince really considered his own; he was himself there, free from any obligation to maintain the formalities of his official position. He puttered in the garden, pruned his trees, blew on his bagpipes. We entertained a great deal, but our guests were always the people we liked to have around—there were no dignitaries, no representatives of state and empire. Our life was quiet, even domestic. It was in fact so tranquil, so uncluttered by complications, that in retrospect there seems very little to say about it. But I did learn that the outward shyness of the Prince masked a whim of iron. I was sublimely happy; the comfortable simplicity was all that I wanted, and I was pleased that we were spared the *Sturm und Drang* that is the traditional background of a love such as ours. Politics were never discussed; political figures never intruded into our private world. I was in love with a man, a shy, sensitive, charming man. That he happened also to be the Prince of Wales, and that he was destined one day to be king, were facts only incidental to my feelings; they were elements of history, not love. I certainly had no desire ever to be queen—such an idea never occurred to either of us.

Our quiet routine may seem unbelievable to readers who expect all royal romances to follow the dramatic patterns of *Mayerling*. There were times, in fact, when my role at the Fort would have appeared to an outsider to be extremely placid.

One day, wandering through the National Gallery, I noticed two flower paintings by the Dutch painter Van Heusen, and it occurred to me that done in petit point they would be lovely subjects for fire screens. I decided to make one for the Prince, the other for myself. (Mine I still have; I wonder what happened to the other one?) The picture I chose for the Prince's screen was of a vase of flowers at the base of which were two large bunches of grapes, one green, the other purple. It took me a good year and a half to complete the piece; in one of the flowers alone I later counted seventy-three shades of yarn I had used. And almost all of this work was done at the Fort. The Prince seemed fascinated by the technique which was involved. One day, watching me, he said, "That looks like fun. Do you think I could do it?"

I was delighted to think that he wanted to share my interest. "I'm sure you could," I said. "Why don't you try?"

We decided that his first project should be a paperweight for his mother, Queen Mary. The idea was ambitious for a beginner; the subject was the royal crown, which required all the colors of the fabulous Crown Jewels. Below the crown were to be the royal initials, M.R., in gold. The Prince worked hard at this; and when it was finished, mounted on its silver base, I must say it was beautiful. The Prince then made me a petit-point backgammon table cover. The background of the board was beige; the points were in the Guards' colors, red and blue. During the war my house in London was bombed and I lost most of my things. Fortunately, this table was saved; it had for me many happy memories. I would have hated to lose it.

There were weekends at the Fort when my father came to stay with us. Papa was always fond of reading aloud. And if a visitor had come upon us on any of these occasions he would have witnessed an unexpected and old-fashioned scene of bourgeois bliss: the Prince and I busy with our needlework, and Papa sonorously reading to us from a novel by Scott or Dickens—once even from *The Wild Party*, a then-popular book whose title was ironically at odds with this setting.

One night we had as a house guest my old friend—and also the Prince's friend—Gav. Our needlework and readings went on as usual. Gav in time became bored with needlework as a spectator sport, and bored as well, perhaps, with Papa's literary renditions, he decided to go to bed. On his way to his bedroom he walked through the Fort's well-lighted halls. Being Scotch, he naturally was appalled by the waste of electricity. Conscientiously he flicked every switch that he could find. Suddenly there was a clanging loud enough to be heard a mile away. Sirens screamed. It turned out that Gav, in his economy drive, had flicked not only light switches, but the fire alarm. Pandemonium broke loose. How we laughed!

During the months after his return to England, the Prince and I saw each other constantly; our relation was no longer a flirtation, but one based on deep-rooted affection. There was then no longer any thought of Duke's joining us; Duke went his way, and I went mine. I spent most weekends at the Fort. At other times the Prince and I would go together to various parties, or dine quietly alone at York House or my house. We also attended together the numerous charity balls.

The Prince's love for Viennese waltzes set the fashion. The outstanding charity event of 1931 was the Strauss Ball at the Savoy. Four couples in costume danced to the "Blue Danube" conducted by the composer himself, Johann Strauss! I was one of the dancers. My gown, a changeable almond-green-and-black taffetta, had a tight bodice and billowing bustles. I wore a bright red wig, as red as Elinor Glyn's hair, ornamented by diamond stars lent me by Cartier. This jeweler also lent me the most exotic earrings, a dangling cluster of diamond grapes. The night before the ball we all rehearsed in costume. My partner and I were whirling around when suddenly, without the slightest indication of having felt ill, the chief of Scotland Yard, who was standing near us, dropped to the floor foaming at the mouth. Before the hotel physician could get to him, he was dead; he had had an epileptic stroke, we were told. We were all so shocked that we wanted to call off the ball, but because the event was for charity —and had been a sellout—the committee decided to go on with the festivities.

The Prince could not come to this ball; that night he had to attend Court. I was to join him later at the Fort. And when the dancing ended, I decided that instead of going home to change I would drive out as I was, in costume. I wanted him to see me in all my finery.

I paid for my vanity. Neither the period gown with its stays and full skirt nor my towering red wig was designed for a low-slung car. All the way to the Fort I had to keep myself propped at an angle between the floor and the roof; it was not possible either to sit up or lie down. What a foolish idea this was! But I was so very young. And the admiration in the Prince's eyes, when he finally saw me, made me feel that my dramatic gesture was not such a silly one after all.

That summer Orman and Betty Lawson-Johnston and I rented a house in front of the famous Cheberta golf course in Biarritz. Our house guests that season were the Prince of Wales, Prince George, and their entourage.

Biarritz is not a great distance from the famous Shrine of Lourdes, which I had never visited. I told the Prince I was anxious to see it.

"Why don't you use my plane?" he said. "You can make it in a day that way." I thought this a wonderful idea. The morning I was to go the Prince decided he would go with me. We stopped at Pau to have lunch with Lady Leveson-Gower, and then motored to the Grotto. The service was impressive. Hundreds of poor, sick, crippled people had come hoping for a cure. As the service progressed, the Prince turned to me and said, "I don't know what to do." I smiled at him and said, "Do just as I do. Remember, I'm a Catholic."

Halfway through the ceremony it started to drizzle. As the priest came by with the Blessed Sacrament, we all knelt, the Prince with the others.

The Prince was recognized by the people who had charge of the management of Lourdes, and they asked him if he would like to be shown around. He said that he would.

The last place they took us to was a one-room house, lined with pictures of people who had been cured at the Shrine. As we opened the door to leave we found ourselves surrounded by hundreds of people. Some had heard that the Prince of Wales was there; some thought a miracle had taken place. Lady Leveson-Gower, an elderly lady, turned pale at the sight of such an enormous crowd. A little girl threw herself at her feet, kissed the hem of her skirt, and said, "A miracle!"

"No, no," poor Lady Leveson-Gower said, "I'm not a miracle, please let me by."

A few days after we returned to London the Prince called me and asked me to come to York House at once. It was important. When I arrived he was surrounded by letters. On the desk, on the floor—everywhere there were letters. "Just pick one up at random," he said.

"Who is this Lady Furness?" This was the greeting of the first letter I opened. "How dare she let our Prince of Wales kneel in the mud at a Catholic ceremony? What is this country coming to? What is behind all this?" I was furious. What did they mean, kneel in the mud! A little drizzle never hurt anybody, not even a future King of England, and a prayer for poor sick people, I thought, would hurt a man much less, no matter what religion he professed.

"Sir," I said, "in your country, at the end of every performance at the theater, moving pictures, night clubs, they play 'God Save the King.' Everybody gets up—foreigners as well as Englishmen—not because they swear allegiance to the King of England, but because of respect for the customs of the country they are in. And that's all that you did." I was really angry.

"That's right, darling," he said. "That's my answer. Thanks." I never heard any more about it. Nor did I tell the Prince about the many letters I got from Catholics all over England asking me to keep up the "good work." I'm afraid they got the same answer.

Much has been written in many books about the famous meeting of the Prince of Wales and Mrs. Simpson, yet none of the accounts I have read is true to fact. Not even the Prince's version in his own book, *A King's Story*, is accurate. Perhaps one should understand and forgive his lapse of memory; the meeting was uneventful, and it took place a long time ago. But the claim to the dubious honor of introducing the two to each other is mine; and in the historical events that followed I was an unwitting catalytic agent.

In the latter part of 1930, or early in 1931, when I was living at 21 Grosvenor Square, Consuelo telephoned one afternoon and asked if she could bring a friend for cocktails.

The friend, she explained, was a young American woman married to an Englishman, Ernest Simpson. "Mrs. Simpson is fun," Consuelo said. "You will like her." And when she and Consuelo arrived later in the afternoon, I found that Consuelo was right; Wallis Simpson was "fun," and I did like her. At that time she did not have the chic she has since cultivated. She was not beautiful; in fact, she was not even pretty. But she had a distinct charm and a sharp sense of humor. Her dark hair was parted in the middle. Her eyes, alert and eloquent, were her best feature. She was not as thin then as in later years—not that she could be called fat even then; she was merely less angular. Her hands were large; they did not move gracefully, and I thought she used them too much when she attempted to emphasize a point.

We talked casually about mutual friends in America and about the London season. I asked her the usual questions about her reactions to England. Later, Gloria arrived, bringing a few friends with her, and our gathering turned into an impromptu party. Eventually the butler came up to me to announce that the Prince had just arrived. I went to the door.

"Oh, a party!" the Prince said, not too happily, as I greeted him.

"No, darling, just a few friends," I said. "You know most of them. Consuelo, by the way, brought a friend of hers, a Mrs. Simpson." Then, repeating Consuelo's description, I added, "She seems to be fun."

We went up to the drawing room. The Prince immediately began a conversation with old friends. I went over to Wallis, took her to the Prince, and introduced her.

This meeting has been the subject of an enormous amount of fiction. It has been written, for example, that the Prince, on being introduced to Wallis, asked her if, in England, she did not miss the comforts of central heating, and that she had answered, "I'm sorry, sir, but you have disappointed me. Every American woman who comes to your country is always asked the same question. I had hoped for something more original from the Prince of Wales."

Had this been true, it would have been not only bad taste but bad manners. At that moment Wallis Simpson was as nervous and as impressed as any woman would have been on first meeting the Prince of Wales.

Another apocryphal story is that when the Prince first met Wallis an electric tension was set up between them, and he then and there decided he could not live without her. This is utter nonsense. Wallis and I became great friends; actually I came to regard her as one of my best friends in England, and the Prince and I often would include Wallis and her husband in our parties.

The Prince, consequently, saw her at least once a week for the next three and a half years. It was only after this that he discovered she was more important to him than the throne.

Early in June 1931 Wallis Simpson was to be presented at Court. We were then warm friends; I shared in her excitement and helped dress her for the occasion. She wore a large cross of aquamarines that I believe she had bought in China when she was married to Spencer. I lent her the same train and feathers I had worn when I was presented. She could not wear my dress, however, because she is not my size; I am taller.

In some odd way word got around about my association with the train and feathers. At the time of the abdication in 1936, Gloria and I had a dress shop on Fifty-sixth Street, between Madison and Fifth, in New York. One day a short, pudgy man came into the place and asked to see me. I was out at the time; Gloria saw him for me.

"Well, Mrs. Vanderbilt," he said as he lumbered into the office, "it's this way. We are told that Lady Furness has the train that Wally wore at the Coronation. We want to buy it."

Gloria looked at him icily. "I was not aware," she said, "that Mrs. Simpson ever attended a coronation. You must mean 'presentation.'"

The visitor stood corrected. "Whatever it was," he said, "we want to buy the outfit."

"What makes you think it's for sale?" Gloria asked.

"Well," the visitor continued, "it's big money I'm offering the lady."

Gloria looked at him in amazement. "I'm sorry," she said. "I'm sure Lady Furness has no intention of selling it. But I am curious, just the same. Why should you want to buy it? Surely you don't expect to be presented."

"Well, Mrs. Vanderbilt, it's this way," he said. "We have bought the house that Wally was born in, in Baltimore, you know. We're turning it into a museum. We have life-size wax figures, beautiful wax figures, Mrs. Vanderbilt—the King and Queen Mary are seated on their thrones. In front of them is the figure of Wally. She is making a deep curtsy to them. That's why we want the train. You see, we want everything authentic; everything just as it was."

"I'm sorry," Gloria said, smiling. "I understand your interest, but you're wasting your time and mine. The train is not for sale."

The man shuffled sadly to the office door, then, turning, said in a pathetic voice, "Please, Mrs. Vanderbilt, think how the shrine is going to suffer."

That was too much for Gloria. "Shrine? Shrine, indeed!" she shouted. "Now, look here. I'm a very religious woman. I only put God and His saints in shrines, and believe me, Mrs. Simpson is neither. Good afternoon!" The man bolted out of the office.

The Prince had an unpredictable and somewhat eclectic interest in both business and economy.

On one of my visits to my family in America I had met Mr. Klein, the owner of the fabulous store on Fourteenth Street in New York, and he seemed surprised that I had never visited his store, which is a New York institution. He explained to me that there was no other store quite like this in America or the world. "We actually sell dresses," he said, "for as little as $2.98."

I was curious to see this "Klein's on the Square," and when Mr. Klein offered to show me through the store, I had taken advantage of his invitation. The store, as Mr. Klein stated, is unique. There were no salesladies. Customers went to the racks, selected their own items, took them to cubby-hole dressing rooms, and made their selections without supervision. And the prices were unbelievably low.

As I had been about to leave, Mr. Klein had said to me, "Won't you please accept some little remembrance of your visit here? Pick out anything you like."

I smiled and thanked him, and chose a black-and-white checkered wool suit, consisting of a skirt and a three-quarter-length coat. The suit was a little loud; you could see it for miles. The material was quite fine, however; the suit was one of Klein's more expensive items, selling for around nineteen dollars.

When I returned to London, I told the Prince about my visit to the store. The Prince seemed fascinated. "I should very much like to see your suit," he said. "Have you still got it?"

This sudden interest surprised me. I had told him about Klein's, thinking that the store would interest him; it did not follow that the suit would concern him. To a man, you would assume, one woman's suit was very much like another.

The next weekend I brought the suit to the Fort. The Prince examined it carefully. Then, to my amazement, he asked, "May I keep it?"

"Of course, darling," I answered. Nevertheless, I was puzzled. "What in the world are you going to do with it?" I asked him.

The Prince did not bat an eye. He spoke as if his idea was totally commonplace. "I am going to have some plus fours made out of it," he said. And he did.

Perhaps the most striking innovation I introduced into the Prince's way of life concerned the keeping of Christmas. It had been his custom to give presents to the members of his staff at the Fort and at York House. But I felt there was something lacking, something rather perfunctory and impersonal, in the way it was done. The selection of presents, too, was, to say the least, unimaginative: an autographed picture, perhaps, for a senior servitor, cuff links for footmen and chauffeurs, money for the rest, and nothing at all for the wives and children! This I determined to change. I went to the Prince and offered to get something personal for each and every one of the staff and families, and not to exceed the expense of previous years. The Prince admitted he had not been too happy with the old system but had not been able to think of anything better. He enthusiastically fell in with my scheme, and we agreed to make a real occasion of the presentation and have a party for the group from both establishments.

I soon realized I had got myself in for something. A quick tally showed I had committed myself to making some hundred individual purchases and on a budget that impressed me as being scarcely princely. I kept a record of each year's purchases (a sheet of which is reproduced elsewhere here). For weeks I haunted the department stores and shops of all kinds seeking out the best buys, always being careful to avoid duplicating the same thing for the same person from one year to the next.

One day in 1932 while I was so engaged I found myself in Harrod's. I looked at my watch and suddenly realized I was already fifteen minutes late for an engagement I had to meet the Prince at York House for cocktails. Now if there is anything the Prince hates it is to be kept waiting, and I knew I was in for some stormy weather. As I dashed toward the door I passed a bargain table piled high with tiny little teddy bears in green and pink. They were two for a shilling. They were so absurd the thought flashed through my mind I might make a joke out of offering a pair of them as a peace offering. A two-shilling piece happened to be uppermost in my purse, and I popped it into the hand of the nearest salesclerk, scooped up four bears, and fled. On the drive to St. James's I wished I had something more impressive for my peace offering but there was no help for it. When I was ushered into his presence, the marks of his irritation were all too plain. I quickly held out the little creatures and said they would speak for me. A smile slowly dissolved the storm clouds from his face; then he chuckled. "I will take a pink one and a green one, and you the same. Whenever we go on a trip away from each other I'll give you my green one and you give me your pink one, and thus we'll always have something of each other." And the exchange of the bears became a ritual of each departure; and in his letters from abroad he rarely failed to say, "My bears send their love to your bears." Faded now almost to a neutral gray but with traces of pink and green still showing, I still have my bears. I wonder if he has his.

The two or three weekends before Christmas at the Fort were package-wrapping time. After dinner each evening all the guests became an informal task force. Shears, paper, ribbon, string were issued to each and the production line started rolling. On the first of these occasions the Prince got down on the floor with his paper and ribbon and manfully struggled through three or four parcels. The results were hardly reassuring: the corners sagged ominously and the ribbons apparently were tied with some sort of knot he had learned to use in securing hawsers during his naval days. I tactfully suggested he could be of the greatest help if he would cut the paper for the rest of us, and this became his special task from then on. I can still see the group sprawled on the floor: Prince George flourishing rolls of ribbon but mostly kibitzing Molly Dalkeith, who could tie rings around him; Wallis Simpson keeping up an animated chatter from one corner, while Ernest stolidly ground out package after package with astonishing skill and artistry. What a boon Scotch tape would have been!

I also suggested to the Prince that I couldn't feel Christmas was Christmas without a tree. He was delighted at this and remarked, "Why didn't I think of this years ago?" Of course it ended up with my having to procure the tree, a big ten- or twelve-footer, nearly unobtainable in the London of those days, and I had to scour the city to find one. Then to Selfridge's for ornaments; being American in origin they always had the best assortment. Finally, a few days before Christmas, we would have a dinner party at York House and afterward all the guests would trim the tree and place the presents about its base in the corner of the big Reception Room opposite the great folding doors. As the grand finale the Prince would mount a ladder and place a tremendous star on the top.

The presentation itself was impressive. The Prince stood beside the tree and then the great doors were thrown open and in order of seniority the whole staff flocked in. As their names were called each stepped forward to receive his or her present, the men bowing stiffly from the waist, the women curtsying. Some of the young girls, I must say, did it with more grace than many a peeress—their mothers must have had them practicing for the whole year, a surmise several of them confirmed as I walked about exchanging pleasantries and good wishes. After the last of the gifts had been distributed and the Prince had wished each and everyone a Merry Christmas, we would withdraw leaving them to enjoy the season's cheer without the rigid formality his continued presence would have required.

After the first Christmas I was relaxed and really enjoyed myself. But how the staid Britishers would react to this newfangled foreign Christmas custom I couldn't predict, and I was scared that first time. To my vast relief they loved it, and the children were thrilled. As the doors folded behind us the Prince remarked, "Good, old girl; you've done it well." I never felt more like Queen Victoria in my life.

Perhaps next to Christmas the biggest event of the year was Ascot. The racing was exciting but even more dramatic was the pageantry, with the Royal Family riding onto the course in the state landaus with the footmen in the special Royal Ascot Livery —the King's racing colors. The men all wore the famous Ascot ties, or stock, and gray toppers, the women their most flowery prints and big hats. The Prince had always had to ride in the landau facing his mother and father, and thus riding backward. He remarked one morning, as he was preparing to leave to join the procession and I was giving his stock a final straightening, that one of the few kingly prerogatives he looked forward to was seeing Ascot coming and not always going away!

Prince George was not the only member of the Royal Family who was a regular visitor to the Fort and formed part of what, for lack of a better term, might be called the Prince's circle. The Duke of York—Bertie as he was called by the family—and his lovely Duchess, Elizabeth, were often there. They lived nearby at Royal Lodge. The Duke was more retiring than the Prince, less effervescent. He was content to live the quiet life of an English country gentleman and found his greatest delight in the bosom of his family. But he had his lighter side, too. I remember one time when the Prince had just received a new shipment of records, which were unusual for the time in that they were made of plastic. The Duke inspected them critically and finally said: "Come on, David, let's see if these are really unbreakable, as the label says."

Thereupon the Prince and the Duke repaired to the Terrace and started scaling them up in the air like discuses and watching them crash down on the flagstones. The Duke soon learned to throw them in such a way that they would soar back again like boomerangs. While the brothers roared with laughter, the Duke had us ducking and dodging like rabbits. Unfortunately the records didn't break, and the game went on until we all fled inside. They followed us in and continued their sport in the drawing room until one of the Prince's most treasured lamps was bowled over by a direct hit and only by the greatest good fortune survived unscathed. The Prince then called a halt.

But the scene I like most to remember is one winter weekend, when Virginia Water, the lovely little pond below the Fort in Windsor Great Park, froze over for almost the first time within living memory. The Prince, his two brothers, the Duchess of York, Mrs. Ralph Stobart, and I were walking along the edge of the frozen water when one of them suggested we all go skating. The Duchess and I were appalled at the prospect as neither of us had ever been on skates before. Neither her exalted station nor my piteous pleas did any good; we were given no quarter. Skates were brought down from the house, our feet were unceremoniously inserted in the boots by the laughing Princes, and we were led onto the ice. At the last minute the Duke took pity on us. From somewhere he produced two kitchen chairs for us to cling to. Hanging on to these sturdy if inelegant supports, the Duchess and I were soon able to navigate around the pond safely if not gracefully. She found the sight of the two of us thus equipped terribly funny and we were both soon off in gales of laughter. The lovely face of the Duchess, her superb coloring heightened by the cold, her eyes wrinkled with the sense of fun that was never far below the surface, made a picture I shall never forget. All her charm, good humor, and character were so evident then as always. I was not the least surprised that she turned out to be such a tower of strength to her husband and country after he ascended the Throne. I remember thinking at the time that if I ever had to live in a bungalow in a small town, this is the woman I would most like to have as a next-door neighbor to gossip with while hanging out the wash in our backyards.

Early in December Duke left for Africa on a second safari. I was to join him after Christmas; I wanted to spend the holidays with our son Tony—and of course the Prince's scheduled semi-official visit to South America had something to do with the timing of my trip.

The Prince and I met in Paris, where we were to separate—he to go to Spain to board ship for South America, I to go to Naples en route to Mombasa. I helped him write a speech in Spanish for delivery in Argentina. But suddenly I came down with appendicitis. The Prince insisted that I return to England and consult Sir Crisp English, the famous surgeon. It was not until I promised that I would that he stopped fretting.

The next morning the Prince left for Spain. I hated to see him go, knowing that it would be months before I would hear or see him again. Consequently, I was even more thrilled than I ordinarily would have been when, that night, I heard his voice on the telephone; he was calling from Santander, where his train had been delayed by an accident.

I cabled Duke about my illness, saying that I was going back to London to see my doctor and that, if possible, I would join him later. I was greatly surprised to get the following cable in answer:

HOPE YOU FEEL BETTER STOP IF YOU FEEL JOURNEY TOO MUCH SAY SO I WILL UNDERSTAND IT IS ALL IMPOSSIBLE STOP I KNOW MY FEELINGS BUT AM NOT NOW CERTAIN OF YOURS STOP THINK IT OVER STOP ALL I CAN SAY MY ONE WISH AND DESIRE IS THAT YOU COME STOP IF YOU DO I WILL TRY AND DO EVERYTHING POSSIBLE FOR YOUR HAPPINESS STOP JUST LEFT MASSAN ON MY WAY TO ADEN WEATHER GLORIOUS HOPE TONY WELL DEAREST LOVE STOP DUKE

I didn't understand anything any more. What was the cause of this sudden change of heart? I was too ill to think.

For the next few days I remained in bed in Paris; then I went back to London and consulted Sir Crisp English. He advised me that I had what is called a "rumbling appendix." The condition is temporarily upsetting but not dangerous, and he assured me that I could certainly go to Africa without an operation. Two weeks later I cabled Duke that I was on my way.

A few days before I left I had a sweet letter from the Prince postmarked Cuba. He damned the Fate that separated us, and told me that his bears sent their love to mine. He went on to say that the Lawson-Johnstons and Betty's daughter and their son-in-law, Jane and Grant Mason, had brought him gifts of rum and records to the ship. He couldn't go ashore. President Machado was in the process of being removed by revolutionaries. A bullet intended for him might hit the Prince. Only the thought that every day brought us nearer together again kept him alive—or so he said!

From Buenos Aires he reported that our work on his speech had paid off. The Argentinians were complimented and surprised when he addressed them in their native tongue, and Stanley

Baldwin had cabled congratulations to him on his pronunciation.

His occasional observations were interesting. However, for the most part he and I were the subject of his letters.

The eighteen days on the ship, on my way to Mombasa, gave me ample time for thought. Duke's cable had upset me. What did he mean, "I know my feelings?" I thought that he had led me to understand only too well what his feelings were, and they had no direct relation to this cable.

After my arrival, we stayed some two weeks in Nairobi. And for a time Duke was solicitous and attentive; but it wasn't long before he reverted to his old mannerisms, and resumed his habitual shouting and swearing. When Rattray, our white hunter, Duke, and I left on safari, I was terribly confused.

One night, as I went to my tent, I realized that this experiment of Duke's had only aggravated our situation. I had come back—to what? I realized then that the damage our marriage had suffered was far too great to mend. My husband asleep in the tent next to mine, less than twenty feet away, was a thousand miles away in feeling, in understanding. But who was I to blame him for his infidelities? Why take it as a fault that he was vulnerable to beauty and passion? Wasn't I to blame, too? Wasn't I just as vulnerable?

When the dawn came, I got up. Duke was already stirring. I slipped on my dressing gown. Perhaps, I thought, we could still talk things out. But as I sauntered toward his tent, I could hear him exploding one oath after another at the bath boy. Instinctively I turned back toward my tent. It's no use, I said to myself; it's too late—we have drifted too far apart.

When we came back from Africa, we brought with us two Grévy's zebras. These zebras, which have a much broader stripe than the more common ones, are very wild and scarce. Rattray and we had quite a time capturing these fascinating beasts.

Andrew Rattray was a man in his sixties who had spent most of his life hunting, all over the world. Duke and I stopped at his house one day, at the foot of Kilimanjaro, in Tanganyika, and I was amazed—this house could only be described as a shack. It consisted of a single room. Half-cured pelts hung on the walls. Empty tin cans—and I don't know what else—littered the floor.

Duke had an idea that these zebras could be domesticated. He thought it would be a novelty—and fun—to harness them to a pony cart and drive them to hunt meets in Leicestershire. So it was arranged that Rattray was to bring them back to England and break them in. When Rattray arrived in England, his presence, however, was a problem. His status in our household was not clear. We weren't quite sure whether he had come to us as a guest or as a retainer. Was his place with us, or was he to be housed in the servants' quarters?

"After all," Duke said, "he is an interesting man, and he probably will have much to say that could be interesting to our friends. So let's have him eat with us."

Averill was enchanted with the zebras. Breaking them in became a challenge to her. The day came when she finally saddled one with Rattray's help. How miraculous, I thought, to be able to tame these wild animals as they had done. They now seemed so gentle. Far from it! As Averill headed the zebra for the riding ring, it suddenly turned and gave her a vicious bite on the leg. But this wasn't a simple bite. Her leg became infected.

Duke had doctors flown in from the four corners of the earth. Each tried to heal this wound which wouldn't heal. Finally Rattray said, "If you will let me do something, I can cure it."

I don't remember the name of the salve he put on Averill's leg —it was something he used in Africa on injured wild animals. But Averill's leg healed. The zebras were taken to the London Zoo, Rattray went back to Africa, and we thought no more of the incident.

DOUBLE EXPOSURE

On our return to 21 Grosvenor Square, I realized that Duke and I could not go on the way we were. Living in the same house under the circumstances had become impossible, and Duke and I agreed to separate. At dinner that night at York House I told the Prince I was leaving Duke. As he took me in his arms, I felt that he, too, realized and understood that the strain we had both been under the past few months had been unbearable and that sooner or later something had to happen. Well, it happened. This decision of mine was not made on the spur of the moment; ever since our half-hearted attempt in Africa to try and pick up the frail threads of what remained of our marriage, I had thought of nothing else. My friends implored me not to be hasty. Gav was furious—"Don't be a fool—don't you know Duke by this time? Oh! you Americans and your divorces." But nothing they said could change my mind. I knew my life with Duke was over. As I leaned my head back on the sofa, the Prince's arms around me, I closed my eyes. What of the future, I thought to myself— what was in store for us? As every woman dreams of an idyllic existence with the man she loves and all that goes with it, so did I; but in my heart of hearts I realized that it was just that—just dreams. As far as I was concerned, the obstacles in our path were insurmountable.

The King was still alive, but I knew the day would come when the Prince would have to take his place on the Throne and all of the responsibilities that went with it. England as well as the British Empire worshiped him. He had endeared himself not only to his own people but to the world. England looked forward, I am sure, as another generation had when Edward VII came to the throne at Queen Victoria's death, to a new era—an era of a young and progressive King—a King who had traveled the world over in their interests.

I wondered what was going through his mind as I sat silently with my own thoughts. He startled me out of my reverie as, holding me a little closer, he said, "Oh, my darling, I am sure you have made the right decision. I am so very, very happy," and at that moment all thoughts of the future went out of my head and I felt secure in his love.

A few days later I went to stay with my sister, Consuelo, in a charming house she and Benny had taken in Farm Street. Just before I left, Duke told me he was taking Averill and Dick on an African safari later that year.

A few days before Duke was to leave, Averill came to me and said, "Thelma, darling, promise me you won't breathe a word of this to Duke, but as soon as I get to Africa I'm going to marry Rattray."

I was shocked. Taking her hand in mine, I said, "Listen, darling, you don't know what you're doing. You don't know anything about him. You have no idea where and how he lives. You couldn't stand it. Why, it's really primitive. I love you, and do care what happens to you. I implore you—don't marry Rattray."

"I don't care how he lives," Averill answered stubbornly. "I love Andy and I'm going to marry him." This speech had a strange sound coming from a girl who had always lived in the center of extraordinary luxury—with personal maids, two or more cars at her disposal, hunters of her own. What was she thinking? After Averill left, the more I thought about it the more I was convinced that, in all fairness to her father, I could not fail to warn him. I sent a hurried note asking him to come to see me.

"Duke, it is none of my business, really," I said on his arrival. "Averill has asked me to promise not to say anything, but I cannot let you go off to Africa without letting you know that she intends to marry Rattray when she gets there."

Duke blew up, but his explosion was not directed at Averill; it was directed at me. "What the bloody hell do you mean? What the hell are you trying to do? I don't believe you. I don't believe a word of it!" he shouted, as he slammed the door.

They all left for Africa the next day.

A few weeks later the London newspapers bore headlines announcing that "the Honorable Averill Furness has married Andrew Rattray, her father's white hunter." Duke in a fury cut her off without a penny. I wired Averill wishing her all happiness. That same day I had a wire from her announcing the marriage. Our cables must have crossed. Within the week came an airmail letter.

"Thelma, darling," it began, "I was delighted to get your wire yesterday and know that one member of the family is sympathetic. We could not let you know that we were getting married as the whole thing was a dead secret."

Life on safari had been terrible and her father difficult.

"Goodness only knows why," she went on. "He insulted us both in every way he could think of. The climax came about a month ago. We had a lovely row, and I demanded to come home on the next boat. After that he was worse than ever and finally sacked Andy. That was the most fortunate thing that could have happened, as it made everything much easier for us."

Rattray left when Duke fired him, Averill followed, and they were married in Nairobi with Averill's maid for a witness.

"I had no idea the papers at home would get hold of it before you got my wire. Of course there is a devil of a lot of talk here, but things are quieting down now, I hope."

Another white hunter, Lunsden, had tried to alert Duke in the jungle. He flew a plane to the spot where the Furness safari was located but a sudden and violent thunderstorm prevented his landing.

"Duke is due in town Friday," Averill continued. "If I come home to Burrough it's only to pack my things. Honestly, Thelma, it is absolutely impossible to exist anywhere near him and keep one's reason. Anyway, all that is past now, thank God, and for the first time in my life I am really happy. Well, my dear, this is rather a bitter letter but you can guess I'm feeling sore in spite of everything else being perfect. Do write to us! Torres Club, Nairobi, will always find us and don't forget I've a new name. You did not in your telegram. How is Tony? Poor old Dick will be the next one to go, I expect. He is never allowed out shooting on this safari, but has to remain in camp washing lorries and building grass banyas [shelters].

"My maid is on her way home to pack up all my stuff at Burrough. I have given her Jumbo, my dog, as she is marrying Taylor [the chauffeur] and I know will look after him. Be an angel and see she gets him. Do write me and let me know how he is. Dearest love, Averill."

What a tragic letter, and I could do nothing about it. Duke cut the poor child off without a cent. Then, suddenly, Rattray died. That piece of news also hit the papers before I heard it. I cabled Averill: "Darling, is there anything I can do? You know my home is yours."

She replied by cable that she was flying out and would be in London within the next few days. Meanwhile, Duke had come home. Averill came straight to me the moment she arrived. I hardly knew her. Although never pretty in a feminine way, she was always meticulously groomed. Her lovely red hair always gleamed from daily brushing, her skin had a well-scrubbed, wholesome look, her nails were beautifully manicured, and her clothes were carefully brushed and pressed. But now she was disheveled, unkempt. Yet lack of grooming was not the only cause of the appalling change in her appearance. She had not only coarsened, but she had suddenly matured—in a thick, ugly way. There was now no longer any resemblance to the slight girl who had been the Honorable Averill Furness. Yet in her trouble she had turned to me, and I wanted to help her.

I telephoned Duke. He wouldn't speak to her. But I was pleased when I managed to persuade him to settle £500 a year on her. However, my efforts were seemingly in vain, for shortly after this she returned to Africa and Rattray's shack, and there she died alone, of a broken heart, I am sure.

CHAPTER XX

"Take Care of Him"

Thelma

Early in January 1934 Gloria asked me to visit her. She was planning to go to California. I had not been to California for years, and we both had many friends there it would be pleasant to see again. I decided I would join her in New York—then go west with her.

I spent the weekend of January 12 at the Fort. As I remember, the guests with us were "G." Trotter, the Prince of Wales' aide-de-camp; the Duke of Kent (Prince George); the Duchess of Buccleuch; and the Lawson Johnsons. General Trotter—"G."—had lost one arm in the Boer War; he had been the Prince's aide for years and was devoted to him. In "G.'s" eyes, at least at that time, the Prince could do no wrong. He would refer to the Prince endearingly as "My Master." The Duchess of Buccleuch, who often stayed at the Fort, was an extraordinary beauty. Betty Lawson-Johnston was an American, like myself, and a great friend; she came from the deep South and would entertain us by singing, in a rich voice, wonderful Negro spirituals, many of which she had collected and written down herself while living in the plantation country. She had a quaint habit of calling everything "little," no matter how large its actual dimensions; in lilting, flutelike tones she would refer casually to the "dear little Southland" or "dear little Buckingham Palace." Ernest Simpson, for once stealing Wallis' thunder, maintained that "dear little Betty must live in the land of the pygmies."

That Saturday the Prince went off to play golf. I had promised to pick him up. Later, on the way back from the links, I decided to broach the matter of my trip to America. "Darling," I said, "I've just had a letter from Gloria asking me to come over for a short visit. I would very much like to go. Would you mind very much?"

The Prince seemed surprised. "Oh, darling," he asked, "how long would you be gone?"

I felt rather guilty. "Just five or six weeks," I answered, trying to make "weeks" sound as insignificant as "days."

His face took on a look of resignation, as if to imply that although this was not to his liking, he would say nothing that might interfere with my pleasure. "Of course, dear. Do what you want." And then he added, "But I will miss you; I will miss you very much."

I was uneasy. It was obvious that the Prince was not too happy about my leaving. I wondered if it was right to go. Little did I know!

Meanwhile, back in London, I busied myself preparing for the trip.

Three or four days before I was to sail, I had lunch with Wallis at the Ritz. I told her of my plans, and in my exuberance I offered myself for all the usual yeoman's services. Was there anything I could do for her in America? Were there any messages I could deliver? Did she want me to bring anything back for her? She thanked me and said suddenly, "Oh, Thelma, the little man is going to be so lonely."

"Well, dear," I answered, "you look after him for me while I'm away. See that he does not get into any mischief."

It was later evident that Wallis took my advice all too literally. Whether or not she kept him out of mischief is a question whose answer hinges on the fine points of semantics.

"TAKE CARE OF HIM"

The day I was to sail, I went to the Fort for dinner. Now that the time had come for me really to go, I had no wish to leave. The Prince seemed so forlorn; I felt so forlorn. When the dinner was over, and my car was at the door, ready to take me to Southampton, we said our farewells. "I'll be back soon, darling," I said as he kissed me. Then reluctantly I got into the automobile.

(It has been said that I went to America to help Gloria in her custody case. This is true, but not of this voyage: I left England on the twentieth of January 1934, and was back in London the twenty-second of March. The disgraceful case Mrs. Harry Payne Whitney instigated did not come up until September 1934—a good six months later.)

A week or so after my arrival in New York, where I had a wonderful time, Gloria and I left for California. It was good to be back in America, but I missed the Prince very much. Yet we were never actually out of contact with each other. He telephoned me constantly; and on days when phoning was not practical, he sent me long, intimate cables in our private code.

The cables were most affectionate, and I loved them; but as the Prince once wrote me, while on a tour in South America, "Cables are also very nice, my darling, but never the same thing, are they?" This was a fairly obvious observation, but love is usually expressed by the perfectly obvious. The language of love is a necklace of clichés.

As the Prince's cables were usually quite long, it took me hours to translate them into intelligible English. How I hated this decoding! When you are in love, you want to know everything at once! But the effort was worth-while, for in code you can say many more things than in bald English, open for all to read, and this way we did not have to leave unsaid all the little sentimental things so dear to the heart of a woman.

In Los Angeles, Gloria and I stopped at the Town House. We were warmly entertained by our old friends, among them

Corinne Griffith, Dorothy di Frasso, Kay Francis, Harry Cohn, Bebe Daniels, Louella Parsons, Marion Davies, Constance Bennett, and William Randolph Hearst. We were constantly busy. Yet, in spite of this, the Prince and I managed to keep our line of communication clear. One day, for example, Gloria and I visited Constance Bennett at the studio. She was that day on the set, doing a scene in a picture called, if my memory is to be trusted, *The Affairs of Cellini.* The three of us had lunch on the lot. We had scarcely begun when somebody came to our table and said, "Lady Furness, there is an overseas telephone call for you. Somebody at Buckingham Palace wants to talk to you."

I dashed to the phone.

Gloria told me afterward that within a few minutes everybody in the restaurant knew that the Prince of Wales was calling me. I had at long last become a star—a star without a studio.

A week later I was in New York, waiting for the ship back to England. Mrs. Frank Storres gave a small dinner party for me. Seated at my right was Aly Khan. At that time Aly was a very handsome, very dashing young man, with great charm—the kind of charm that makes women feel important. Aly told me that he was on his way to Florida to look over some horses for his father. The late Aga Khan owned some of the finest horses in the world and had, I believe, won the English Derby five times. Aly turned his battery of charm on me. I was flattered, although at the time certainly not interested. In the course of conversation I mentioned to Aly that I was leaving in a few days for London. I was most surprised when he said to me, in all seriousness, "I'm sailing in ten days. Can't you put off your trip for a week? We could sail on the same ship."

"Certainly not," I answered. "I can't. I've promised to get right back—I've been gone long enough."

Aly seemed disappointed. "Well, then," he said, apparently to salvage something from his efforts, "will you dine with me tomorrow night?"

I saw nothing impractical in this. "I think that would be very nice," I answered. "Telephone me in the morning."

The following morning a large box of flowers arrived with a note saying, "Will call you at eleven thirty." It is odd, Gloria and I both have a passion for flowers, and most men who have admired us have always by some intuition announced their interest in us with notes attached to impressive masses of flowers. I was pleased.

We dined together that night; we talked; we danced.

When I sailed, Gloria and some friends came to see me off. When we got to my cabin, I was surprised to find that it was massed with red roses: there were roses on the dresser, roses against the walls, on the floor. My friends exchanged knowing looks. And when I read the many cards that were attached to the various flower arrangements, I found a series of somewhat extravagant notes: "See you in London, Aly"; "Love, Aly"; "You left too soon, Aly."

I winked at Gloria, then dismissed the issue from my mind. Aly, I thought, was certainly persistent; he was certainly attractive; but it so happened I was not interested.

The following morning I was having my breakfast in bed when the telephone rang. "Hello, darling," said a voice I couldn't quite place. "This is Aly. Will you have lunch with me today?"

I took this as a joke. "Where will it be, Aly? Palm Beach or New York?"

"Right here," Aly said, laughing. "I'm on board. I finished my business and flew back just in time to make the ship. Did you like the flowers?"

All this, I admit, was very gay, very flattering. And every woman is susceptible to flattery, particularly when it comes from a man as debonair, as decisive, and as imaginative as Aly. Aly had—and probably still has—a way with women; this comes from his combination of good looks, self-assurance, and sensitivity to subtleties. As a consequence, he is an arbiter of excellencies. He follows in the tradition of men who sat on peacock thrones and constructed Taj Mahals for the women they loved. This quality of romantic largesse obviously adds to his attractiveness and conjures up the splendid images and dramatic pageants whose forms are sketched in the books notably translated by Sir Richard Burton.

I dined with Aly that night—and the remaining nights of the voyage. But as the pleasant days and nights went by, I realized that Aly's attentions were getting a little more serious than anything I was prepared for—or anything I wanted—at that time.

When we were approaching England, I told him that my car was meeting me at Southampton, and that I was driving to London. He asked me if I could give him a lift. Naturally I said yes; the trip from Southampton to London is not long, but is more fun if you don't have to make it alone.

The night before we landed I was called to the telephone. The Prince's voice came over the wire. Was I going to London by train or car? If by car, would I stop at the Fort and have dinner?

"No, darling," I said, "I can't stop. I've promised a lift to a friend."

I was in a delicate spot. I had promised Aly this lift, and I was not quite sure that the Prince liked Aly. To mention his name might have created an issue. I don't know that I avoided the issue by not naming him, but in my confusion over the phone I was not able to find a tactful solution to the problem.

"Oh," said the Prince. "Very well. Then shall we dine at your house?"

The Prince arrived at my house in Regent's Park that night, Thursday, March 22, 1934. He seemed a little distrait, as if something were bothering him. At dinner the conversation seemed to me somewhat stiff; there was not the easygoing, re-

"TAKE CARE OF HIM"

laxed talk we always had had. And when coffee was served, I noticed that he looked at me oddly. Suddenly he said, "I hear Aly Khan has been very attentive to you."

I thought he was joking. I couldn't understand this abrupt shift in the conversation. What could the Prince know about the flirtation Aly had attempted on the ship? This was really silly, I thought.

"Are you jealous, darling?" I asked. I could well afford to joke; there could have been no possible basis for any real jealousy. But the Prince did not answer me. We sat silent for some time, then we made small talk.

What had happened? Was the Prince trying to tell me something—something that he found difficult to say? Or was there something else that was bothering him? I was in no position to know.

It took me exactly twelve days—from March 22 to April 2, 1934—to find out.

Just before he left my house, the Prince asked me if I would come down to the Fort the following day, Friday, the twenty-third, for the weekend. "Of course, darling," I said, "I'd love to." Later, as I was getting ready for bed, my mind went back to the earlier scene. How could the Prince be jealous of Aly? It must be only my imagination.

But the weekend told another story. At the Fort, the Prince, although formally cordial, was personally distant. He seemed to want to avoid me. I knew that something was wrong. But what? What had happened in those short weeks while I was away?

When I got back to London, I telephoned Wallis. I needed a friend's advice. I told her I would like to see her that afternoon; I was worried; perhaps she could help me. In retrospect, it is quite evident that I chose the wrong friend.

When I arrived at Bryanston Court, where Wallis had a flat, Kane, her maid, answered the door. She showed me to the drawing room. Wallis said to her, "We don't want to be disturbed for any reason. Please answer the phone."

I told Wallis about the night of my arrival, my talk with the Prince, the odd reference he had made to Aly Khan. What had happened? Did she know? Had she heard anything? I was certain that if there were any tangible reasons for the Prince's change in attitude, Wallis would know about them and tell me. But the only answer I got to my questions was the saccharine assurance, "Darling, you know the little man loves you very much. The little man was just lost without you."

Empty as these sentences were, they were a kind of emotional bulwark. Here was Wallis, my friend and my confidante, assuring me that everything was what it had been. After a while I said, "Wallis, the Prince has asked me to come to the Fort next weekend. It's Easter weekend, you know. Would you and Ernest care to come down? It might help."

"Of course," Wallis replied warmly, "we'd love to."

At that moment Kane came back into the room and told Wallis that she was wanted on the telephone. Wallis was irritated. "I told you," she said, "I did not want to be disturbed."

Kane's face was a study in confusion. "But, Madam," she said hesitantly, half in a whisper, "it's His Royal Highness."

Wallis looked at me strangely. "Excuse me," she said, and left the room. The door was left open. I heard Wallis in the next room saying to the Prince, "Thelma is here," and I half rose from my chair, expecting to be called to the telephone. There was no summons, however, and when Wallis returned, she made no reference to the conversation. This omission would have been surprising at any time; it was all the more surprising at a moment when the Prince was the point of our conversation. The call became a punctuation mark, yet it was not clear whether the mark was an exclamation point or a period.

There was no further discussion. I left Wallis, after arranging to pick her and Ernest up that Friday afternoon to drive with them to the Fort.

The weekend was negatively memorable. I do not remember who was there, other than the Simpsons; there were about eight of us in all. I had a bad cold when we arrived; I was, in fact, miserable. I went to bed early that night, hoping that a good rest would make the cold less annoying—and less conspicuous. Most of Saturday passed without incident. At dinner, however, I noticed that the Prince and Wallis seemed to have little private jokes. Once he picked up a piece of salad with his fingers; Wallis playfully slapped his hand. I, so overprotective of heaven knows what, caught her eye and shook my head at her. She knew as well as everybody else that the Prince could be very friendly, but no matter how friendly, he never permitted familiarity. His image of himself, shy, genial, and democratic, was always framed by the royal three feathers.

Wallis looked straight at me. And then and there I knew the "reason" was Wallis—Wallis, of all people. And this was the friend I had asked, jokingly, to look after the Prince for me while I was away—the friend to whom I had gone for advice, and who had assured me "the little man" missed me very much. I knew then she had looked after him exceedingly well. That one cold, defiant glance had told me the entire story.

I went to bed early that night, without saying good night to anyone. I wanted to be insulated from the world; I wanted privacy, and I wanted to think. So much had so suddenly cascaded on my head. I was still not prepared to accept as a final truth what I had been witness to; the logic of my brain was contradicted by what I wanted to believe—the logic of my heart.

A little later the Prince came up to my bedroom. Was there anything he could have sent up for my cold?

The cold by now was a negligible issue. I searched his face for an answer to the central question. Would *his* expression be as outspoken as Wallis'?

"Darling," I asked bluntly, "is it Wallis?"

The Prince's features froze. "Don't be silly!" he said crisply. Then he walked out of the room, closing the door quietly behind him.

I knew better. I left the Fort the following morning.

CHAPTER XXI

Little Gloria Grows Up

Gloria

When the smoke had cleared from the battleground of the trial, I went with Mr. Burkan to see Surrogate Foley and told him I didn't want any of the Vanderbilt money. Judge Foley suddenly became protective. "Mrs. Vanderbilt," he said, "you will regret this decision for the rest of your life. Nobody is asking you to do this."

"Surrogate Foley," I answered, "I have not got my Gloria. I do not want her money. I will manage somehow." Of course I could no longer afford the East Seventy-second Street house, so I rented a small apartment at the Southgate, on East Fifty-second Street. I sold most of my furniture, keeping only enough to make Wann, my devoted maid, and me comfortable.

Then came other problems. The Court had decided that Gloria was to be with me every weekend—and the month of July. But my new apartment, in Surrogate Foley's eyes, was not adequate. "You can't take Gloria there," he said. "It's not large enough for you and Gloria and Gloria's governess and Gloria's bodyguards." The Surrogate insisted that Gloria should be surrounded with an entourage which would do credit to a Medici in a time of civil war.

"Very well, Your Honor," I replied, "if you will allow my lawyers, or Mrs. Whitney's lawyers—or whoever you want—to engage an apartment at the Hotel Sherry Netherlands for our weekend use, I'll take Gloria there."

Although this arrangement cost $21,000 a year, including the July visit, it met with no objection from Judge Foley.

What followed belongs in a musical comedy. Every Saturday morning Wann would pack my traveling case and we would taxi the seven blocks north and six blocks west to the hotel. My ten-year-old daughter had her own car and chauffeur; and around noon each Saturday she would be driven in this car, together with her nurse and her private detectives, to meet me. Every Sunday afternoon, precisely at sundown, this pageant would be staged in reverse.

Naturally, a situation as artificial as this was not only nerve-racking for Gloria as well as for me, but it tended to give Gloria a somewhat exaggerated sense of her position in life. There was, for example, the Saturday my brother Harry and Edith, his wife, and her three children were in New York. They had planned to go to the Bronx Zoo, and they invited little Gloria to join them. Gloria was delighted, but the nurse and the detective insisted that all make the trip in Gloria's car. When the party reached One Hundred and Tenth Street, Gloria announced that she wanted an ice-cream cone. The nurse immediately turned to the chauffeur and said, "Drive back to Sherry's at Fifth Avenue and Fifty-eighth Street."

"Why do we have to go back?" one of the other children asked, astonished. "Why don't you go to a drugstore?"

The nurse sniffed haughtily. "Gloria," she said, "only likes Sherry's ice cream."

Back they went.

During one of the weekends, when Gloria was about twelve, she asked me if I wouldn't make up with her grandmother. As much as this went against my grain, I realized how much this would mean to Gloria, and I reluctantly went with her to see

Mamma. The meeting, as can be imagined, was very strained. Little Gloria did most of the talking. My only compensation for the trying ordeal was that Gloria, going down in the elevator, squeezed my hand and said, "Thank you, Mummy dear. It was very nice of you, and you have made me very happy."

Gloria at that time was movie struck; a good part of each weekend was spent at the pictures. In time I think I became the world's greatest authority on the B and C movies of the 1934-35 period. To me this interminable movie-viewing had its advantages, because in the theaters at least we could sit in happy silence. Yet there was one continuing problem this routine raised: avoiding the press. We were news. Photographers followed us everywhere we went. They would wait for us in theater lobbies; sometimes they would slip into the orchestra and take flash shots of us in our seats. Gloria then would tremble and hide her face. Eventually, I worked out ways for us to slip into movie houses like characters in a spy thriller. We went into most of the Times Square theaters through side doors. We entered the Capitol through Mesmore Kendall's apartment, which had a private entrance to one of the theater's boxes.

One Saturday I suggested that we vary our routine by going for a drive. Gloria had never seen the George Washington Bridge; I told the chauffeur to go up Riverside Drive, then turn and cross the bridge. Suddenly, just as we were in the middle of the bridge, it dawned on me that we were crossing into New Jersey—an act that would violate the court order. Gloria was not permitted to leave the state. I had the car stopped at once. I sent one of the detectives ahead to the Jersey end of the bridge to explain the situation to the authorities, and to ask if they would allow me to make a U-turn and reverse my tracks to New York. This they considerately allowed me to do, and we returned to New York as slightly frustrated but law-abiding citizens.

When Gloria was fourteen, she asked me if I couldn't do something to have the court order changed. As things stood, she was a ward of the state of New York; she could not leave the state without special permission from the Court. If Gloria's friends asked her to stay with them in Connecticut, or her cousins invited her to Newport, we would have to get a court order before she could go, and even then she would have to be back with me for the weekends. And she was also bound, whether she liked it or not, whether I liked it or not, and whether Mrs. Whitney liked it or not, to spend weekends with me—those famous, horrible weekends—and the month of July. Gloria wanted the Court to allow her to come to me when she really wanted to come, or when I wanted her to come, and not when a visit was required arbitrarily according to the Court's timetable. The existing arrangement was as hard on Gloria as it was on me.

Emotionally and legally this situation was exceedingly strange. It was something you would expect in a fantastic novel, not in the midst of a normal flesh-and-blood family. Our family, it seems to me, was very much flesh and blood, but as far as "normal" behavior was concerned, it was distinctly amiss. "I'm in a very difficult position, Gloria," I said. "I'm damned if I do and I'm damned if I don't. Your aunt with her battery of lawyers might come back into the picture and say, 'You see—even the weekends are too much for her. She doesn't want the child.'"

I also told Gloria that I agreed with her. "But," I asked, "what will your aunt say?"

"Auntie Ger," Gloria said, "will do anything I ask."

"Well, go and ask her, and if this new arrangement is agreeable to her—and she will back me up—I will apply for a new court order."

At any rate, the order was amended and it was decreed that Gloria should come to me whenever both of us so wished. The atmosphere between us immediately changed; there was warmth and friendship and understanding between us. I was a mother Gloria turned to for advice and for help in her little conspiratorial plans. She was beginning her teen-age romances and suddenly she discovered that I was most sympathetic.

When the court order was changed, $21,000 was made available to me to cover both my normal expenses and those which were incurred whenever little Gloria said, "Mummy, I'd like to come and spend the night with you."

Provided with this new freedom of movement, I went, at the beginning of 1940, to California.

CHAPTER XXII

Dick

Thelma

Early in 1939 my twin and I took a little house called Piccola Bella, which was in a small village above Cannes. Gloria later went back to America, and I stayed on alone. One evening, to my amazement, I had a call from Duke. He was staying at the Carlton in Cannes, and asked if I would have lunch with him the following day. "Where is Enid?" I asked, referring to the woman Duke had married after I divorced him.

"I'll tell you all about that at lunch," Duke replied.

The next day he sent his car for me, and I picked him up at his hotel. We drove to St. Paul and lunched in the same restaurant we had visited during our romantic honeymoon. "Enid has left me; a divorce is in the offing," he stated, without making further explanation. I let the subject drop. We talked then of Tony, of Dick, and of many of our old friends. And again I felt very close to Duke. Our past differences now seemed remote and immaterial.

While we talked I noticed that Duke seemed extremely jittery. His movements were abrupt and jerky, and he seemed to exaggerate his old mannerism of tucking his handkerchief in his sleeve. As we drove back to Cannes, I noticed that Duke was biting his knuckles. Obviously, he was in pain. I tried to get him to tell me what the trouble was, but he wouldn't tell me.

We went up to Duke's suite, and there, Duke called for his

valet; but the valet was not to be found anywhere. Then Duke took off his coat and asked me to give him an injection—a *piqûre*. I couldn't do this because I did not know how; I had never handled a hypodermic needle. Finally, he asked me simply to pinch his arm, and he gave himself the injection. I realized then that he was obviously quite ill and required some special kind of medication; exactly what it was I didn't know.

During the days that followed Duke was extremely ill. He was kept in bed at the hotel, and almost every day I would visit him, having either lunch or dinner with him in his room.

One day while we were having lunch the telephone rang. The call was from Duke's secretary in London. He told Duke that Enid was back in London, that she had tried to commit suicide, and was then in a London hospital. She was asking for him. Would he come at once?

Ill as he was, Duke got out of bed and flew to London in his own plane. Dick told me afterward that the so-called suicide was nothing more than a rest and beauty treatment.

A few months later Duke's secretary phoned me in Cannes to say that Duke had had a very serious operation and was not expected to live. Enid, Lady Furness, had left him, "this time for good, she says," and had gone to America. "Lord Furness," said the secretary, "is asking for you. Will you come?" Immediately I flew back to London. I was with Duke until he recuperated. We spent a few days together at Guildtown, and then I returned to the Villa Piccola Bella.

The Riviera in the spring of 1939 was memorable for its divine weather. The mimosa bloomed early, turning gardens and hills into gold. The skies had never been so blue, the sun never so bright. As spring gave way to summer, Dick arrived by car with his valet. My handsome, gay, debonair stepson seemed more charming than ever.

On August 23 Dick gave me a birthday party. It was a gala

party, the last we would know on the Riviera for a long, long while. The following morning a somber-faced Dick met me on the terrace. He had a telegram in his hand; he had been ordered to report immediately to his regiment. War was at hand. Dick, Tony, our personal servants, and I left by car for Paris the following day.

When we arrived in Paris, we found that it was not easy to get transportation back to England; people were fleeing the city in such numbers that all travel facilities were jammed. Dick took over. Could passage be had on a Channel boat for his stepmother, his ten-year-old half-brother, and himself?

On August 29 the Consul General crowded not only us, but our cars, into an already-overcrowded boat. There were no chairs, no cabins. We slept on deck, as Gloria, Mamma, and I had slept, under similar conditions, in the ominous days of World War I.

It was past noon when the boat nosed up to the dock at Dover. Dick drove the car off, we all piled in, and made for the nearest hotel to clean up. As we walked into the lobby, loud-speakers were blaring reports on the present crisis. We freshened up and hurried back to the car; the sooner we got to London the better. Early in the morning of September 1 Germany invaded Poland, and on September 3, at 11:15 A.M. the Prime Minister announced that war had been declared.

Dick reported at once to his regiment. Not long afterward he dashed over to my house to say good-by. His regiment was off to France.

Tony returned to Summerfield, his school.

An ominous quiet hung like a pall over London. The chill of war gripped the city. I longed for noise, for activity, for the sounds of life. Everybody was waiting, tense, for the bombs which, as yet, had not been dropped. It was like waiting for a second shoe to fall. I lived in terror of bombs falling in the country—on Tony.

DICK

Some five months later my maid announced that Lieutenant Furness was downstairs. I rushed to Dick and threw myself in his arms. How good it was to see him! Here was a link to a brighter past. "Can you put me up?" he asked.

Could I? Dear Dick, as if I would let him stay any place but in my home. His father, I was told later, was really quite upset about this. Duke still lived in the south of France, and he had counted on having Dick spend his leave with him. But, instead, Dick came to England, although not entirely because he wanted to see me, I'm sure; he also wanted to do some hunting.

The war had turned everything into a queer, unreal, looking-glass world, with everybody and everything topsy-turvy. Yet Dick seemed still the same old Dick—gay, happy, without a care in this world. Whatever he saw was a "jolly good show," even the war. With gas rationed we couldn't drive out into the country, but we did take long walks; and always there were many memories, so many reminders of the past. When he went back to France, I saw him off. He had two greyhounds on a leash.

"Dick, what in the world have you got these two greyhounds for," I asked, "when you're going to war?"

He grinned. "Look at the collars."

On the collars was printed, "By order of Lord Gort."

"While we're sitting over there doing nothing"—this was during the first months of the "phony war"—"we might just as well have some coursing."

How handsome he looked in his uniform, leaning out of the train window waving his cap, the wind rumpling his auburn hair.

That was the last time I ever saw him.

A couple of days later London got its first honest-to-goodness air raid.

My basement was large. Air-raid officials made it a public air-raid shelter. People would dash in off the street; sometimes I would find fifty or sixty there. Day and night the bombing continued. Everybody who could was leaving London. My lawyer urged me to take Tony and go to America. My maid and I packed to the accompaniment of bombs. I put all my favorite possessions down in the basement—the crepe-de-Chine sheets I had made myself, rugs, silver, furniture. I left my chauffeur, his wife, and their children in the house as caretakers, and once more Tony and I boarded a Channel boat. In my pocketbook were one-way steamship tickets to America; but the south of France, from which we had fled ten months before, was our immediate destination.

Soon after Tony and I left England, a bomb fell on Green Street, and the drains of London began emptying into my basement. What few of my possessions were not ruined by water were sent to Burrough Court.

Tony and I stayed in Cannes with my brother Harry and his wife Edith until our ship sailed.

Duke was living with Enid in a villa he had bought near Monte Carlo. Since we did not expect to return to Europe for a long while, I called him up and asked if he would like to see Tony. Duke was hesitant; he explained that it would be difficult for him to get away. "I'll tell you what I'll do," he said finally. "I'll tell Enid I'm going to the dentist's."

What had happened to Duke? Since when did he have to make excuses to get out of the house? His voice had sounded so tired, so ill.

He came over to the house for a few minutes, saw Tony, and visited with Harry, Edith, and myself. He looked pale, unhappy. "Oh, Duke," I said impulsively, "what are you doing here? Come to America with us."

"I only wish I might," he said, "but that is impossible. My place is in England, but I am too ill to go there now."

Harry cut in. "Thelma leaves day after tomorrow, Duke. I'm giving a luncheon for her at a little pub in Monte Carlo. Why don't you join us?" Duke mumbled that it would not be easy to get away, then finally promised to come.

The day we left for Monte Carlo, Davis, Duke's chauffeur, called up. "Lord Furness is terribly sorry. He cannot come. It is impossible for him to get out."

I felt very sad. So did Tony. We went to the little restaurant, about twelve of us, including Tony. When we returned to the Hôtel de Paris where I had left our luggage, I saw Davis standing outside near Duke's car.

"Is Lord Furness here?" I asked.

"Yes, His Lordship is in the hotel. He wants to see you."

I hurried in. Duke was waiting in a little private sitting room. I've never seen a man look so frail, so mixed up, so ill. I cried, "Oh, Duke, if I could only put you in my pocket and take you away."

Tears spilled down his cheeks. "If you only could, Thelma," he said sadly.

Tony and I never saw him again.

Daisy Fellowes had offered her yacht, the *Sister Anne*, to take Duke and Enid across, as well as Davis, the chauffeur. Enid refused to let Duke go on the grounds that he, as a prominent shipping magnate, would be bait for the German submarines. However, Davis did go, and made it safely to England.

Tony and I crossed the Atlantic safely.

On my arrival in New York, Gloria and I decided to make our home in Beverly Hills, California.

We were about to leave the house one day when Wann, Gloria's maid, handed me a cable. It was from Duke's office. Dick was reported missing in action. Good God! I thought, not Dick, too! The memory of the happiness and understanding those dear children—Averill and Dick—had brought to my brief married life surged back to me. And now they were both gone!

The report from Dick's regiment, though detailed, left doubt as to whether Dick was killed or taken prisoner by the Germans. He had been in command from May 17 at Arras. His battalion formed part of the garrison. Taking the offensive, he led his platoon in surprise attacks on the enemy. On the twenty-third of May, while heading a patrol, he was wounded, but insisted upon remaining at the front instead of going along with other wounded to a field hospital in the rear. The enemy advanced. Dick, in spite of his injuries, went forward with three carriers to the enemy lines. All three carriers were hit. Dick fought on, forcing the Germans to retreat. His desperate fighting saved not only British supplies and equipment but the lives of many. Following the German withdrawal, what was left of his regiment returned to gather up its dead. Neither Dick's body nor his identification tag was ever found.

Duke exhausted every avenue of search to find out whether Dick had been killed or captured. He clung to the hope that Dick might have lost his memory, or was being held in a Nazi prison camp and would reappear when the war ended.

Dick was posthumously awarded the Victoria Cross.

In his book, *Welsh Guards at War*, E. F. Ellis has this to say of Dick:

A section of the Carrier Platoon under Lieutenant the Honorable Christopher Furness was with the column and some light tanks [at Arras]. Furness (who had been wounded earlier that night) told the quartermaster that he must turn the transport and get away quickly. I explained that it was impossible to turn quickly, in that narrow road, forty vehicles including three-tonners. The mist was rising. We should be seen by the enemy—and it had been impressed on us that the Germans were not to know that Arras was being evacuated. Furness replied, "Don't worry about Jerry. I'll go shoot him up and keep him busy while you turn and get out."

DICK

This remark was so characteristic of Dick. To the very end life for him was a great adventure, a "jolly good show."

But to return to Duke—what would the news of Dick's fate do to him? How would he take it? Halfway across America I got the tragic answer. We had driven into Albuquerque, signed the register at The Fonda, and got to our rooms, when my phone began ringing. The United Press calling; the Associated Press calling; the local papers calling. Did I know that Lord Furness was dead? I sat there on the edge of my bed, gripping the phone, trying to be composed, to speak calmly when the ache in my heart was so great I could hardly stand it. I'd had so many shocks—Averill, the war, Dick, and now Duke.

That evening I walked out alone. I thought of Duke as I had first seen him, as I had last seen him. It all seemed far away and long ago. It was a cool, moonlit night. In the distance loomed dark blue snowcapped peaks. I kept on walking until I came to the edge of the desert. For a long time I stood there, then turned back to the hotel. The mountains and stars had eased my sorrow.

The next blow was Burrough Court. It was burned to the ground accidentally while the Canadian Air Force was billeted there. When the airmen on guard saw the house going up in flames, they got panicky. It is odd what the excitement of a fire does to human thinking, and the way it impels people to make quick and irrational choices of objects to be saved. There were no firemen, and the soldiers, trying to be helpful, saved what they thought most valuable. They ignored the pictures; they ignored the family treasures and the silver and linens; instead, they saved the grand piano. One soldier, observing that everything would be lost, walked over to the piano, now sitting on the lawn. Casually he sat down and played, "I Don't Want to Set the World on Fire."

Mr. Wilson, the trustee of Duke's estate, cabled me, "Sorry to say property destroyed by fire. You haven't got even an umbrella left." I suppose he thought he was very funny. I cabled back: "I never owned one."

Burrough Court was gone. But somehow it no longer mattered. A house means little when it no longer belongs with those we love. Averill, Dick, and Duke were gone; they lived now only in my heart and my memory. And this and Tony were all that now mattered.

Among the many friends Gloria and I saw again in California were June and Edward Hillmans, who live in Montecito, a township near Santa Barbara. June was the Marilyn Miller of the English stage; she still has beauty, the charm and grace for which she was famous at the height of her career. She was formerly married to Lord Inverclyde. The nicest thing I can say about Eddie—and there are many—is that when I think of friendship, I think of him.

When I was back in London, in 1946, Tony was summoned to Buckingham Palace to receive, at the King's hands, the Victoria Cross posthumously awarded to Dick. He asked me to accompany him.

On a Tuesday morning—the day and time officially set aside for Investitures—Tony and I entered the Grand Hall of the Palace. Some fifty or sixty people who were also to receive decorations were already seated. Because of the rank of Dick's decoration, the V.C., we were ushered to the front row. Colonel Sir Piers Legh, the Master of the Household, then addressed us, instructing us in the procedure. I knew Piers Legh well; he had been one of the Prince's aides-de-camp, and had naturally been with us on many occasions.

When Piers Legh finished his address, he came over to me and asked me to go into the garden with him. "I have a message for you from the King," he said.

I was startled. And as I followed him into the garden, I was more than a little nervous. I had not talked with the King since his brother's abdication. I did not know how he felt about me at this time—and in the back part of my mind I even believed that he might resent me for the unwitting part I played in the events that led to the abdication.

When we were alone, Piers said, "The King has asked me to tell you that he and the Queen would so have liked to have you and Tony for a glass of sherry after the Presentations. But the press are all about—and he was afraid singling you out might cause talk. He hoped you would understand."

I was touched that the King had taken the trouble to send a message to me and I replied, "Of course I understand. Will you tell Their Majesties how touched I am at their gracious thought."

Later, as I curtsied to the King, he said, "Thelma, did you get my message?"

I was deeply moved. It did not require imagination to picture the brother standing in his place. I contented myself with saying, "Thank you, sir." Then I saw the Victoria Cross in Tony's hand. And suddenly I realized that all that was left of a precious part of my life, all that was left of years of friendship and happiness, was just a cross in my son's hand.

The reporters, as the King had surmised, were avidly searching for any tidbit they could enlarge into gossip. They had observed the King talking to me; and when Tony and I left Buckingham Palace, they rushed up to me. "What did the King say?"

"He said that it was nice to see me again," I answered—and walked away.

At a party at Dorothy di Frasso's I met Edmund Lowe. Edmund greeted me with the line, "Where have you been all my life?" I quipped back as brightly, "Looking for you." And this corn-fed dialogue started one of the happiest and gayest friendships I have known.

Edmund's chosen profession was the right one for him. He was a born actor; and he was a very fine and famous one. His characterization of Sergeant Quirt in *What Price Glory?* has remained in the memory of thousands of movie-goers—as have many of the other roles he has played on Broadway and on the screen. He is a graduate of Santa Clara College in California. His enthusiasm for his religion is as wholehearted as is his love for baseball and women, and his knowledge of all three could qualify him for "The $64,000 Question." His unbounded enthusiasm for everything that interested him was catching. In his company I, too, became a baseball fan.

David Butler, the famous motion-picture director, and his wife, Elsie, lifelong friends of Edmund's—and later to become mine as well—were also baseball fans. Together we made a gay and happy foursome.

CHAPTER XXIII

Little Gloria Marries

Gloria

I had not been on the West Coast more than a year when little Gloria called me and said, to my amazement, "Mummy, I want to come and live with you for good." Gloria was then sixteen. I said to her, "Now come, Gloria, this is just a little more complicated than the business of your visiting me at your 'discretion.'"

"Oh, no," Gloria answered. "I've already talked about this with Auntie Ger ... and everything can be arranged."

I said, "I think I had better come to New York and we can talk this over."

I went to New York. Gloria announced that she was fed up with "Auntie Ger," and that she should have stayed with me all along. Could I do something? I explained that there was not much that I could do. "It's up to you to act," I said. "If you really want to come and live with me, you will have to make a court application through Mr. Crocker."

Gloria went to see him. There was no opposition. In my opinion, Mrs. Whitney was by then so fed up with Gloria, and with the whole continuing mess, that she was only too glad to wash her hands of her responsibility. After all, the original court order was even harder on her than it was on me; I had to be in New York every weekend, but she had to be there the whole week. If she ever dared set a foot out of the state during the days she had Gloria in charge, I could have said, "Oh, if the Court thought I was neglecting the child, look at her!" Mrs. Whitney was well aware of this possibility; every time she really wanted to go anywhere, she first had about ten doctors sign statements claiming that she was practically dying, and that the trip was necessary for her health.

Gloria thus finally came to live with me. California became her home.

Meanwhile, Gloria had a series of adolescent "loves." Gloria had many "loves." She was first in love with Geoffrey Jones, whose home was in New York. This was the first "love of my life," and she was going to "kill herself" if she didn't marry him. When she came to live with me in California, Jeff was her "dream boat," the "man of my dreams." She was going to marry Jeff as soon as he graduated from Princeton. Gloria described him as the quintessence of everything that was wonderful.

Gloria had a telephone installed in her bathroom. Lying in luxury in her bubble bath, she would call her friends in New York—or Princeton—and talk for hours. In one month alone she had a phone bill of $900.

Time passed. One night Gloria came into my room and announced that she wanted to get into bed with me. In my bed, in the dark, she said, "Mummy, I'm not in love with Jeff any more— I'm in love with Van Heflin, and I'm going to marry him." This was an unexpected switch. I don't know what happened here, but Van Heflin apparently did not have long staying powers as Gloria's "love of my life." A month or so later Gloria asked me to meet Howard Hughes; she was in love with him and going to marry him. I asked her if this was serious; she insisted that it was, and informed me that Howard Hughes was coming to see me that afternoon.

Howard Hughes arrived. Incidentally, I found him a rather odd man: he never lets go of his hat. The butler made the usual effort to take a visitor's hat, but he said, "Oh, no!" and strode into the drawing room with his hat firmly in his hands. He continued to hold it while we talked. Howard Hughes is a brilliant man with an extraordinary personality, but his mannerisms are exceedingly strange. There is an old Russian folk tale about a magician whose soul is contained in an egg; Howard behaves as though his were boxed in his hat.

He and I talked of various things. He explained that the details of their wedding plans were entirely up to Gloria. Whatever she wanted was agreeable to him.

After Howard left, I asked Gloria if she had written Mrs. Whitney about her engagement. Gloria told me that she had. She added that Howard intended to be in New York in a few days, and that she would like to be there at the same time, to introduce him to "Auntie Ger."

"Please, Mummy," she said, "come with me."

Two days later Gloria and I, together with Gloria's phonograph —without which at this time she never traveled—a half-dozen bags, and a vast collection of records, were on our way to New York by plane.

Gloria immediately told Mrs. Whitney the happy tidings. I never learned what Mrs. Whitney thought of the marriage, because two days later Gloria suddenly rushed up to me at our apartment at the hotel and announced that it was important for her to go to Chicago at once. "Why?" I asked. "Isn't Howard expected here any day now? Have his plans been changed?"

Gloria smiled, as if to imply that nothing in life was as simple and clear cut as it seemed. "Oh, no," she said, "this has nothing to do with Howard Hughes. I want to go to Chicago to see Pat di Cicco."

There are limits to the understanding even of a worldly and sympathetic mother. "What does Pat have to do with all this?" I asked. All I knew about Pat was that he was a pleasant young man who in one vague way or another seemed to be running interference for Hughes. "I don't understand," I continued. "I thought you were unofficially engaged to Howard Hughes. Has the wind suddenly changed? Is it Pat di Cicco you are now in love with?"

"The more I think of it," Gloria answered, "the more I am convinced that I'm in love with Pat."

For once I put my foot down. "You can't possibly go traipsing off to Chicago after any man," I said to her. "You had better wait and see what happens."

In any event, Howard Hughes came to New York. I have no idea what each said to the other, or how serious this engagement had ever been in Howard Hughes' mind, but at this moment the whole thing blew up.

As I recall, a day or so later Pat di Cicco arrived in New York, and from then on I saw practically nothing of Gloria; she was always out. Finally, she told me she was going to marry Pat. Again I said to her, "You'd better tell your aunt." Gloria did. She went to Mrs. Whitney and told her she was going to marry Pat di Cicco. Apparently all hell broke loose, because Gloria came dashing to my room and said, "Mummy, I want to go right back to California!"

"What happened?" I asked.

"Well, Auntie Ger doesn't approve at all. But I don't care what she says. After all, you are my mother. You have the right to let me marry him if I want to. I'm going to marry him, anyway, and I'd like to be married in your house. Besides, I never want to see Auntie Ger again."

I then saw Frank Crocker, Mrs. Whitney's lawyer. Mr. Crocker said Mrs. Whitney under no circumstances would approve of this marriage, and that if Gloria married Pat, Mrs. Whitney would "wash her hands of Gloria once and for all." If I approved, Mr. Crocker continued, that was my own affair.

The first time I met Pat was at lunch, without Gloria. He was very tall, very good-looking—a charming man. He talked quite sensibly. "After all," he said, "I am several years older than

LITTLE GLORIA MARRIES

Gloria. I don't think this marriage is wise. I am very much in love with Gloria, and I think she is very much in love with me, but she *is* very young and I don't think she realizes what marriage really is. I think it would be better if we waited—at least six months—to see how things work out." He also pointed out a very significant psychological fact: that although he was quite capable of supporting Gloria, he could not possibly compete with Gloria's money, and that this difference in income would probably be a drawback to a successful marriage.

I agreed with Pat. I thought his attitude was quite sensible. I felt that his thinking was thoroughly honest and thoroughly realistic; I had spent seventeen years competing with Gloria's money, and I knew what an insidious, destructive force it could be.

It was decided between them, at first, that their marriage should wait. But Gloria, on second thought, declared that she would not hold up this marriage for anything; nothing was more important. It was then agreed that they would be married in December; she was to be eighteen in February.

The marriage took place in Santa Barbara. Why in heaven's name Gloria insisted on Santa Barbara when we lived in Beverly Hills I will never know; possibly she thought a wedding there would be more romantic, with the mission as a stage prop and the ocean nearby, pounding on the rocks. But at any rate all the guests had to drive up the coast a good one hundred and twenty miles. I had asked my brother Harry to give Gloria away, but when he heard that Gloria had insisted that her nurse, Keislich, was to be there, he refused point-blank even to attend the wedding. Harry had not forgotten or forgiven any of the witnesses against me at the trial. I had not seen the nurse since the day Judge Carew discharged her, but I did not want to mar any part of Gloria's happiness on her wedding day, so I resolutely put my own feelings aside.

After the ceremony a reception was held at my house on

Maple Drive. All ended well except for one minor note: we were held up. Veneta Oakie, Jack Oakie's wife, Edmund Lowe, Melba Meredith, Thelma, and I were gaily discussing the wedding and the reception. All the other guests had left. Suddenly a George Raft gangster type of man strode into the living room and, at gun point, said "This is a stickup. Fork it over." Thelma and I got up simultaneously and faced him, hoping that Veneta Oakie, who had on a fortune in jewels, would use the moment to hide them in the sofa cushions. Pointing at me, the man said gruffly, "Lady, hand over that diamond brooch." As I did so, I noticed Thelma giving Edmund Lowe a swift and surreptitious kick. I could almost read her mind. I knew she was hoping that Edmund would not take this particular moment to play the big hero.

"You know this house is surrounded by detectives," I said to the robber. He took me at my word and bolted, taking with him nothing more than my diamond brooch, which was recovered and returned to me by the New York police months later.

A few months after their wedding war broke out. Pat enlisted, and in time was sent to Officers' Training Camp in Manhattan, Kansas. Gloria went with him and did her best to set up housekeeping as a soldier's wife. It must have been an incongruous picture, Gloria, who had never in her life been without a retinue of nurses, maids, chauffeurs, and detectives—much less put her hand to a pot—now cooking, sewing, cleaning, and otherwise keeping house like any *Saturday Evening Post* American girl. Here was a solid, though banal, movie scenario: the little rich girl who discovers that love is not something to be bought and that rough hands sometimes pull hardest on the heartstrings. But I suspect that Gloria only enjoyed play-acting the simple life; as a novelty it was fun. Marie Antoinette for a single afternoon enjoyed the role of a milkmaid.

A short time later Pat came down with a streptococcus infection in the blood stream. He was brought back to New York for treatment. Gloria immediately called me in California. "Pat," she said, "is dying. Please, Mummy, come to me." I flew East at once to be with her. I was certain that Pat's condition was hopeless; only a few years before Consuelo's husband, Benny Thaw, had died from the same type of infection—streptococcic septicemia.

About three weeks after I arrived in New York, Pat passed the critical stage of his illness; penicillin and other wonder drugs had done their work. Gloria was radiant. She seemed to be going through a change, deepening, maturing. As soon as she heard the good news, she dashed to Pat's side, at the same time asking me to see her grandmother and tell her. I really believe that, in her new happiness, or new maturity, or reasonable facsimile of each, Gloria wanted to bring about a *rapprochement* between my mother and me. For at that time, even though Mamma and I were on speaking terms, the scars of the trial were still on me.

During the next three years, everything between Gloria and me was perfect. I was so pleased and proud when in some articles she was writing for the New York *Journal-American* she referred to me affectionately as "the most beautiful woman in the world." We were all great friends—Gloria, Pat, and I. But I also knew that Mamma was not at all pleased by the understanding that seemed now to exist between Gloria and me. Mamma never approved of Pat, whom she called, in reference to his father's business, "the broccoli king." Her fear of losing an infinitesimal part of Gloria's love was pathological.

On my part there was not only a resentment of Mamma because of what she had done, but a very real and persistent fear of what she still might do. I had only to close my eyes to see again the dreadful scenes at court, to see Mamma frantically clutching at her crucifix and screaming to the world the sordid details of her daughter's "shame." Her whole disordered mind, with its weird fantasies and its caricatures of piety, centered in a single, obsessive drive: to keep Gloria and me apart.

Nevertheless, I went to 14 East Sixtieth Street, where my

mother had lived since 1932. Difficult as this visit might be, I was determined to fulfil my obligations both as a mother and as a daughter. It gives me an odd feeling to write these words. Why should a woman who once had loved her mother, and who always had loved her daughter, find life so patterning itself around her that when she does what should be a normal, instinctive thing, she must say, in all sincerity, "fulfil my obligations"? I, who have wanted all my life only to love and be loved, ended as a courtier, currying favor with my own mother and my own daughter.

Mamma was not at home. I wrote a note, telling her the news about Pat; then, at loose ends, I had half a mind to go to the Plaza Theater and see a movie. But as I walked, I found myself in front of the Chalom Art Gallery; I remembered Maurice Chalom from Paris; I had not seen him for years. Acting on a sudden impulse, I went into the gallery and asked for Maurice. Little did I suspect that this impulse was to open a new, warm chapter in my life.

Maurice was not handsome or even good-looking. He was short, as American men go. He had been badly wounded, a head wound, in the war of 1914, and because of this he wore a black velvet patch over his right eye. The patch was not unattractive—on the contrary, it gave him an air of "the man of distinction." He spoke English well, although with a very strong accent.

Over a cocktail Maurice and I reminisced on the past. I told him about Pat. Time flew. He asked me to dine with him that night—but naturally I wanted to get back to Gloria, so, after promising to be with him the following night, I went home.

Upon my arrival, Orlando, Gloria's butler, told me Mrs. di Cicco had phoned to say that she was staying at the hospital for a bite of dinner with Pat. Here I was alone again. Remembering Maurice's invitation, I called him. He was delighted. I went up to my room and asked Wann to put out my new blue Ceil Chapman evening dress.

That night we dined at Le Pavillon. The dinner was the first of many, many happy dinners we were to have.

The next morning Gloria was sitting on my bed, talking about Pat while I was having my breakfast, when the most gigantic plant of mimosa was brought in. It took our breath away.

"Well," said Gloria, "what gives? What have you been hiding from me?" Handing me the card, she added, "Who's the dream boat?"

"Really, Gloria," I said, laughing, "what expressions! I can hardly understand you. The flowers are from an old friend I dined with last night."

Cutting me short with a hug and an "Oh, yeah?" she left me to my mimosa.

People have often asked me why I have never remarried. There are a number of reasons. After the trial my situation became awkward. Because, much as I might have been tempted to fall in love, what man who called himself a man would accept a life of court-supervised weekends—and the month of July—when I was legally bound to be a combination of real mother, proxy mother, nursemaid, and companion. And whatever I might have done spontaneously could have been used against me to prove that I was not a fit mother for my own daughter. Everything snowballed to curtail what might have been the normal inclinations of a young woman. By the time Gloria had grown up and married, it was too late. I had lived so long alone that it was difficult for me to conceive of marriage. I had more or less made up my mind that I would never remarry; I thought of myself as too set in my ways. This was 1944, and I was forty.

CHAPTER XXIV

Spanish Interlude

Thelma

London had a charity, sponsored in times past by the Prince of Wales—The League of Mercy. Actually it was a kind of small-scale united hospital fund; its purpose was to provide whatever facilities the hospitals might require in emergencies. Each year The League of Mercy gave a ball. Although well supported by society, the ball was never proved very profitable. By the time the costs of a ballroom at the Savoy or the Dorchester, and the costs of printing, catering, and entertainment, had been deducted, the net amount raised was deplorably small, about £800.

Two years before my ominous last weekend at the Fort I had the bright idea of getting a moving picture then being made in England and showing it at a gala preview, thus collecting a really substantial sum for The League of Mercy. The picture was *Lily Christine*, written by Michael Arlen. Beautiful Corinne Griffith, whom I remembered with such affection from my Hollywood days, was the star. We had a meeting of the organizing committee at York House, St. James's Palace, which the Prince had kindly lent us for the occasion. I believe this was the first time York House had ever been used for such a purpose. I got the management of the Plaza Theater to give us the use of the theater at midnight—after the regular showing. Our first meeting was a huge success. There were some ninety-two seats in the Royal Circle, which I sold at ten guineas a seat. When I found that all the seats there had been sold, I kept right on selling. My secretary was frantic. "Don't worry," I whispered, "I will think of something." Later, I telephoned the Prince and asked him if he would mind very much if we made the balcony into the Royal Circle. It must have been the first time royalty sat under the rafters.

The Hungarian Restaurant generously donated after-theater suppers. I got the big wine merchants of London to donate champagne. And by the time The League of Mercy party and parties ended—which was around four in the morning—we had made £11,000 net, or about $55,000.

The following year I was able to repeat the procedure. This time the feature was a newsreel anthology I assembled of all the interesting newsreel movies made of the Prince of Wales—including pictures I had shot during the Prince's lion hunt in Africa. I also arranged to have the newsreel cameramen take pictures of the members of the audience as they entered the theater. These were developed while the main feature was on, then put on the screen before the audience left the house. To make this possible, I had to get the cooperation of the police department, which waived all traffic restrictions to let the newsreel people get to the laboratories and back in time. This turned out to be a surprise and a great success, as most of the audience had never seen themselves on the screen.

This time we greatly increased our earnings of the previous year: we netted around £16,000.

Naturally, I was delighted over my success as an entrepreneur. I thought of myself as Little Miss Fix-It. And for the coming season I planned an even more ambitious undertaking. I would produce a picture from beginning to end. My idea was to show the dramatic history of a five-pound note, as it passed from hand to hand. There would be a series of episodes; and I planned to have each developed, in a distinctive way, by a well-known writer-director-star. This was to be a gigantic project.

After my break with the Prince, however, the whole plan slipped from my mind; I was too full of my own problems to think about motion-picture production.

One night, while I was in Paris, I suddenly remembered with horror that I had not done anything about The League of Mercy. Immediately I put a call through to the Prince in London to ask him if he would get somebody else to take my place. I explained the situation to him. To my surprise, I found that the Prince had abandoned all his customary warmth and courtesy. He was at this moment an official prince, talking officially. "As far as I am concerned," he informed me, "I have not the slightest interest in who puts this performance on, nor am I in the least concerned with how it is done."

I suddenly saw red. "Sir," I said, "I have put a tremendous lot of work into this project. And I'm now in a very embarrassing position, because I've asked, in your name, Sir, for all the co-operation which has been promised. I suppose the King can do no wrong. I have never hung up on anybody before, but I'm going to do so now. Good-by!" Then I banged down the receiver.

At that precise moment Aly Khan walked into my room. My hand was still on the telephone. "Come, Aly," I said, "we're going to Spain."

I don't know what made me think of Spain, but I wanted to go somewhere quickly. And I knew Aly—part of his attraction was that he was one of the few men in the world ready to do anything anywhere, any time. He had no ties, and he was adventurous. My gesture at this moment was one of defiance more than anything else, and I'm sure Aly knew it.

Aly was always untroubled. He gave me the impression that he thought himself tops—the best rider, the best dancer, the most attractive man on the international scene. Hence he took everything in stride.

The following morning, accompanied by his valet and my maid, we motored to Barcelona. Aly drove, sometimes pushing the speedometer on his high-speed car above one hundred miles an hour. Once we narrowly skidded away from death. But I was fascinated both with the speed and with Aly. This was the escape I needed. I made up my mind that I was not going to indulge myself in that delicious, if somewhat foolish, luxury of self-pity. I was going to live. And Aly was the ideal person with whom to do all this. He was gay, attentive, impetuous, jealous. There is in Aly, however, a strong Eastern quality that is not realized except by women who have known him well. His ways of thinking, his desires are, in his mind, unquestionably "right" where women are concerned. He makes demands that he expects to have unquestioningly accepted. I don't mean to imply that he treats women as slaves; I have in mind only what I believe to be an Oriental assumption—that there is an inherent and unalienable superiority of the male.

We spent several exciting, tempestuous days together in Barcelona, then we went on to Seville. We arrived there during festival week, a time that fitted well with my mood; I, too, was festive—I felt like Carmen, just after her moody Don José had been replaced by the toreador. Aly made a good Escamillo. Unfortunately, a day or so after we were encamped in Seville Aly received a cable saying that his grandmother in Persia was dying. He had to leave Seville, taking care, however, first to engage for me a suitable "guide." Whether this gesture was an expression of thoughtfulness or of jealousy was never quite clear to me. Was this to be a guide, or a guard? I thought my Spanish quite adequate.

Fortunately, as it turned out, Aly's grandmother did not die; he rejoined me the next week in London. And from then on we were inseparable. We flew to Paris, Ireland, Deauville; and we went together to every important race meet on the Continent.

One night in London Aly gave a ball at Claridge's. At about two in the morning I was called to the telephone. To my surprise, the voice was Gloria's; she was calling from New York. She explained that she was having trouble with Mamma and with Mrs. Whitney about little Gloria and that she needed me at once. Would I come? "Of course," I said. "I'll be on the next ship." I quickly called my house, told my maid to pack whatever she thought I needed, then to take the boat train to Southampton and meet me on board. I was having such a wonderful time at the party that I stayed on. Then, still in evening dress, I motored to Southampton, met Elise, and was on my way to America.

I stayed with Gloria only a few weeks, then sailed back to London. That summer I rented Aly Khan's villa at Deauville. I had as my first house guests Aly, of course; Gloria, who came over in the middle of the summer; Sir Hugh Seely; Chris Stobart and her husband. My son Tony was also there. With the house I took over Aly's servants, all of whom, with the exception of the cook, were Persians. Wann, Gloria's maid, as I remember, was terribly afraid of the Oriental contingent. This fear, of course, was altogether without basis; the Persian servants were friendly, courteous, and extremely competent.

The summer passed quickly. It was a gay, exciting time, filled with varied and delightful moments. We spent our mornings on the beach, our evenings entertaining and being entertained, or gambling at the Casino. At the Deauville Sales Aly went so far as to buy me a horse, a gesture which officially entered me in the arcana of the elect. The gesture, I'm afraid, was an empty one, although certainly charming and sentimental; at this time I was in no position to stable a horse—the hotels I stopped in were no longer inns on a post road. I reluctantly had to give him back to Aly.

It is not easy, in retrospect, to disentangle all the subtle emotional drives which made me turn to—and from—Aly; nor do I think, at this time, that it is necessary. I suppose the crux of the matter is that I was never really in love with him.

As the summer came to a close, I returned to America. And little by little Aly and I drifted apart.

SPANISH INTERLUDE

After Gloria's case ended, I remained with her in New York for some time, then returned to my house in London. It was not long after this that King George V died, and the Prince of Wales became Edward VIII. Eleven months later the world was rocked by the news that the new King had abdicated to marry, as he put it, "the woman I love." I was shocked—as were millions of others.

I had thought, as many did, that because the Prince of Wales was only Prince of Wales, without actual authority, and because King George V had a very strong upper hand over his family, his latent qualities were suppressed. And I assumed that when he acquired his royal authority he would use it dynamically and progressively—to the best interests of England and the whole world. Or perhaps he really never wanted to be king.

It is my belief that at this time the new King made the celebrity's fatal mistake of believing his own publicity. He had been presented to the world as England's Ambassador-at-Large. He had been the Prince Charming of the Empire, a man everybody loved. And, as Prince of Wales, he fulfilled successfully the requirements of this image. But when he became King, he believed that he was so popular, so powerful, so firmly supported by the people that he could make them accept him on his own terms. It seems to me that he should have known that the British Empire could not and would not accept as their King a man who deliberately flouted the most deeply rooted traditions of Church and State.

CHAPTER XXV

The Maestro

Gloria

One day when little Gloria and I were both in New York, she called me.

"Mummy, darling," she said, "I have to see you at once. Something very important has happened. Can I come over?"

On arrival her first words to me were, "Mummy, I'm divorcing Pat." I was stunned. I had always thought that this was such a happy marriage. In nothing that she had ever said was there any hint of a disagreement between them. "Oh, darling," I said, "are you quite sure that this is what you want to do?" Her answer was "Yes." I asked her if there was anyone else. "No," she said, "there's no one else." I did not press her for details. It seems strange, I know, that a mother should be so fearful of asking anything that might trigger an emotional outburst. But the psychological fact, no matter how you treat it, is that this was the case; I had had enough emotional wound stripes, and I moved, now, as if I were walking on eggs, fearful that any questioning on my part might raise a barrier and again close her heart to me.

About two months later I had a telephone call from Mrs. Marcus, the mother of Carol Saroyan, who was then the wife, or ex-wife, of the playwright and one of Gloria's close friends. Mrs. Marcus said that she was giving a dinner dance at her Park Avenue apartment and asked if I would come. For the moment I was off balance; I hardly knew Mrs. Marcus. I told her I was terribly sorry, but I had a previous engagement. I was dining that night with Maurice Chalom.

About half an hour later Gloria called me in great excitement. "Oh, Mummy," she asked, "didn't Mrs. Marcus call you?"

"Yes, she did," I said. "I'm so sorry I can't go to her party."

"Oh, but you must," Gloria insisted. "This is the most important thing in my life. I've got a wonderful surprise for you."

"I love surprises. Come over and tell me about it."

"I can't." Gloria seemed ecstatic. "I can't show you the surprise—except at that party. You must come."

"But, Gloria," I explained, "this is a little awkward because I refused Mrs. Marcus' invitation only half an hour ago."

"Please, Mummy," Gloria said breathlessly, "you must fix it up in some way. You must come!"

I told Gloria that if she really wanted me at the party that much, I would find a way of arranging matters diplomatically. First I called Maurice Chalom and explained the situation to him. We had planned to dine quietly in some little restaurant, and later to go to a movie. I asked Maurice if he minded changing the plans and going to the Marcus' after dinner. He said he'd be delighted to go.

I then called Mrs. Marcus. I told her that I had talked with Gloria, that Gloria was most eager that I should be at the party, and that I was, of course, eager to come, but that I did have this dinner engagement which I couldn't break. Would she mind if I came after dinner and brought Maurice Chalom?

Naturally, Mrs. Marcus said that she would be delighted.

So, instead of dining quietly in a little French restaurant that we adored, we wound up at the Colony. Around eleven we arrived at the party. Gloria met us at the door.

"Oh, Mummy darling," she bubbled, "I'm so glad you've come! You look beautiful! Now wait till you see...you're going to die when you see my surprise."

I was impatient. "Where is it?" I asked. "Show me."

"Oh," she said, "*it* hasn't arrived yet."

Gloria conducted us to one of Mrs. Marcus' smaller rooms and we sat down. Next to us was Pat di Cicco's niece. We all talked, more or less casually. Meanwhile, I tried to get Gloria to tell me what the "surprise" was. I couldn't wait.

Suddenly Gloria broke off our conversation, jumped up, dashed across the room, and took hold of the arm of a rather elderly gentleman with a mane of white hair. As she reached me, she said, "Mummy, *this* is *it*. This is Leopold Stokowski, and I'm going to marry him."

When I heard this, naturally I was jolted. If I hadn't been sitting down, I think I should have fallen. If Gloria had wanted to surprise me, she had succeeded. What I heard was unbelievable; she could as well have told me that she had just invented antigravity, or that she was going to live in a tree. I thought that the surprise would be Pat and the news that he and she had made up. At any rate, with Pat di Cicco's niece listening to this conversation, she explained that as soon as she got her divorce from Pat she was going to marry Stokowski. The "Maestro" stood by with Olympian disdain, oblivious to this chatter about marriage and divorce.

Finally, when Maurice tactfully led Pat's niece off to the dance floor, Gloria's enthusiasm rushed out like champagne from a bottle just uncorked. "Isn't he wonderful, Mummy? This is the love of my life. I've never really been in love before." This was a speech which by now was as familiar to me as the opening lines of Lincoln's Gettysburg Address.

Stokowski sat down.

At this moment, as if by prearrangement, Mrs. Marcus joined us, then took Gloria away. Leopold Stokowski and I were left alone.

"Mr. Stokowski," I said, bracing myself to face the inescapable, "this *is* a surprise."

"Oh, yes," he replied disinterestedly. "I intend to marry

Gloria." From his tone you would imagine that nothing more serious was involved than ordering a new station wagon. You picked up the phone, specified the delivery date, and that was that.

"I'm a little confused by all this, Mr. Stokowski," I said. "Will you bring Gloria to tea tomorrow afternoon?"

Stokowski got up and with brazen coldness said, "Mrs. Vanderbilt, it is quite unnecessary that we meet. I intend to marry your daughter. This is a statement of fact. I assume that you are still old-fashioned in your notions about such matters. I am not asking for her hand in marriage. I intend to marry her. It is not necessary for us to have any kind of meeting."

"As far as I am concerned, Mr. Stokowski," I answered, "the arrangements will be whatever Gloria wants them to be." By then I was livid. I went in search of Maurice. When I found him, I was shaking.

"What has happened?" he asked.

"Don't talk to me now," I answered. "I'll cry."

Maurice understandingly guided me to the ballroom, and I forced myself to dance until I had calmed down. Finally I saw Gloria. "Darling," I said, taking her hand, "we're leaving now. Call me in the morning."

Early the next morning Gloria phoned. "Isn't it wonderful, Mummy?" she said, bubbling like one of the Rhine maidens in a Stokowski recording. "I'm the happiest woman in the world!"

"I'm happy that you are happy, dear," I said, doing my best to hide my anxiety. "Come and see me this afternoon."

As soon as she arrived, she told me that she was leaving for Reno in a few weeks to establish residence, and that as soon as she obtained her divorce she and Leopold would get married some place in Mexico.

"Darling," I said, "do you want me to come with you?"

"Oh, no, Mummy," Gloria said "If we both go, there will be nothing but publicity. The case will be rehashed all over again.

It's going to be bad enough as it is. Anyway, you have planned to go to England with Thelma. As soon as we are married we are flying to Europe, and we can all meet there."

"Dear, I'm terribly disappointed," I said, "but I do understand."

When I got to England, the first news I had was that Gloria had taken Carol Marcus Saroyan with her as "chaperone." Then I learned that Leopold Stokowski was on his way to Reno to stay with her in the cottage she had rented. This struck me as ludicrous, and a great deal more. Here she was in Reno getting a divorce and presumably avoiding publicity, and her future husband was going to her cottage as a house guest.

The gods, who seem to have a keen sense of humor, were keeping jaundiced eyes on Gloria's retreat from the press. Gloria had just learned to drive. And when Stokowski arrived at the station in Reno, Gloria proudly drove to meet him. Stokowski walked behind the car to get in on the side opposite the driver. At this precise moment, with the gears in reverse, Gloria suddenly stepped on the gas. The car started back, bumping into Stokowski and practically running over him. Naturally, there was great excitement. The newspapers had a field day. Headlines all over the country were emblazoned with the news that Gloria, in a frenzy of anticipation, had run down her future husband.

Accidents seem to run in pairs. I heard that a few days after Stokowski moved into Gloria's house he came down with shingles. Again the newspapers got hold of the facts, and the hush-hush Gloria wanted so much was replaced by a stream of bulletins on the progress of Stokowski's recovery.

Meanwhile, Gloria turned twenty-one. Simultaneously she acquired the legal right to administer her own money.

To explain the significance of what follows, it is necessary to outline my financial position at this time. Gloria had been giving me $750 a month. When she had been living with me, I received $21,000 a year. After she married Pat I naturally did not need so much, nor did I want it. And it had been agreed very pleasantly that my income should be continued on that diminished basis.

I was sitting in Thelma's apartment in London a few days after Gloria's marriage when I got the following cable:

LOOKING THROUGH MY BOOKS AND ACCOUNTS, OWING TO HEAVY EXPENSES, I CAN NO LONGER CONTINUE YOUR MONTHLY ALLOWANCE. GLORIA.

I was frantic. Here I was without a penny—in a desperate situation. I wired her back:

DEAR GLORIA: WHAT YOU TERM "MONTHLY ALLOWANCE" IS MY SOLE MEANS OF LIVELIHOOD. PLEASE RECONSIDER. LOVE, MUMMY.

Gloria replied with a terse letter in which she said there was nothing to reconsider, and that there was no reason why she should support me at all. And that was that.

I decided to go to New York at once. The war had been over only a short time and it was difficult to get reservations of any kind. Plane seats were booked for months in advance. On all sides I was frustrated. Suddenly I remembered that in my youth I had known Juan Trippe, who had since become president of Pan-American Airways. Twenty years at least had passed since I had last seen him. Nevertheless, I wired him telling him of the situation I was in, and asking him if he would do what he could to get me on one of his planes. The following morning the Pan-American office in London called me, saying that they had a cable from Juan Trippe announcing that I was to be on the next plane leaving for New York. This plane, they informed me, left at noon—in three hours. This was a wonderful gesture on Juan Trippe's part, and I shall never forget it.

I arrived in New York but with no place to stay. Maurice Chalom had just remodeled and decorated an apartment to rent, and he let me have it as a temporary residence. As soon as I had unpacked, I tried to reach Gloria. This turned out to be a formidable operation. I had her old telephone number, but in the interim she had had it changed, I discovered, to a new and unlisted number. I did not know Stokowski's unlisted number. I called up his agents, but they would give me no information. I called my mother. Even she refused to give me Gloria's number. The door was closed wherever I turned.

My immediate problem was survival. The only thing I owned that had any cash value was my diamond engagement ring. I went to a wholesale diamond merchant whose name I think was Brock. "How much will you offer me for this ring?" I asked. The Brock experts examined the stone and said, "Thirty thousand dollars." I accepted.

A few months after I sold the ring, an article appeared saying that Gloria had offered to buy it for $300,000. Somebody apparently had tacked on a few zeros. My mother was very funny about this; she thought I had been cheated and that the diamond had really been worth $300,000. In fact, by the time the press got through with the story you would have thought that this was the Cullinan diamond, the Kohinoor, and the Star of India all rolled into one. And you would have believed that Gloria actually made this offer which, of course, was ridiculous. Some reports gave the figure as $100,000, some $150,000, and some the full $300,000. The price varied with the imagination of the writer. By the time the full force of the press was evident, the diamond had passed into the hands of a Mr. Jack Werst of Dayton, Ohio, a man whose publicity agents could be said literally to leave no stone unturned.

Here is a typical item from a story by-lined by Justin Gilbert in the New York *Daily Mirror*, March 15, 1956:

> Gloria Vanderbilt Stokowski has offered as high as $100,000 for the 16½ carat pear-shaped diamond ring her mother, Mrs. Gloria

Morgan Vanderbilt, sold to a Dayton, Ohio, gem dealer last month, after her daughter had cut off her $21,000 yearly allowance.

The *Mirror* yesterday learned exclusively that Gloria, Jr., to whom the ring has a great sentimental value, sent two gem brokers from New York and California to offer the large sum to Jack M. Werst, Dayton dealer, who bought the ring for $30,000 from her mother.

"I don't like to disappoint Gloria, but the ring isn't for sale at present," Werst said. "I'm going to hold it for at least a year." ... and he predicted its value would increase because large-size diamonds are disappearing from the market....

He told how Mrs. Vanderbilt had put out a feeler for the sale of the famous gem early last February. "She wanted $75,000," Werst said, "and I turned it down. After a few weeks of waiting she accepted an offer of $30,000 from my broker!"

The real value of the diamond, I was later to learn, was in the publicity it brought Mr. Werst. It was exhibited in almost every city in America. It even turned up on display in the lobby of the Capitol Theater in New York, an *advertisement,* by some remote association, for the motion picture, *King Solomon's Mines.*

A letter later written to Mr. Werst by Guy Wadsworth of the Dayton *Journal-Herald,* and reprinted in one of Mr. Werst's brochures, had this proud comment to make: "You will be happy to know that my exhaustive research on diamonds reveals that the Vanderbilt diamond which you own has received more newspaper and magazine publicity than any other gem in the world since the turn of the century."

Meanwhile, with Maurice Chalom as partner, I started a perfume house. Two years passed. Then one morning, while I was in Pennsylvania seeing a bottle manufacturer, Gloria called me at home. My maid took the message.

When I got home at nine o'clock that night I called Gloria. And as if nothing at all had ever happened over the intervening years, Gloria purred, "Oh, Mummy darling, Stokie"—by that time she was calling him Stokie, not Leopold—"Stokie and I are sitting in our little apartment... in front of the fireplace... and we're having a drink. Wouldn't you like to come down?"

"I'm terribly tired," I said. "I have just come back from Pennsylvania, and I really don't feel up to getting dressed and going out again. Can't you come up here?"

"Seriously, Mummy," Gloria went on, "Stokie and I really want to see you. He's not dressed. Can't you come here?"

I said to myself: Here we go again! Once more I'm damned if I do and I'm damned if I don't. If I don't go there, then, later, Gloria will say, "Well, I asked her to come and she didn't." I could almost hear Stokowski saying to Gloria, "If you want to see your mother, let her come down here." I decided I would never give her a chance to say she had asked to see me and I had refused to meet her. So at ten o'clock that night, tired as I was, I went to their apartment.

The place was somewhere in the West Fifties—a brownstone in which they had the top floor. You took the elevator as far as it went, then walked up a circular iron staircase to their apartment, which consisted of one room and a terrace.

I was so very happy, after these long years, to see Gloria again. She looked so lovely as she embraced me. We chatted for a bit, then, sitting me down beside her, she said, "Mummy, darling, I think all this money business has been very silly. Can't we work out some arrangement?"

"Of course, darling. I would like to feel that I could have my own apartment and Wann. I'm sure that $6,000 a year would be adequate. Don't you?"

Gloria said nothing.

I continued: "If you will set up a trust fund that will give me $500 a month for my lifetime, and which will revert to you after my death, we will never again have to discuss money."

Stokowski during this conversation had said nothing. But now, when I had finished what I was saying, Gloria looked at him questioningly, as if seeking guidance. The only thing Stokowski did was close his eyes. Immediately Gloria turned back to me and said, "I don't believe in trusts."

I fixed my eyes on Stokowski. "Mr. Stokowski, you must realize that when I say 'a trust to revert to Gloria at my death,' she is risking nothing."

Stokowski did not bother to answer. He merely looked at Gloria. Gloria then added, without further explanation, "I just don't believe in trust funds."

This statement was ridiculous. "Listen, Gloria," I said, "if it weren't for a trust fund your grandfather left, neither you nor I would be sitting here talking about trust funds. You would have nothing."

"No, no!" Gloria repeated, again looking at Stokowski, "I just don't believe in them."

"Now, look here, Gloria! You are the one who said you wanted to do something about all this. We seem to be getting nowhere fast. Suppose you talk to your lawyer. I'll talk to mine. Then let both lawyers meet. Let's see what arrangements the two of them can make."

"Sure," Gloria agreed. "Let the lawyers work out the details."

We talked about other things—her travels, the place they had in Connecticut. Then I left. Stokowski, still in his dressing gown, saw me to the elevator.

The following morning I called Mr. Kaufman, my lawyer since Mr. Burkan had died, and asked him to get in touch with the Stokowskis' lawyer.

About six o'clock that evening Mr. Kaufman called back. He was in such a rage he could hardly get his words out. "Wait a moment," I said, trying my best to calm him. "What's happened?"

"Well," he said, "I've just... I've never in my life heard anything like this. Mrs. Stokowski's lawyer came to my office, and sitting opposite me, said blandly, 'These are the instructions I have from Mrs. Stokowski: She is willing to give Mrs. Vanderbilt $6,000 a year—paid monthly—provided that Mrs. Vanderbilt will be willing to receive it if, and when, and where Mrs. Stokowski chooses to give it. In other words, if Mrs. Stokowski chooses to give it to her in China, then Mrs. Vanderbilt will have to move to China.'"

"This is incredible," I said.

Mr. Kaufman continued telling me what his rejoinder had been.

"In other words, what you are telling me is that Mrs. Stokowski proposes to hold a sword of Damocles over her mother's head?"

And Gloria's lawyer answered, "Yes. That is exactly what she is doing. Those are my instructions. And if Mrs. Vanderbilt will not accept the money on these terms, Mrs. Stokowski will not give her anything."

"I'll call Gloria up in the morning, Mr. Kaufman," I said, and hung up.

When I got her on the phone her voice had lost all the warmth and affection of two nights before.

"Gloria," I said, "I understand that our lawyers did not seem to get on very well."

"No," Gloria said, "they didn't."

"Well," I asked, "what are you going to do about it?"

"My lawyer was right," Gloria answered coldly.

"Do you mean to tell me that you told your lawyer that you gave him authoritative instructions to say to my lawyer that you want to hold a sword of Damocles over my head... or else?"

"You're damn right," she said. "That's exactly what I mean."

"I'm terribly sorry, Gloria," I answered. "I think it was a mistake that I went to see you at all. But if this is the way you feel about it, don't even bother to remember that I'm alive. Good-by."

A few days later Gloria called a press conference. It seemed to me that our money differences were our private affair, but

THE MAESTRO

Gloria considered them, like the reports of the President's health, matters of national and international concern. She hired a press agent. And he invited reporters from all the papers and wire services to a meeting at her apartment on Fifty-fourth Street. Stokowski was not on hand, leaving Gloria and her publicity man to justify her position in this mother-daughter dollar diplomacy.

The papers came out the next day with banner headlines featuring the news: "Gloria says: 'My Mother Can Work or Starve.'"

I did not hear from Gloria again for five years. At this time my lawyer called me and said, "Mrs. Vanderbilt, Mrs. Stokowski, it seems, has instructed her bank to deposit $250 a month in your bank."

"I don't want it," I answered. "I won't accept it. I think this is insulting."

"Mrs. Vanderbilt, please think it over; this may be her way of opening the door to a better understanding. You never can tell what this will lead to; you'd better take it."

"Very well, then," I said, "accept it."

Her lawyers opened an account in my name and each month the $250 was deposited in it. I never thanked Gloria for this "kindness." All during this time Thelma had been supporting me.

357

CHAPTER XXVI

Together

Thelma

In 1947, when I was in London, my twin telephoned me from New York saying she was going to have an operation for some internal disorder. I was worried and planned immediately to fly over. Gloria assured me that this was not necessary, as the operation was not serious. I came over, in spite of what she said. Meanwhile, she had the surgery; the results appeared to be satisfactory, and she was sent home.

One Sunday evening, about a month later, Gloria and I were sitting quietly in her apartment listening to the radio. About halfway through the program, Gloria told me that she was feeling tired and not too well and that she thought she would go to her room and go to bed.

"I'll just finish the needlework I'm doing," I told her, "then I'll come in and say good night."

About half an hour later I went to Gloria's room and there I found her biting her hands in agony. Her hands were bleeding, the pillow was covered with blood. She had not wanted to worry me, she didn't want to call out. As this was a weekend, it was not easy to get a doctor immediately. Finally, after much telephoning I located Gloria's doctor. He came over, gave her sedatives, but seemed puzzled about the cause of the pain.

It was then long after midnight. "Doctor," I said, "I'm worried."

"I am, too," he said. "I think we should get Mrs. Vanderbilt to a hospital at once; and we should have a consultation with a specialist."

The doctor sent for an ambulance to take Gloria to Harkness Pavilion, at the Medical Center, and arranged to have a specialist meet us at the hospital. In the dead of night we strapped Gloria to a chair; the elevator in Gloria's building was too small to hold a stretcher. We got her to the ground floor this way, then transferred her to a waiting stretcher. I rode with her in the ambulance. Meanwhile, Gloria kept saying to me, "Darling, what is the matter with me? Am I going to die? I think I'm dying." What terrifying words to hear from a person you love, from a twin whose life is part of your very own. I felt as if I myself were dying as I repeated, over and over, "Of course not, darling! You're not going to die!" and other empty reassurances which I needed as much as Gloria.

At the hospital a team of doctors went to work making emergency examinations and taking a variety of tests. I sat through the long night in one of the side rooms, trembling, waiting to hear frightening news.

About six o'clock in the morning the consulting doctors came out of surgery. Their faces were grim. "I think you had better send for the family," one said. "There isn't much chance."

A general feeling of numbness came over me. I was sure Gloria was not going to die. I wouldn't let her. This couldn't happen; it was unthinkable. I couldn't accept it. I would will her to live. But I was too numb to analyze or reason. All feeling had gone out of me. I went back to the apartment, had a cup of coffee, then called my brother Harry, who was in California. I called Consuelo, who was in Palm Beach. Then I called my mother. I asked Mamma for the telephone number of little Gloria. Mamma pretended she didn't know it. She must have had Gloria's number, because she talked to her practically every day. She obviously had been instructed not to give it to me.

Finally I called a friend who worked on a newspaper and told her of the situation. I asked her if she could get the number for me. She did; it was in Connecticut. I reached Gloria and told her that her mother was dying, and that the doctors had asked me to send for the family. Gloria said she would come in at once.

The doctors informed me that they were going to operate. Gloria was taken to surgery, and I was ushered into a small waiting room outside. And there I sat from nine o'clock on, dying myself by slow degrees. The hours passed. There was no word. And I, in my cold sweat, asked myself unreasonably why some doctor did not come out and let me know what was happening. Around eleven, little Gloria arrived looking gay and quite beautiful in a very long mink coat. "What's the matter?" she asked.

"Your mother is being operated on," I said. "I don't know what's happened, or what kind of an operation it is. All I can tell you is that it is an emergency, and she has already been in the operating room two hours. Oh, Gloria, dear, I am so worried!"

Gloria was quiet. I sat staring out the window.

A while later Gloria broke the deadly silence. "Thelma," she said, "by the way, you've been in Europe a lot recently.... Stokie and I are going there on a concert tour. What should I take over as far as food is concerned, and clothes? I hear they're all starving there. And of course Stokie must have proper food. Should I take canned goods and cigarettes?"

I stood this as long as I could. Then I said, "Listen, here, Gloria! Your mother may be dying at this moment, and you've got nothing better to do than to start worrying whether or not you're going to have enough to eat. Really, if at this time you can't talk about your mother, don't talk about anything."

About a quarter to twelve a nurse came in and announced that the operation had been successful and that now there was hope that Gloria would pull through. Until then I had held myself in quite well, but now I burst into tears. Little Gloria got up, put on her coat, looked at her watch, said, "I have an appointment at the hairdresser," and left.

Gloria was in the hospital three months; and during all this time her survival was a matter of touch and go. It appeared that an aftereffect of her previous operation was an abscess which, in turn, had caused peritonitis. Yet in this whole desperate period there was no further word from little Gloria—not even a phone call.

The doctors' bills and the hospital bills were, of course, enormous. I used all the money I had, but my money came from England, and it was extremely difficult to get any but a token amount out of Great Britain. I went to my mother and asked her if she could help me. She did—not very much, but she did help. I decided to write to young Gloria and tell her that these bills had to be met, and that I simply didn't have enough actual cash with which to pay them. If she would lend me the money, I would repay her just as soon as the English regulations would allow my reserves to be drawn on in this country. I wrote her a letter saying exactly this, and sent it to her by messenger. The letter was returned, unopened.

I was furious. I decided that if she would not answer my letter, I would go and face her.

One morning, at about ten o'clock, I rang her doorbell. The door was opened by a woman who, I assume, was Stokowski's secretary. I walked right in before she realized who I was. "I am Lady Furness," I said, "and I want to see Mrs. Stokowski."

"Just a minute," the woman answered. "I'll see if she's in." Meanwhile, she ushered me into the drawing room, a large room whose chief feature was a library of Stokowski's recordings. I sat and waited. Shortly after, the doorbell rang, and in walked Stokowski. The secretary, who had opened the door, must have told him that I was waiting, and as he entered the hallway, he strode past the open archway that led into the room in which I was sitting.

"Oh, Mr. Stokowski!" I called out to him. "May...."

Stokowski did not even turn his head. He walked straight on and disappeared in the back part of the house. I then heard his voice and Gloria's in the back room.

I was stunned by his rudeness. My instinct was, of course, to leave at once. But love for my twin was a more compelling force than pride. I said to myself, "They have to pass me if they want to get out, and I'm going to sit here just as long as they hide in the back."

But nothing happened; nobody came near me. About an hour later I rang the first bell I could find. Orlando, the butler, whom I knew well from happier days when Gloria was married to Pat, came in.

"Orlando," I said, "will you please tell Mrs. Stokowski that if she doesn't come in here to see me I'm going into the back to see her?"

"I'm terribly sorry, Lady Furness," Orlando answered, "but Mr. and Mrs. Stokowski went out the back door."

I was terribly angry, both at them and myself. First, I considered that I had been stupid enough to sit quietly waiting when I should have marched straight to where Gloria was hiding. Second, I was incensed that Gloria and Stokowski should be so insulting and so cowardly as to sneak out of their own house through the back door, to avoid facing me.

It is amazing the temperament that little Gloria has. How can a normal girl possibly be as affectionate as she seems to be at one moment, then the next day for no apparent rhyme or reason not speak to you? The change is what you would find in a book of short stories. You read one, and say to yourself, "This is charming." You put down the book. The next day you read another story, and you find that the action has nothing to do with the life of the central character in the first story; it is the account of another person—quite the reverse of charming. One day Gloria would be overaffectionate, sentimentally tender; everything would be "Oh, Mummy darling this," and "Oh, Mummy darling that"; and then, suddenly, without any understandable cause, she would turn and send a wire like the one she sent Gloria saying, "Looking through my books and accounts... I can no longer continue your monthly allowance." It doesn't make any sense.

I could not understand such a mental turnabout without any provocation. If my twin, for example, had said something cutting, such as "I think this marriage is ridiculous," or "What do you mean, marrying a man old enough to be *my* father?" little Gloria's hostility would make sense. But Gloria didn't do anything of the sort. On the contrary. She said, "Darling, if this is what you want, and this means your happiness, go ahead and do it, and you have my blessing." Now you can't get angry at a mother who does everything she can to make it possible for you to have whatever it is you think you want.

I think she must be either strangely influenced at such moments, or she had an odd flight of ideas.

In 1950, when Tony was about to turn twenty-one, Gloria and I were together in London. We all wanted to make Tony's coming-of-age a festive event; we wanted to stage something different from a run-of-the-mill party. But what? London at this time was a network of rations and restrictions; even ordinary parties posed a vexing problem.

My darling Tony came up with a brilliant idea. He proposed that we should pack up the friends he wanted at the party— and fly them all to Paris for a long weekend. Most of them had never been to France before, because of the war.

It was arranged. The girls stayed at the Hôtel Monceau, with

Gloria and me as chaperones. Tony and the boys were billeted at another hotel. The first night we took them all to the theater—then to a night club for supper and dancing. The following evening I gave a beautiful dinner—for some forty or fifty—at Maxim's. The young people were placed at one end of the table. At the other end Gloria and I sat, with our friends. It was a happy, festive evening; and everyone applauded when Tony's birthday cake arrived, decorated with the Furness coat of arms.

After church, Sunday morning, we all went, in a fleet of cars, to Maurice Chalom's beautiful château at Maule, where he had invited us to spend the day and evening. No one I know gives more enchanting parties than Maurice; and this day he outdid himself. About sixty of us sat down to a delicious lunch. Later we were given *le tour de la propriété*. The gardens were lovely; the spring flowers were in bloom. At teatime, children from the village, dressed in their colorful native costumes, entertained us with folk songs and dances.

Soon after we returned to London, Tony took his seat in the House of Lords. My heart was pounding when Gloria and I entered the House to hear him make his maiden speech. To make matters worse for me, Gloria and I were seated in different places: Gloria was taken to the distinguished visitors' gallery; I, as a peeress, was required to sit in the Peeresses' Gallery. When Tony got up to speak, I said a little prayer. But my worry was unnecessary. Tony showed no sign of nervousness; he spoke clearly and with authority. I was very proud of him. And I was pleased when, some time later, Lord Hawhe wrote in the *Official Report of the Parliamentary Debates* that he wished to congratulate his "noble friend, Lord Furness, on the magnificent way in which he carried off his maiden oration." Gloria left for New York shortly after this.

Tony now is an active member of the House, and takes great interest in the legislative affairs of his country.

TOGETHER

Gloria

One day, after I had returned from London—where I had visited Thelma—I went to see Mamma. Mamma spoke of her "precious little grandchildren"—my grandchildren. For the past year or so, ever since there were two of little Gloria's children, Mamma would talk to me, each time I saw her, about "my precious little grandchildren"—totally effacing me, the actual grandmother, from the picture. She repeated this phrase until I thought I would go out of my mind. I had never seen my grandchildren and Mamma knew it. One day I reminded her of this fact.

"I'll tell you what, Gloria," she said with the air of someone conferring a special favor, "my precious babies are coming to see their *grandmamma* tomorrow at three. Why don't you sit downstairs in the lobby—but be sure it's way in the back—and watch them go by?"

"Mamma," I said, "how heartless can you be?"

My mother looked at me as though she had no idea of what I was talking about, and as though she had made a perfectly reasonable suggestion for which I was too unreasonable even to be grateful.

Suddenly a thought flashed through my mind: what a difference between the feeling of Mamma and the spontaneous thoughtfulness of Ceil Chapman, a devoted friend who, immediately on hearing over the radio that my first grandson had been born, telephoned me in Barcelona where I had gone to see Dr. Arruga, the famous eye specialist, because of my failing sight. Her one idea was that I might be hurt if I learned of it through the newspapers. Mamma never did let me know, and now she was suggesting that I do a Stella Dallas in order to see my own grandchildren.

DOUBLE EXPOSURE

In 1955 Thelma decided to move to Nassau, B.W.I., and of course I went with her. Some seven or eight months later Mamma wrote us saying she was desperately ill. Could we come to her? She needed us. She said she had no idea where little Gloria was. She was all alone in her hotel, and afraid. Naturally, we went to her at once. Our feeling was that no matter what Mamma had done to us, she was, after all, our mother, and if she needed us, our place was with her.

On our arrival the doctor advised us that she should be taken to the Doctors Hospital for blood transfusions.

Mamma had never before been a hospital patient, and the moment she was settled in her bed she began to complain. "Of course," she said, "you, twins, would put me in the oldest hospital in New York."

We were indignant. "Your doctor chose this hospital, Mamma," I said, "not Thelma or I. And this doesn't happen to be the oldest hospital in New York. It's one of the best and most modern."

"Look at this bed," Mamma groaned, "it's so old it's broken in three parts."

The bed was the type of hospital bed whose parts are hinged so that they can be raised or lowered for the patient's comfort. Mamma never accepted our explanation of this and insisted, until the day she went back home, that this was the oldest hospital in town and the beds the most antiquated. Yet it was only a few hours after Mamma returned to the hotel that she began to miss her comfortable "antiquated" bed. And to the relief of the nurses who had to lift her and listen to her complaints, we immediately got one in.

From that time on Mamma was bedridden. It was heart-rending to see this dynamic, high-spirited woman gradually fade away. Toward the end she would ask us to lift her hands, saying, "They are beautiful, aren't they?" And the only expression left in her once flashing eyes was a look of pleading helplessness.

TOGETHER

Mamma had always been a very vain woman. She had not had her hair dyed in months and at this time she was completely gray; she was too ill to keep up appearances. She was, however, quite cute about the change. Just before she died, she asked for a mirror. We brought one to her. Looking at herself, she said, "Oh, my darlings, you see, all these shocks have turned my hair gray overnight."

Mamma died a month later, in her own bed, at the hotel. She was buried from the Lady Chapel in St. Patrick's Cathedral, where she had been married. Little Gloria came to the service with Carol Saroyan, and we were shocked to observe that she sat on the side opposite to ours. She left as soon as Mass was said.

The only people at Mamma's grave were Thelma, Wann, and I. The grave is marked by a simple white shaft on which is carved the inscription she requested: "I implore eternal peace."

Mamma left me $80,000 in her will. Once it was paid to me, Gloria sent word through her lawyer that she once again was discontinuing any personal contribution to my support.

A short time after the funeral Gloria married Sidney Lumet.

I hoped that in her new-found happiness Gloria might find it in her heart to share a little of it with me. But this was not to be. Even the ceremony itself was kept hidden from me. One night Thelma and I were watching television and I saw Gloria and Sidney Lumet at their wedding reception, and I realized, to my horror, that this spectacle was being flashed from coast to coast. At this moment I couldn't help but think back to that memorable time when Gloria, then about to marry Stokowski, expressed a desire not to have me go with her to Reno, saying, "Please, Mummy darling, think of the publicity."

Years ago, in the Twenties, when we were in Paris, we had the good fortune to meet the renowned chemist, Dr. Alexander Farkas. At that time he paid us the charming compliment of blending an exquisite fragrance just for us. At a party shortly before Mamma died we again met this brilliant man and we were delighted when, a few days later, we received two of the most divine and exciting fragrances together with a note: "With the compliments of Alex Farkas to the charming and glamorous *jumelles.*"

We were so excited and thrilled with the beautiful perfumes that we telephoned Dr. Farkas at once, not only to thank him but to ask him if he would make up some more for our use. Our friends all asked us where we had obtained these enchanting fragrances. The idea then gradually grew on us that these blends should be on the market. And thus it was that the company, Parfums Jumelles, was born.

Thelma

Gloria and I are now businesswomen. We live together quietly in a small apartment in New York. We divide our time between our office and traveling about the country visiting our outlets. And we are delighted, and sometimes a little sorry, that we seem to have less and less time to ourselves. But every day we are encouraged to believe that American perfumers, like American designers, can match and exceed anything the Old World can produce.

This life is a vast change from the rounds of balls we knew as young girls. Our world is no longer that of safaris, holidays on the Riviera, stalking in the Highlands, the Newport season, racing at Saratoga, and the great balls of London between the wars.

The events in our lives, like all events in all lives, were the outcome of that always unpredictable blend of chance and temperament. If we had our lives to live over again, we should probably proceed exactly as we did in the past, making the same mistakes in different ways.

Ours was an age this world will not see again, at least not in the same forms. It was an age of splendor and extravagance, of great projects and great follies. Between the two World Wars many changes have occurred: the great fortunes have dwindled, the great balls and parties have disappeared from the social scene, "society" has become a word of ambiguous meaning. Meanwhile, new industries and arts have risen; prohibition has come and gone; and the age of air and space travel and of nuclear fission has replaced the F. Scott Fitzgerald age in which we spent our youth.

We belong to the present as well as the past. We look back with no nostalgia, except for the sense of loss that comes with the passing of those we loved. Every age has its charm and its moments of beauty. And it is of these that we have tried to write, framing their special quality in the events that shaped our lives.

As Lord Byron wrote:

> "All who joy would win
> Must share it—happiness was born a twin."

(Continued from front flap)

of the period. The Edwardian era had its Lily Langtry, the Napoleonic its Josephine, the eighteenth century its Du Barry and its Lady Hamilton—and so on back to antiquity. In our time, among those women who have come close to fitting this role are Lady Furness and Gloria Vanderbilt.

From childhood each had the elusive qualities that characterize the *femme fatale*. Both knew the love of many men, both suffered deeply, and now both have happily risen above the vicissitudes of their checkered careers and face the future with gallantry, humor, and without rancor or bitterness over the past. In this spirit, and with all sincerity, they have set down the story of their lives.

In *Double Exposure,* we are given a matchless picture of life among the great—and the near-great—in the now-vanished world between the two wars. Above all, we come to know the minds and hearts and philosophy of life and love of two fascinating women, and something of the nature of fascination itself.

The painting of Thelma Lady Furness and Gloria Morgan Vanderbilt reproduced on the jacket is by Paul Trebilcock and used by his permission.

DAVID McKAY COMPANY, INC.
New York

CPSIA information can be obtained
at www.ICGtesting.com
Printed in the USA
LVHW081913200323
742069LV00002B/135